M000222859

THE TERMINATOR
SECONDARY OBJECTIVES

BASED ON A PLOT BY MIKE RICHARDSON
AND RANDY STRADLEY

writer	JAMES ROBINSON
penciller	PAUL GULACY
inker	KARL KESEL
letterer	PAT BROSSEAU
colorist	GREG WRIGHT
cover	PAUL GULACY
series editor	DIANA SCHUTZ
collection editor	JERRY PROSSER
collection design	EGON SELBY
publisher	MIKE RICHARDSON
vice - president of operations	NEIL HANKERSON
executive editor	RANDY STRADLEY
managing editor	BARBARA KESEL
marketing director	BOB SCHRECK
controller	BRAD HORN
production director	CECE CUTSFORTH
production manager	CHRIS CHALENOR
DTP manager	SEAN TIERNEY

printed in Singapore
through Palace Press

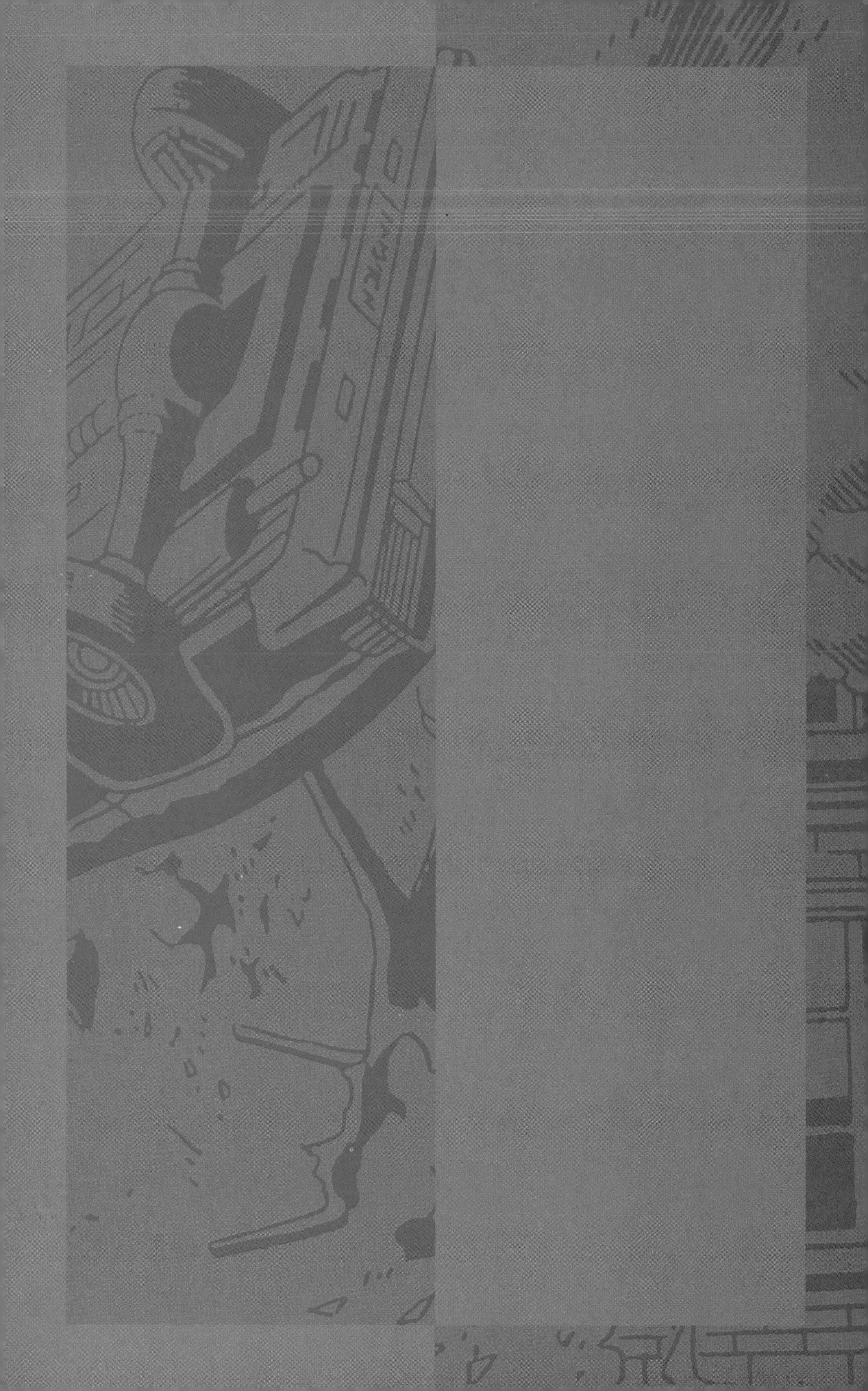

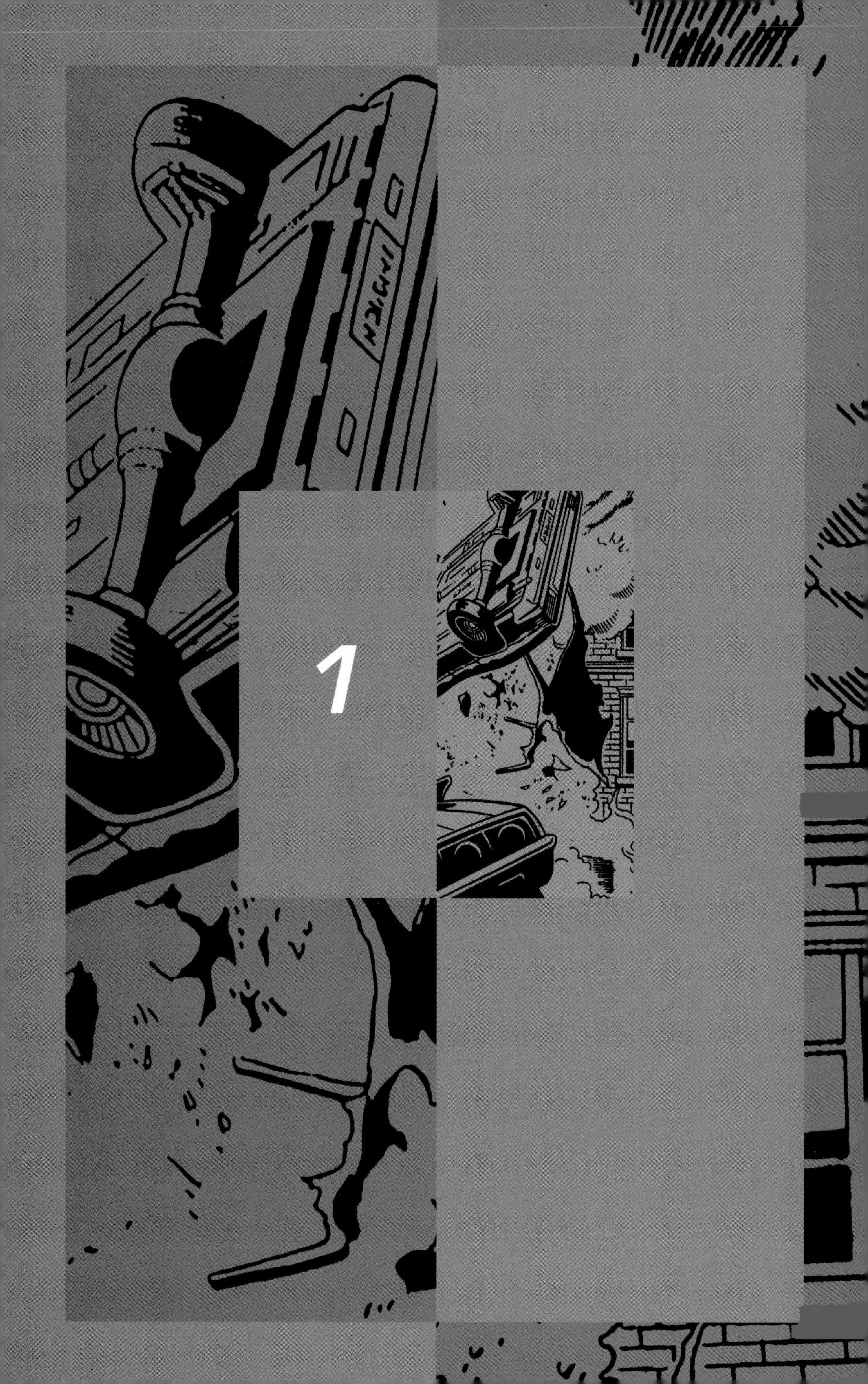
1

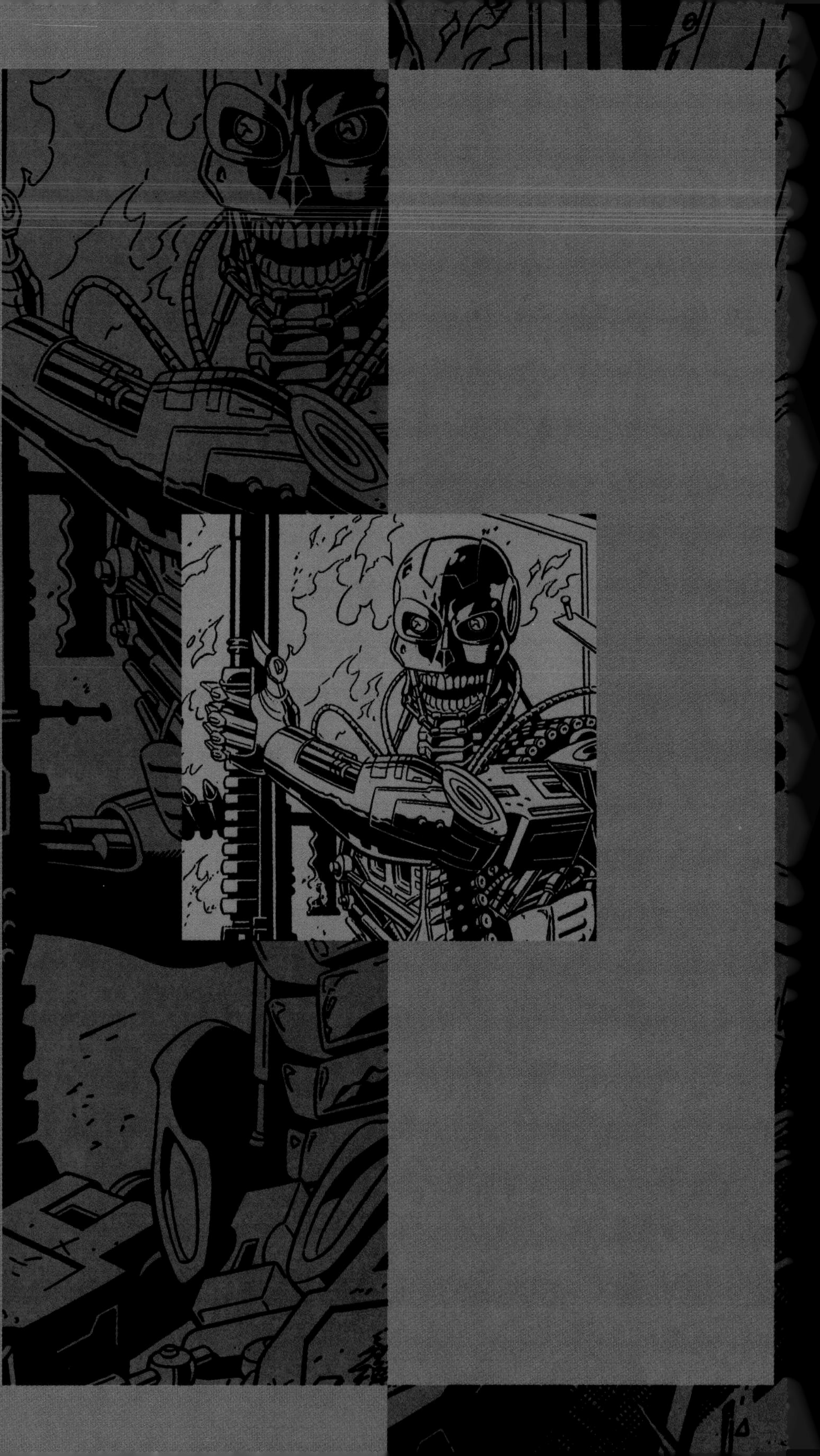

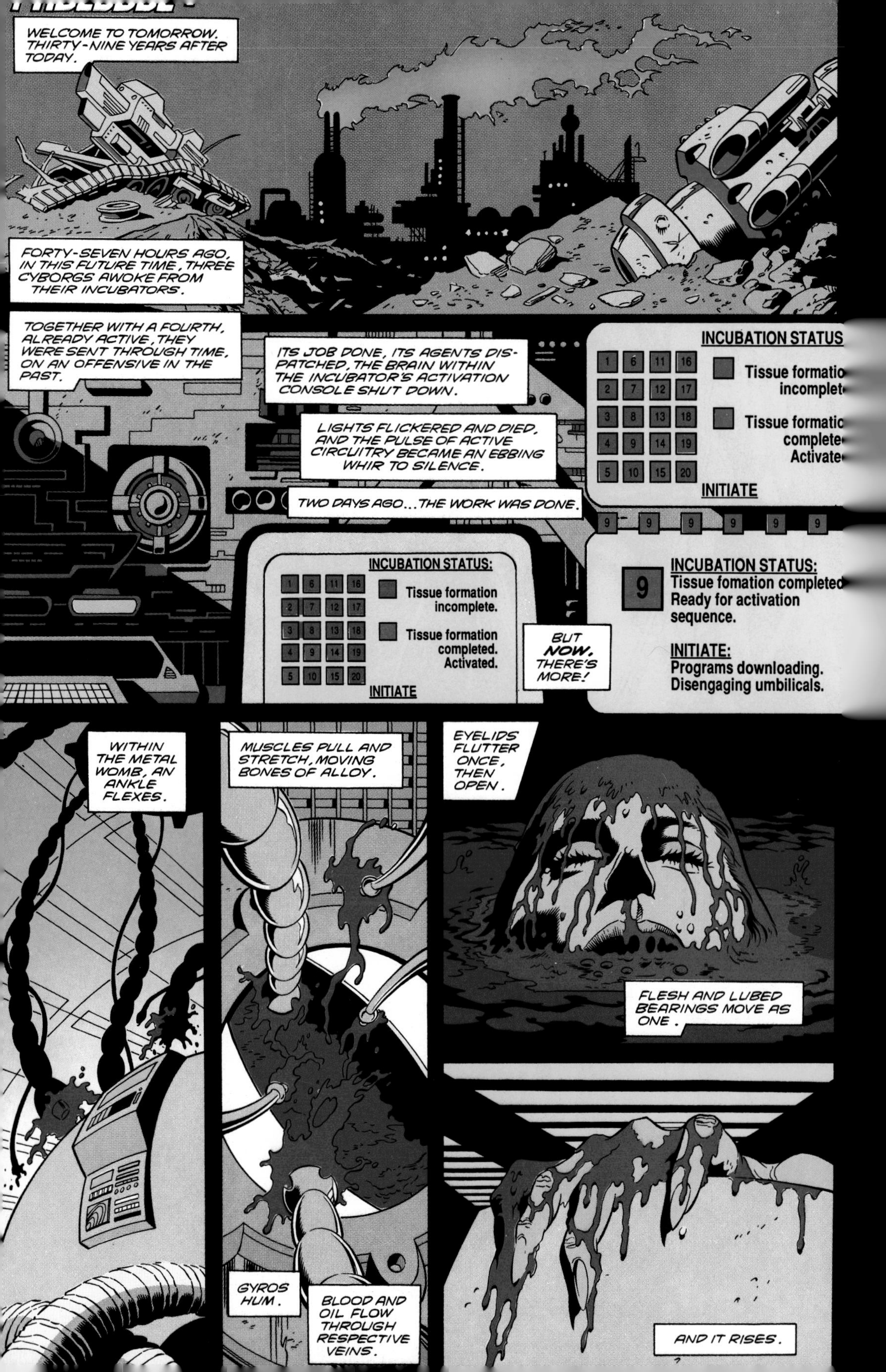

WELCOME TO TOMORROW. THIRTY-NINE YEARS AFTER TODAY.
FORTY-SEVEN HOURS AGO, IN THIS FUTURE TIME, THREE CYBORGS AWOKE FROM THEIR INCUBATORS.
TOGETHER WITH A FOURTH, ALREADY ACTIVE, THEY WERE SENT THROUGH TIME, ON AN OFFENSIVE IN THE PAST.
ITS JOB DONE, ITS AGENTS DISPATCHED, THE BRAIN WITHIN THE INCUBATOR'S ACTIVATION CONSOLE SHUT DOWN.
LIGHTS FLICKERED AND DIED, AND THE PULSE OF ACTIVE CIRCUITRY BECAME AN EBBING WHIR TO SILENCE.
TWO DAYS AGO... THE WORK WAS DONE.
INCUBATION STATUS
1 6 11 16
2 7 12 17
3 8 13 18
4 9 14 19
5 10 15 20
Tissue formatio incomplet
Tissue formatic complete Activate
INITIATE
9 9 9 9 9 9
INCUBATION STATUS:
1 6 11 16
2 7 12 17
3 8 13 18
4 9 14 19
5 10 15 20
Tissue formation incomplete.
Tissue formation completed. Activated.
INITIATE
BUT NOW, THERE'S MORE!
9
INCUBATION STATUS:
Tissue fomation completed
Ready for activation sequence.
INITIATE:
Programs downloading.
Disengaging umbilicals.
WITHIN THE METAL WOMB, AN ANKLE FLEXES.
MUSCLES PULL AND STRETCH, MOVING BONES OF ALLOY.
GYROS HUM.
BLOOD AND OIL FLOW THROUGH RESPECTIVE VEINS.
EYELIDS FLUTTER ONCE, THEN OPEN.
FLESH AND LUBED BEARINGS MOVE AS ONE.
AND IT RISES.

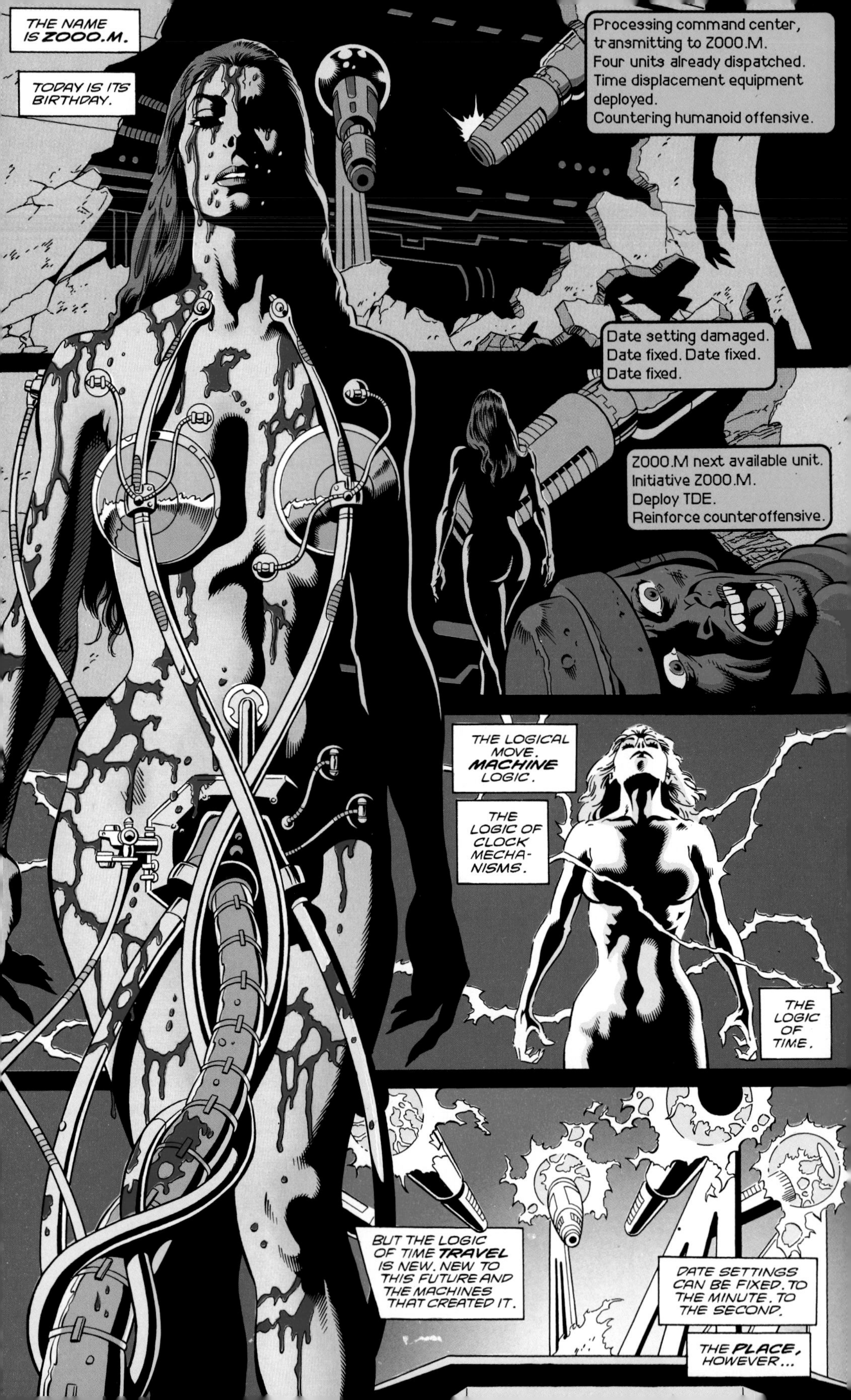
THE NAME IS ZOOO.M.
TODAY IS ITS BIRTHDAY.
Processing command center, transmitting to ZOOO.M. Four units already dispatched. Time displacement equipment deployed. Countering humanoid offensive.
Date setting damaged. Date fixed. Date fixed. Date fixed.
ZOOO.M next available unit. Initiative ZOOO.M. Deploy TDE. Reinforce counteroffensive.
THE LOGICAL MOVE. MACHINE LOGIC.
THE LOGIC OF CLOCK MECHA-NISMS.
THE LOGIC OF TIME.
BUT THE LOGIC OF TIME TRAVEL IS NEW. NEW TO THIS FUTURE AND THE MACHINES THAT CREATED IT.
DATE SETTINGS CAN BE FIXED. TO THE MINUTE. TO THE SECOND.
THE PLACE, HOWEVER...

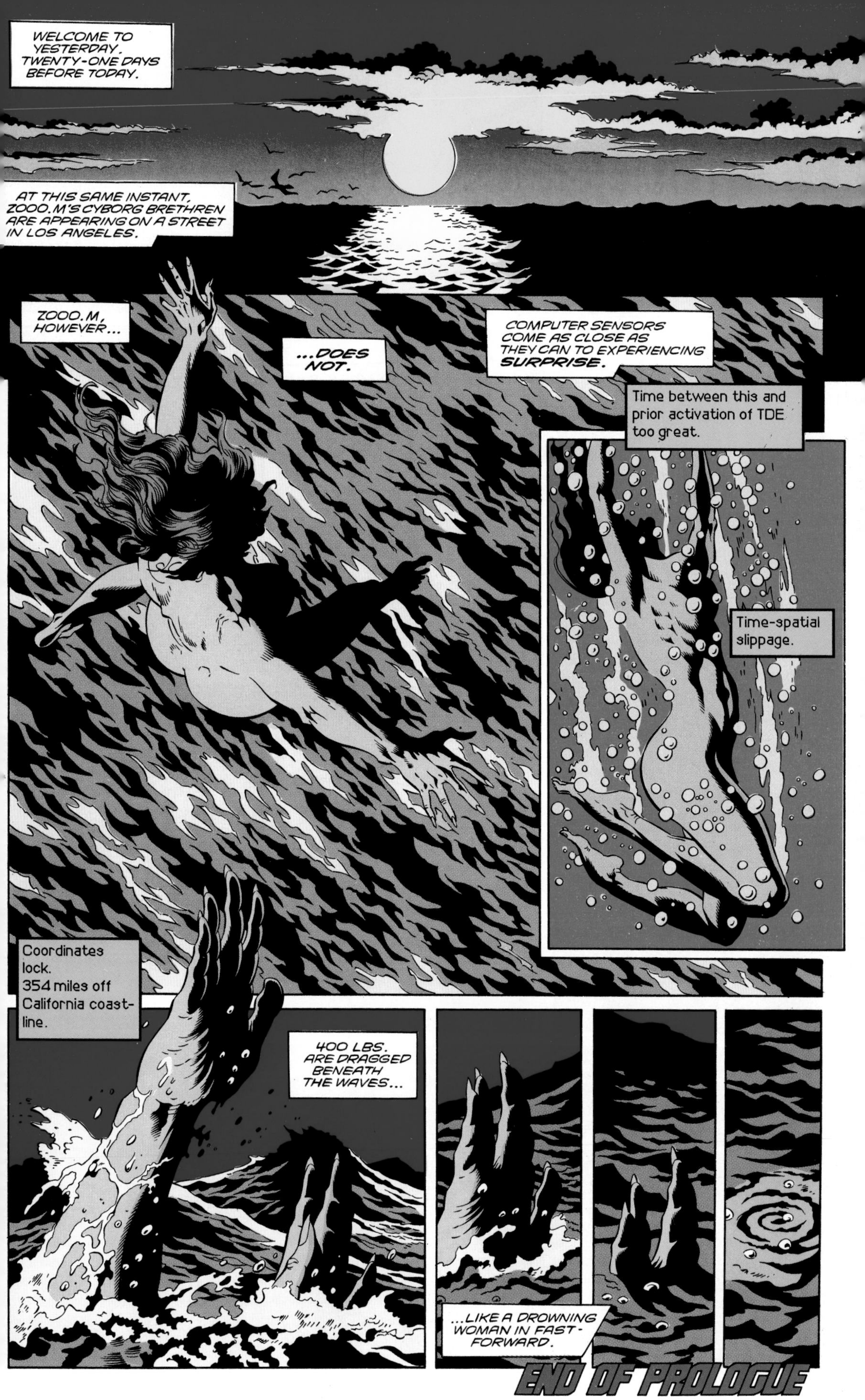
WELCOME TO YESTERDAY. TWENTY-ONE DAYS BEFORE TODAY.
AT THIS SAME INSTANT, ZOOO.M'S CYBORG BRETHREN ARE APPEARING ON A STREET IN LOS ANGELES.
ZOOO.M, HOWEVER...
...DOES NOT.
COMPUTER SENSORS COME AS CLOSE AS THEY CAN TO EXPERIENCING SURPRISE.
Time between this and prior activation of TDE too great.
Time-spatial slippage.
Coordinates lock. 354 miles off California coast-line.
400 LBS. ARE DRAGGED BENEATH THE WAVES...
...LIKE A DROWNING WOMAN IN FAST-FORWARD.
END OF PROLOGUE

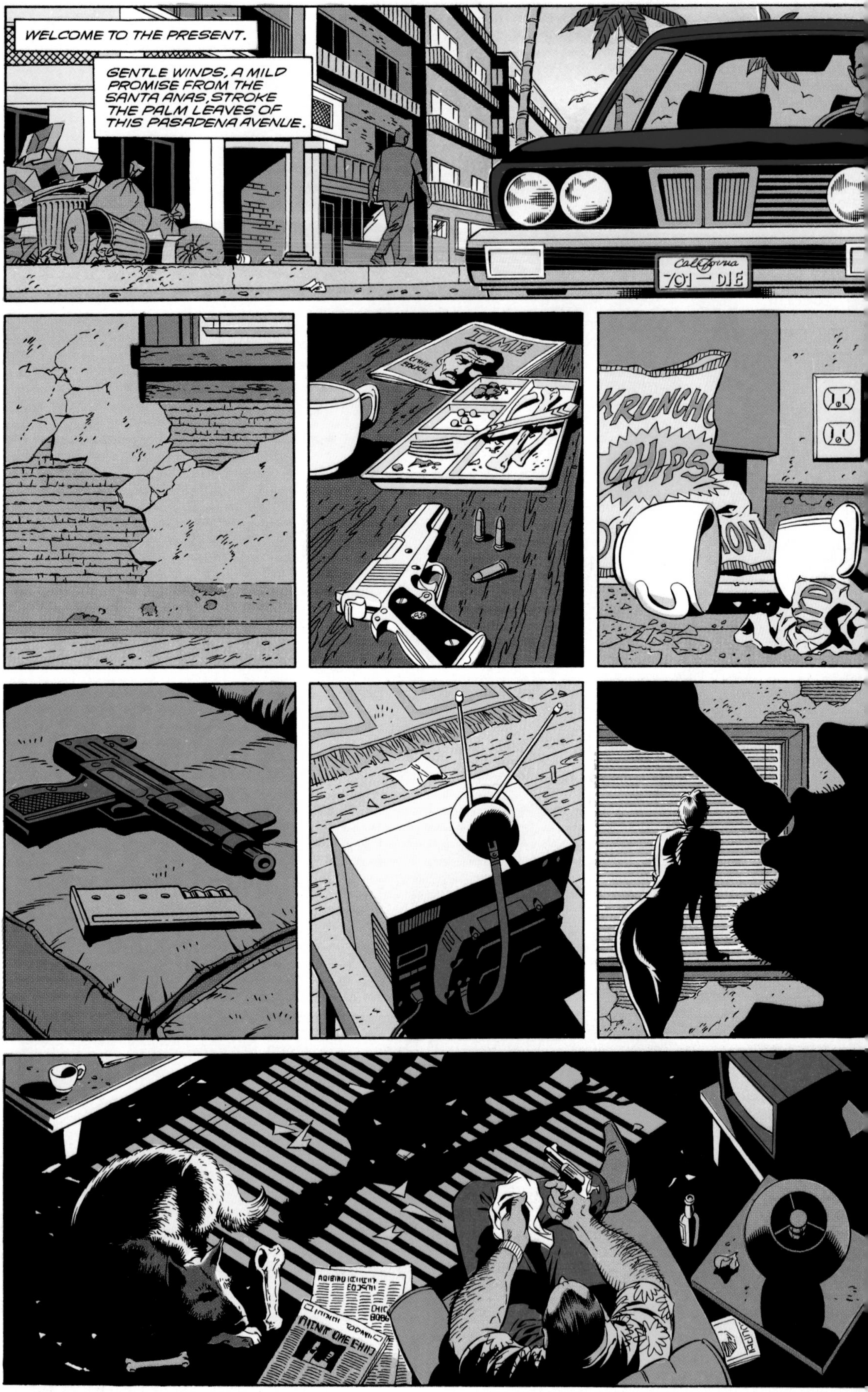
WELCOME TO THE PRESENT.
GENTLE WINDS, A MILD PROMISE FROM THE SANTA ANAS, STROKE THE PALM LEAVES OF THIS PASADENA AVENUE.
California
701 — DIE
TIME
KRUNCHO
CHIPS

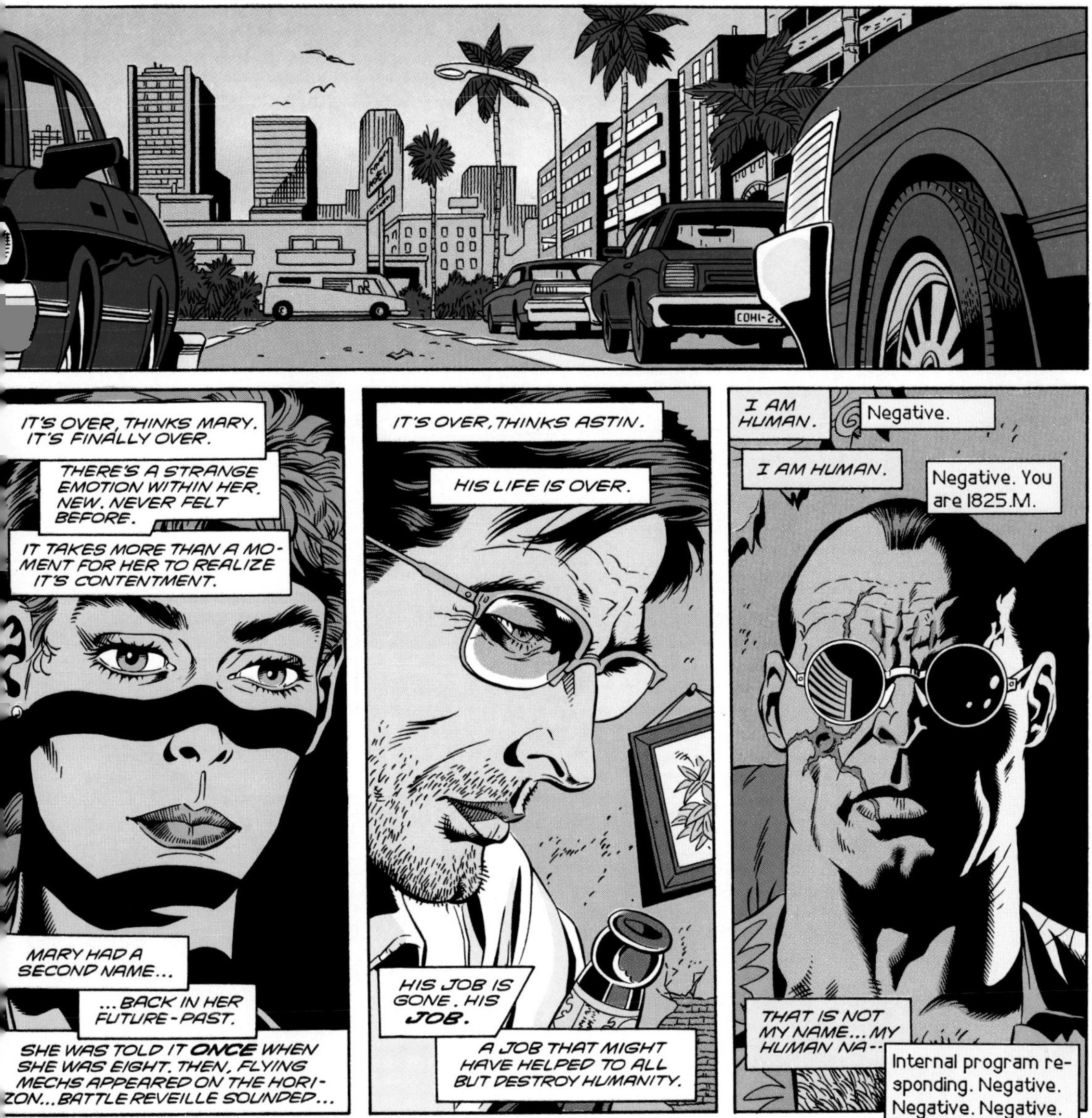
IT'S OVER, THINKS MARY. IT'S FINALLY OVER.
THERE'S A STRANGE EMOTION WITHIN HER. NEW. NEVER FELT BEFORE.
IT TAKES MORE THAN A MOMENT FOR HER TO REALIZE IT'S CONTENTMENT.
MARY HAD A SECOND NAME...
...BACK IN HER FUTURE-PAST.
SHE WAS TOLD IT ONCE WHEN SHE WAS EIGHT. THEN, FLYING MECHS APPEARED ON THE HORIZON... BATTLE REVEILLE SOUNDED...
IT'S OVER, THINKS ASTIN.
HIS LIFE IS OVER.
HIS JOB IS GONE. HIS JOB.
A JOB THAT MIGHT HAVE HELPED TO ALL BUT DESTROY HUMANITY.
I AM HUMAN.
Negative.
I AM HUMAN.
Negative. You are 1825.M.
THAT IS NOT MY NAME... MY HUMAN NA--
Internal program responding. Negative. Negative. Negative.

...AND SHE FORGOT IT.

SHE'S A **WOMAN**-- ALTHOUGH SHE WAS BEGINNING TO FORGET THAT AS WELL.

IN THE FUTURE TIME, THAT HOPEFULLY NOW WILL NEVER COME, SHE WAS A **SOLDIER.**

FIRST, LAST, AND EVERY WAKING SECOND.

BUT NOW, NO LONGER. IT'S OVER.

IT'S FINALLY OVER.

MISSION ACCOMPLISHED. HER TEAM DEAD... ALL OF THEM... BUT THEIR GOAL ATTAINED.

THERE WOULD BE NO DEVELOPMENT OF CYBORG TECHNOLOGY.

NO ARTIFICIAL INTELLIGENCE. NO TERMINATORS.

MARY LOOKS OUT, AT A DUSK DAPPLED GREY-GREEN BY THE SMOG.

AND SEES A BEAUTY... A TRANQUILITY IN IT, THAT NO NATIVE OF THIS TIME COULD HOPE TO.

HE'D WORKED FOR A DESPOT HE HATED... BUT...

...THE DESPOT HAD PAID WELL. THE **JOB** HAD PAID WELL.

THE POLICE... THEY PROBABLY WANT HIM. HE'S SCARED TO GO TO HIS APARTMENT FOR THAT REASON.

AND GOD **KNOWS** WHAT'S HAPPENED TO HIS MOTORBIKE.

ALL HE'S BEEN THROUGH. ALL HE'S SEEN. SUCH KILLING. **SUCH...**

ASTIN'S FOREHEAD IS WRINKLED WITH WORRY.

THE ANKLE HE THOUGHT WAS BROKEN HAD PROVED MERELY SPRAINED. NEVERTHELESS, THIS HASN'T HELPED HIS MOOD.

HE'S BEGUN BITING HIS FINGERNAILS AGAIN. HE'D STOPPED THAT IN SIXTH GRADE.

AND THE **DAMN** SMOG HAS GIVEN HIM A MIGRAINE.

I'VE HELPED PREVENT CYBERNETICS FROM EVER TAKING HOLD OF THE WORLD.

I'VE DONE A **GREAT** THING.

Negative. Unit has countermanded directive.

Rectify.Rectify.

Eliminate humanoid threat.
Resume counteroffensive.

NO!

NO... I'M HUMAN. I'M NOT GOING TO...

Negative. Negative.
You are 1825.M.

...SAM BRADDOCK FOR L.A. ACTION NEWS...

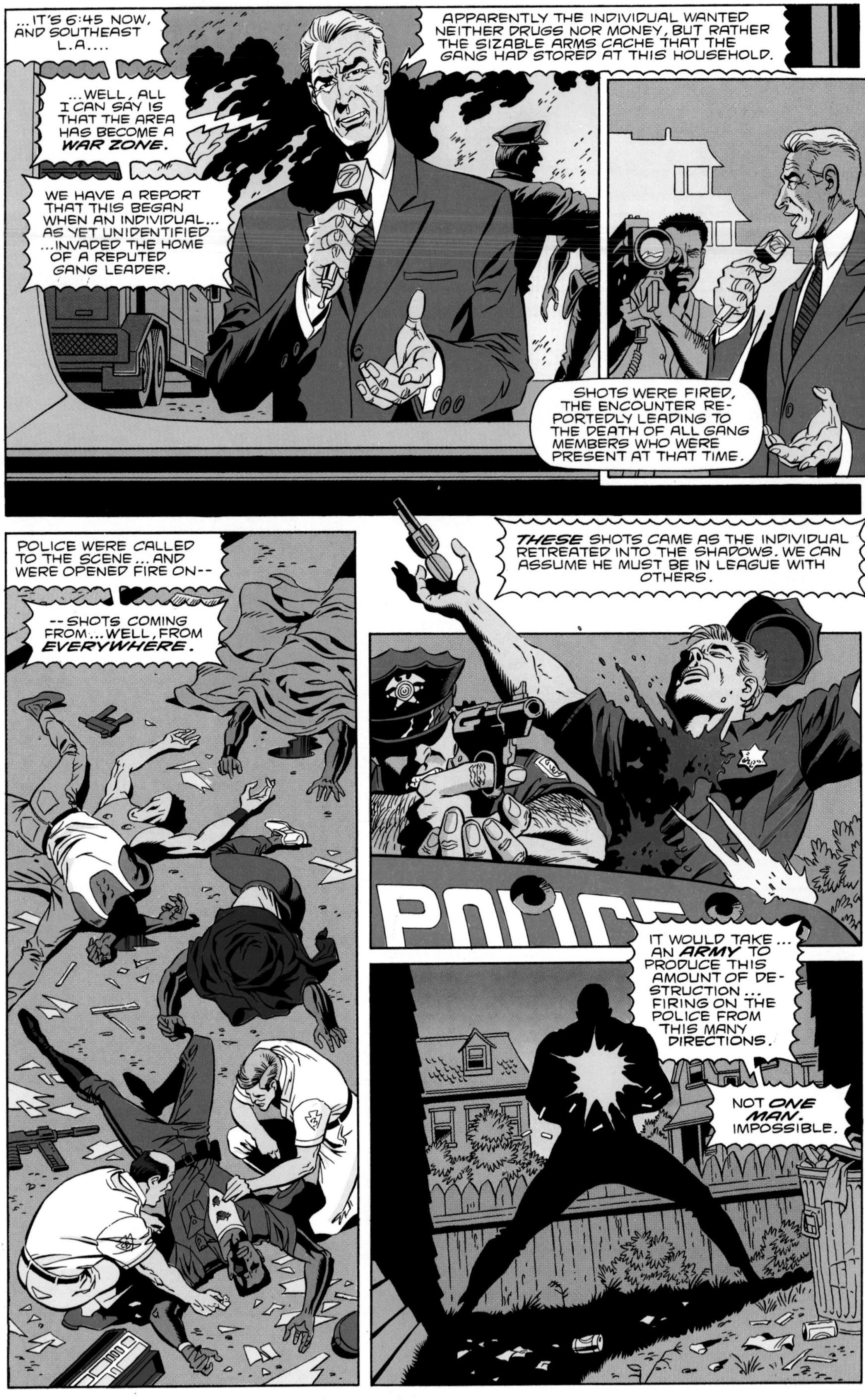

...IT'S 6:45 NOW, AND SOUTHEAST L.A....
...WELL, ALL I CAN SAY IS THAT THE AREA HAS BECOME A WAR ZONE.
WE HAVE A REPORT THAT THIS BEGAN WHEN AN INDIVIDUAL... AS YET UNIDENTIFIED ...INVADED THE HOME OF A REPUTED GANG LEADER.
APPARENTLY THE INDIVIDUAL WANTED NEITHER DRUGS NOR MONEY, BUT RATHER THE SIZABLE ARMS CACHE THAT THE GANG HAD STORED AT THIS HOUSEHOLD.
SHOTS WERE FIRED, THE ENCOUNTER REPORTEDLY LEADING TO THE DEATH OF ALL GANG MEMBERS WHO WERE PRESENT AT THAT TIME.
POLICE WERE CALLED TO THE SCENE... AND WERE OPENED FIRE ON--
--SHOTS COMING FROM...WELL, FROM EVERYWHERE.
THESE SHOTS CAME AS THE INDIVIDUAL RETREATED INTO THE SHADOWS. WE CAN ASSUME HE MUST BE IN LEAGUE WITH OTHERS.
POLICE
IT WOULD TAKE... AN ARMY TO PRODUCE THIS AMOUNT OF DESTRUCTION... FIRING ON THE POLICE FROM THIS MANY DIRECTIONS.
NOT ONE MAN. IMPOSSIBLE.

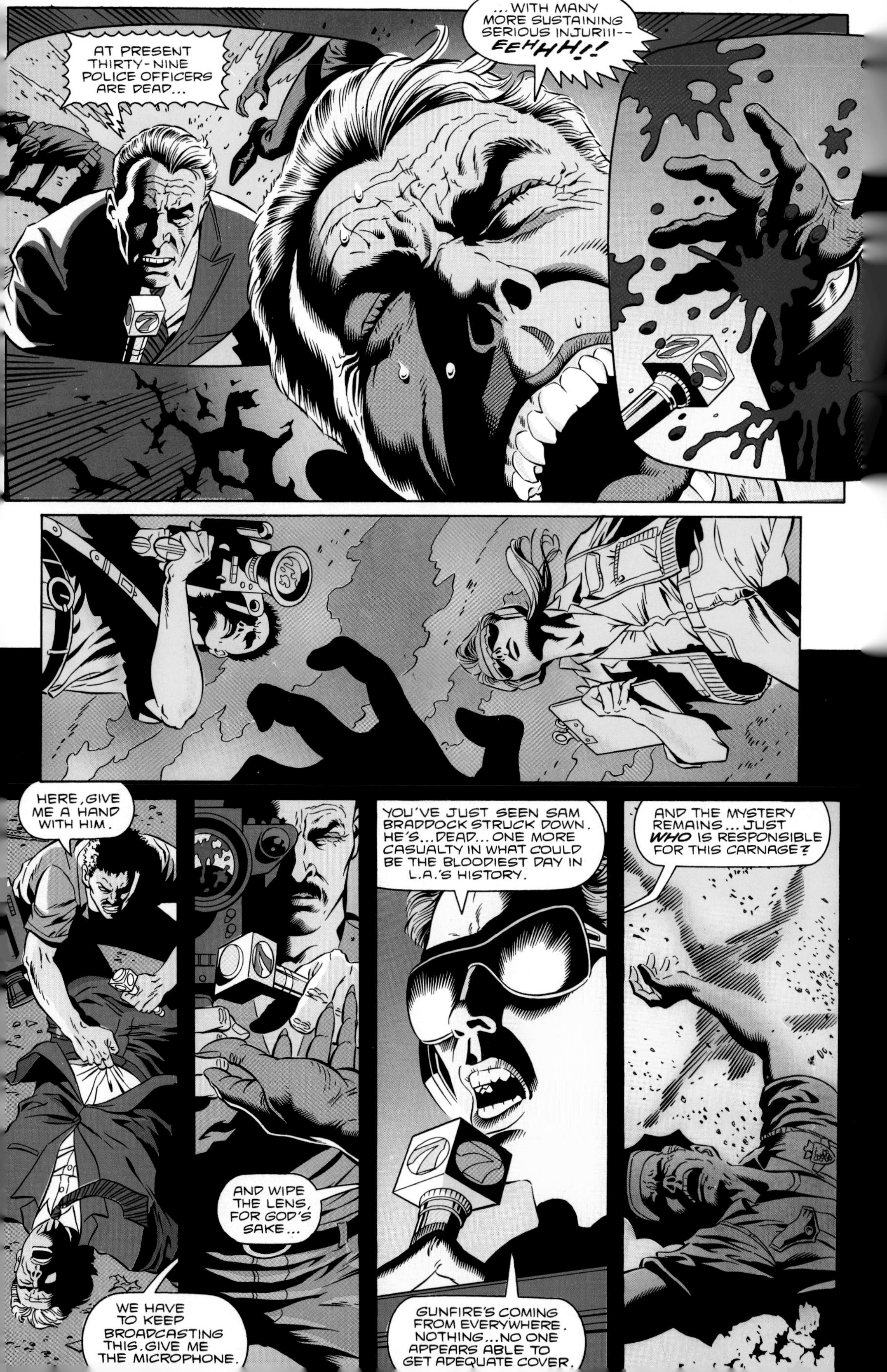
AT PRESENT THIRTY-NINE POLICE OFFICERS ARE DEAD...
...WITH MANY MORE SUSTAINING SERIOUS INJURIII-- EEHHH!!
HERE, GIVE ME A HAND WITH HIM.
WE HAVE TO KEEP BROADCASTING THIS. GIVE ME THE MICROPHONE.
AND WIPE THE LENS, FOR GOD'S SAKE...
YOU'VE JUST SEEN SAM BRADDOCK STRUCK DOWN. HE'S...DEAD...ONE MORE CASUALTY IN WHAT COULD BE THE BLOODIEST DAY IN L.A.'S HISTORY.
GUNFIRE'S COMING FROM EVERYWHERE. NOTHING...NO ONE APPEARS ABLE TO GET ADEQUATE COVER.
AND THE MYSTERY REMAINS... JUST WHO IS RESPONSIBLE FOR THIS CARNAGE?

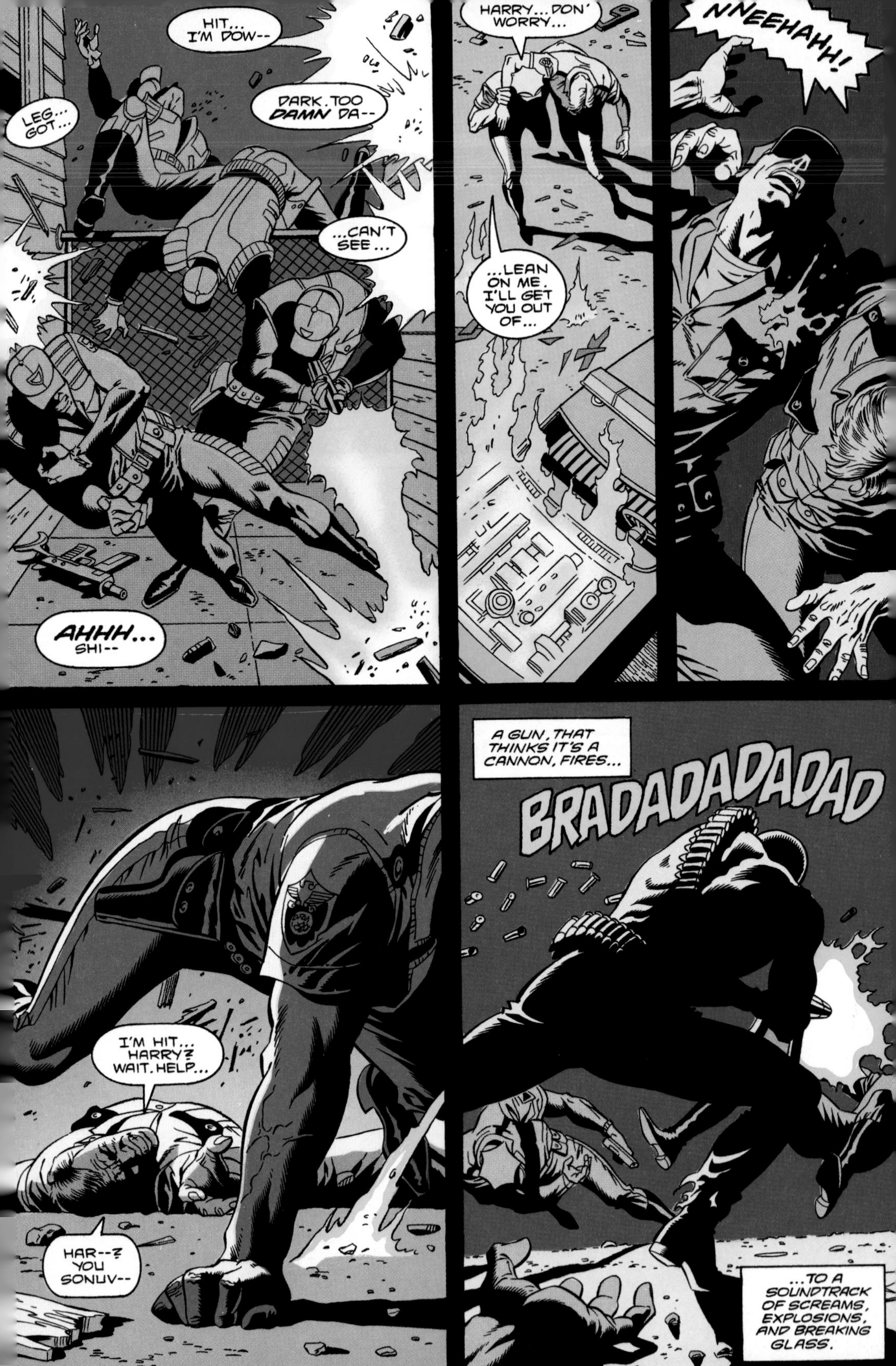
LEG... GOT...
HIT... I'M DOW--
DARK. TOO DAMN DA--
...CAN'T SEE...
AHHH... SHI--
HARRY... DON' WORRY...
...LEAN ON ME. I'LL GET YOU OUT OF...
NNEEHAHH!
I'M HIT... HARRY? WAIT. HELP...
HAR--? YOU SONUV--
A GUN, THAT THINKS IT'S A CANNON, FIRES...
BRADADADADAD
...TO A SOUNDTRACK OF SCREAMS, EXPLOSIONS, AND BREAKING GLASS.

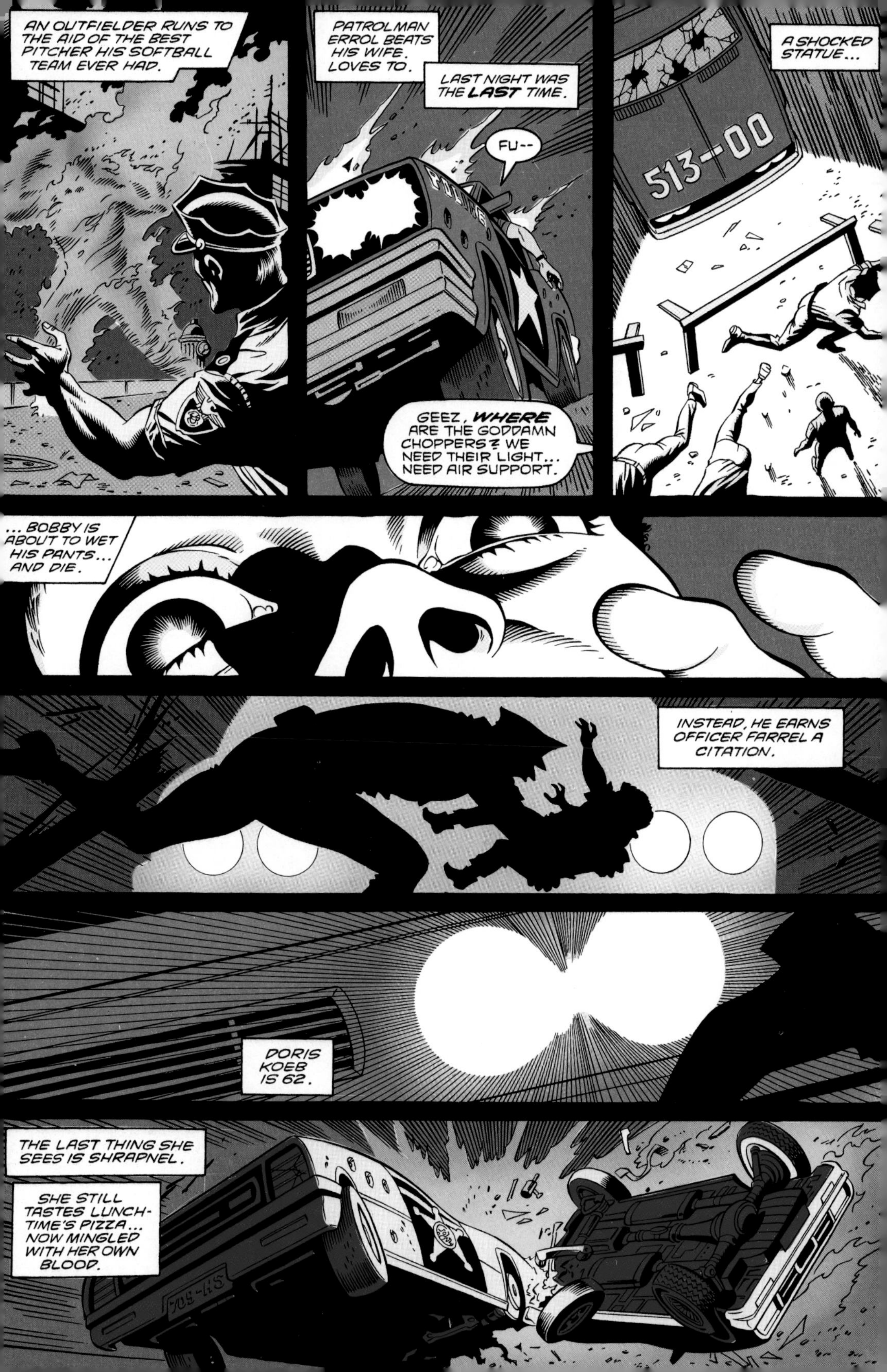

AN OUTFIELDER RUNS TO THE AID OF THE BEST PITCHER HIS SOFTBALL TEAM EVER HAD.
PATROLMAN ERROL BEATS HIS WIFE. LOVES TO.
LAST NIGHT WAS THE LAST TIME.
FU--
POLICE
GEEZ, WHERE ARE THE GODDAMN CHOPPERS? WE NEED THEIR LIGHT... NEED AIR SUPPORT.
A SHOCKED STATUE...
513--00
... BOBBY IS ABOUT TO WET HIS PANTS... AND DIE.
INSTEAD, HE EARNS OFFICER FARREL A CITATION.
DORIS KOEB IS 62.
THE LAST THING SHE SEES IS SHRAPNEL.
SHE STILL TASTES LUNCH-TIME'S PIZZA... NOW MINGLED WITH HER OWN BLOOD.

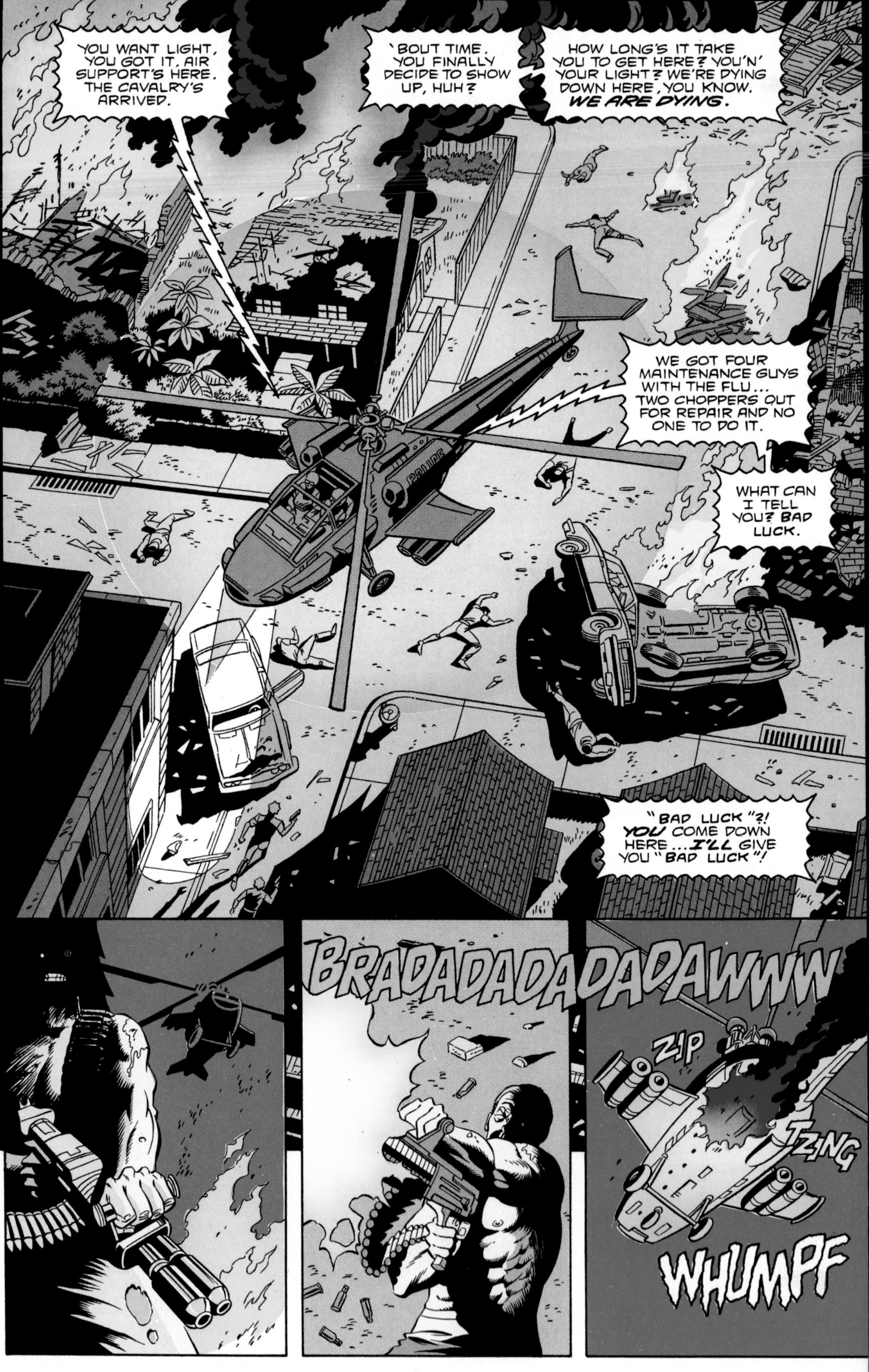
YOU WANT LIGHT, YOU GOT IT. AIR SUPPORT'S HERE. THE CAVALRY'S ARRIVED.
'BOUT TIME. YOU FINALLY DECIDE TO SHOW UP, HUH?
HOW LONG'S IT TAKE YOU TO GET HERE? YOU'N' YOUR LIGHT? WE'RE DYING DOWN HERE, YOU KNOW. WE ARE DYING.
WE GOT FOUR MAINTENANCE GUYS WITH THE FLU... TWO CHOPPERS OUT FOR REPAIR AND NO ONE TO DO IT.
WHAT CAN I TELL YOU? BAD LUCK.
"BAD LUCK"?! YOU COME DOWN HERE... I'LL GIVE YOU "BAD LUCK"!
POLICE
BRADADADADADADAWWW
ZIP
TZING
WHUMPF

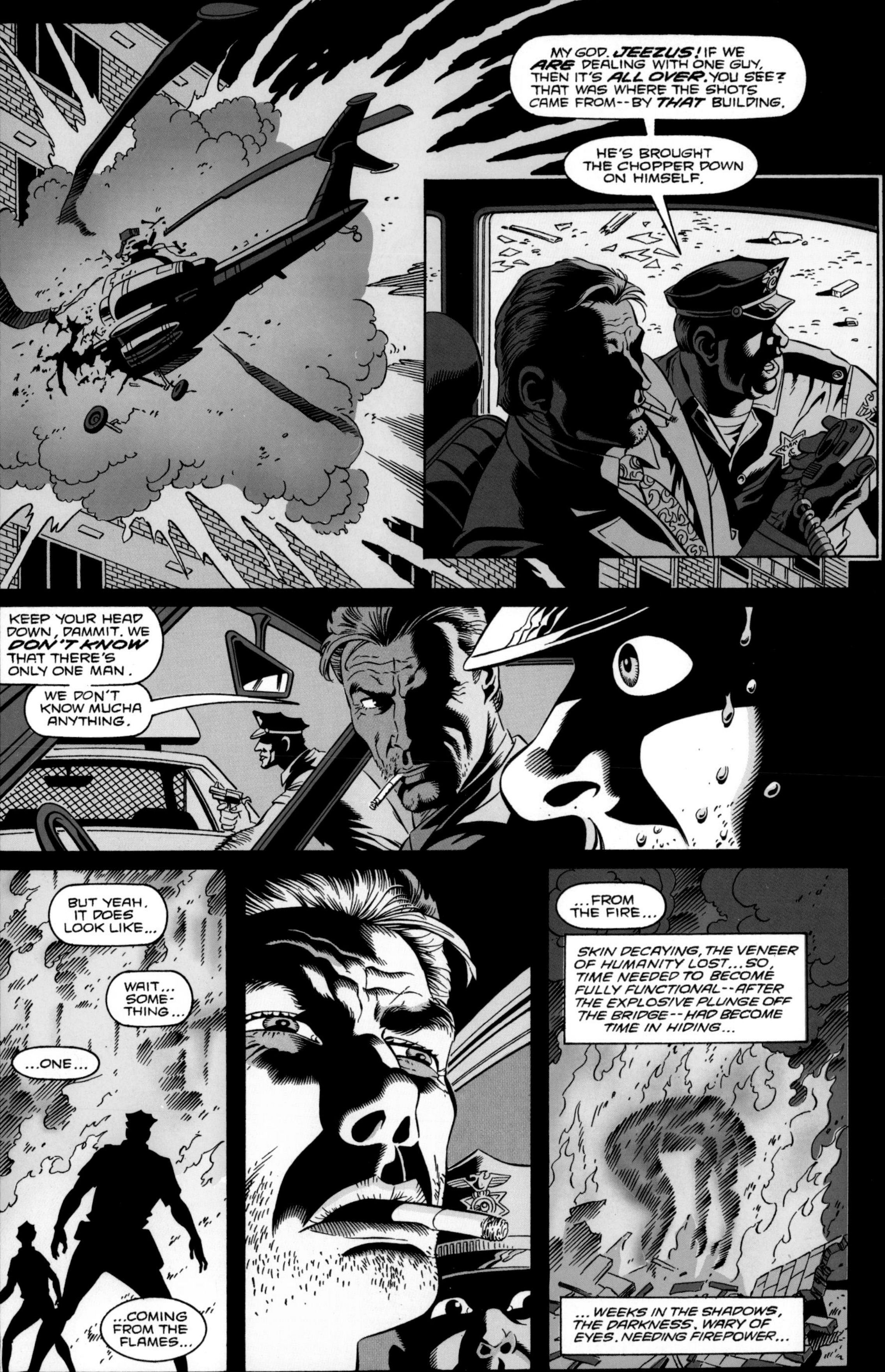
MY GOD. JEEZUS! IF WE ARE DEALING WITH ONE GUY, THEN IT'S ALL OVER. YOU SEE? THAT WAS WHERE THE SHOTS CAME FROM--BY THAT BUILDING.
HE'S BROUGHT THE CHOPPER DOWN ON HIMSELF.
KEEP YOUR HEAD DOWN, DAMMIT. WE DON'T KNOW THAT THERE'S ONLY ONE MAN.
WE DON'T KNOW MUCHA ANYTHING.
BUT YEAH, IT DOES LOOK LIKE...
WAIT... SOME-THING...
...ONE...
...COMING FROM THE FLAMES...
...FROM THE FIRE...
SKIN DECAYING, THE VENEER OF HUMANITY LOST... SO, TIME NEEDED TO BECOME FULLY FUNCTIONAL--AFTER THE EXPLOSIVE PLUNGE OFF THE BRIDGE--HAD BECOME TIME IN HIDING...
...WEEKS IN THE SHADOWS, THE DARKNESS, WARY OF EYES. NEEDING FIREPOWER...

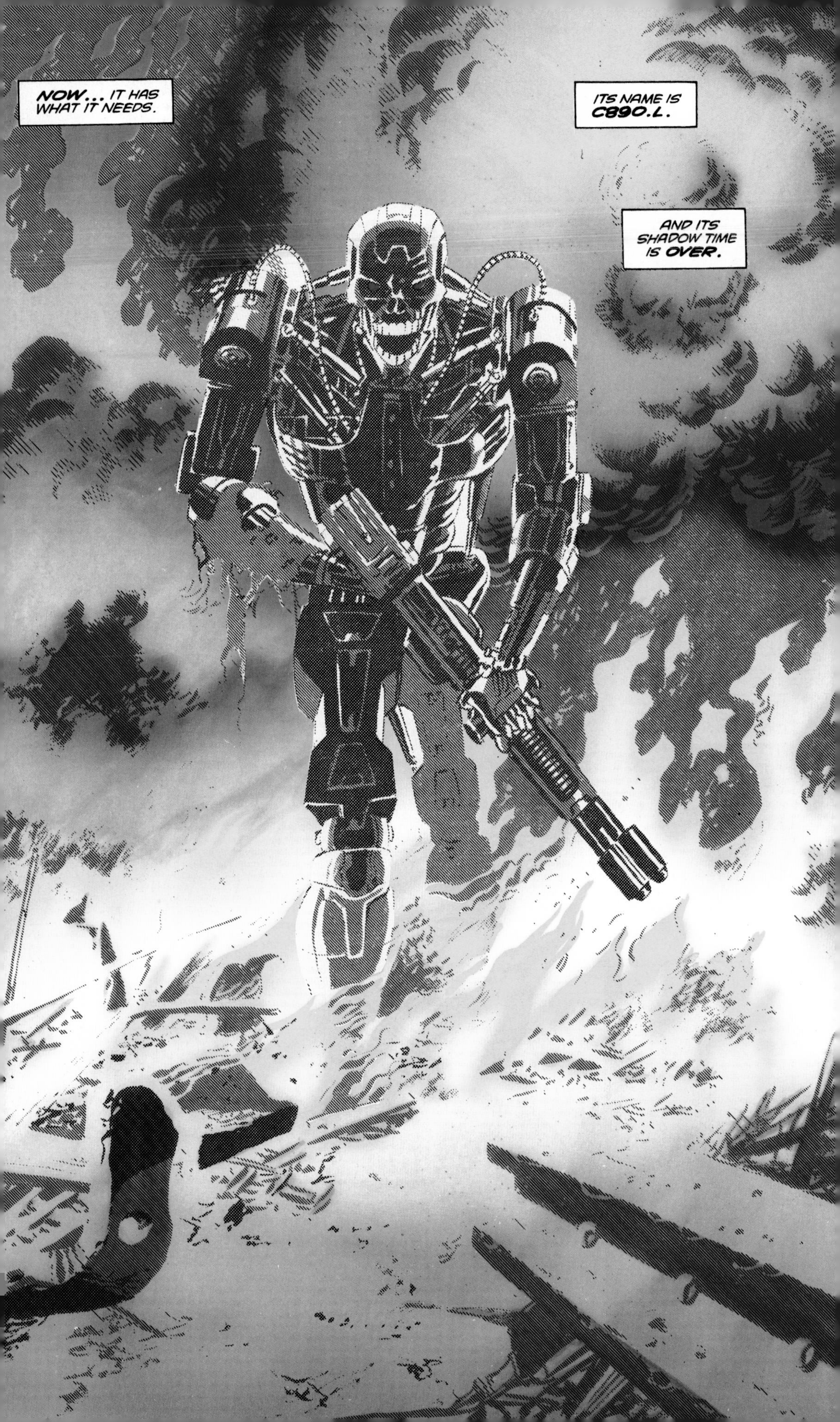
NOW... IT HAS WHAT IT NEEDS.
ITS NAME IS C890.L.
AND ITS SHADOW TIME IS OVER.

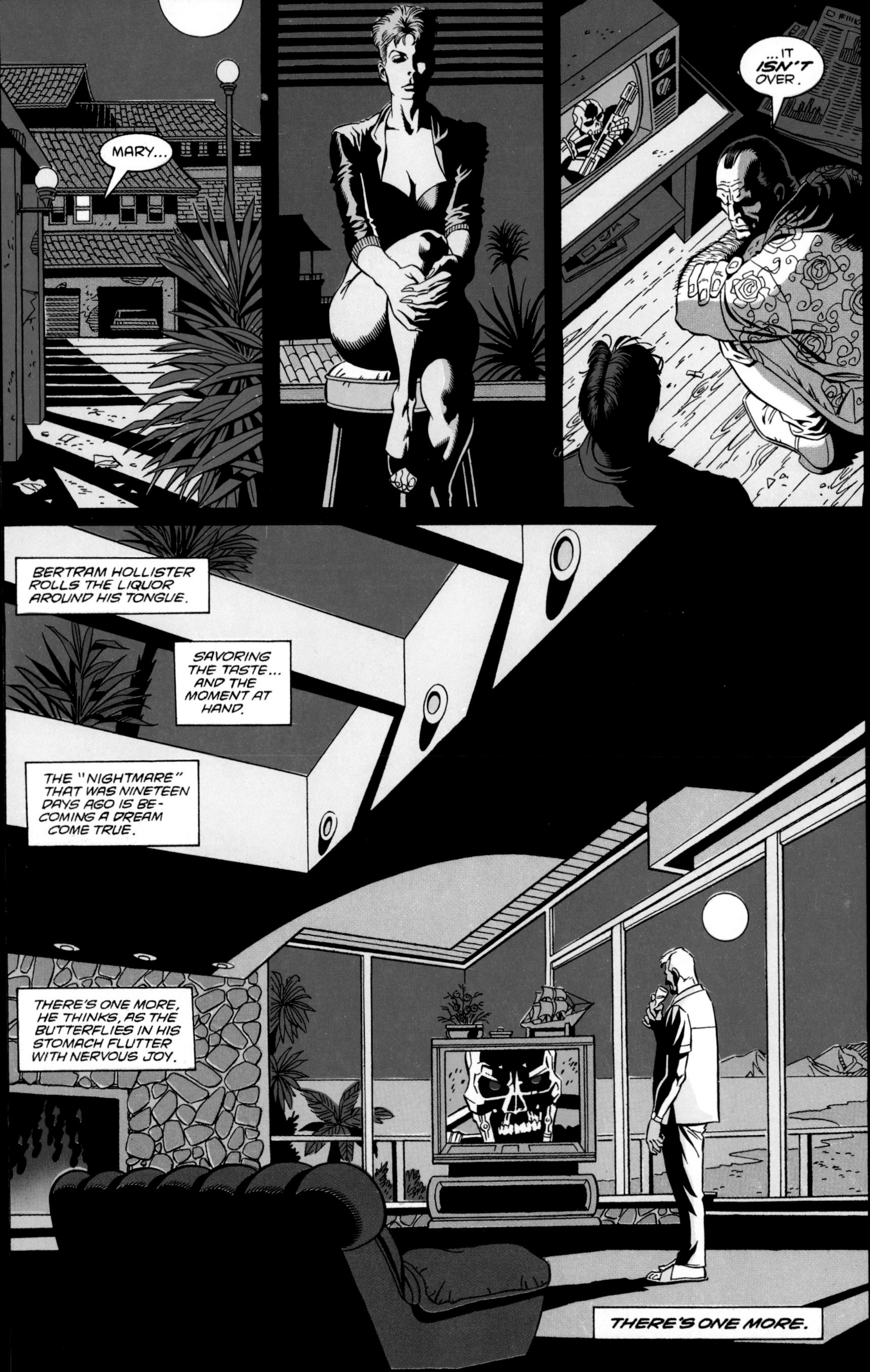
MARY...
...IT ISN'T OVER.
BERTRAM HOLLISTER ROLLS THE LIQUOR AROUND HIS TONGUE.
SAVORING THE TASTE... AND THE MOMENT AT HAND.
THE "NIGHTMARE" THAT WAS NINETEEN DAYS AGO IS BE- COMING A DREAM COME TRUE.
THERE'S ONE MORE, HE THINKS, AS THE BUTTERFLIES IN HIS STOMACH FLUTTER WITH NERVOUS JOY.
THERE'S ONE MORE.

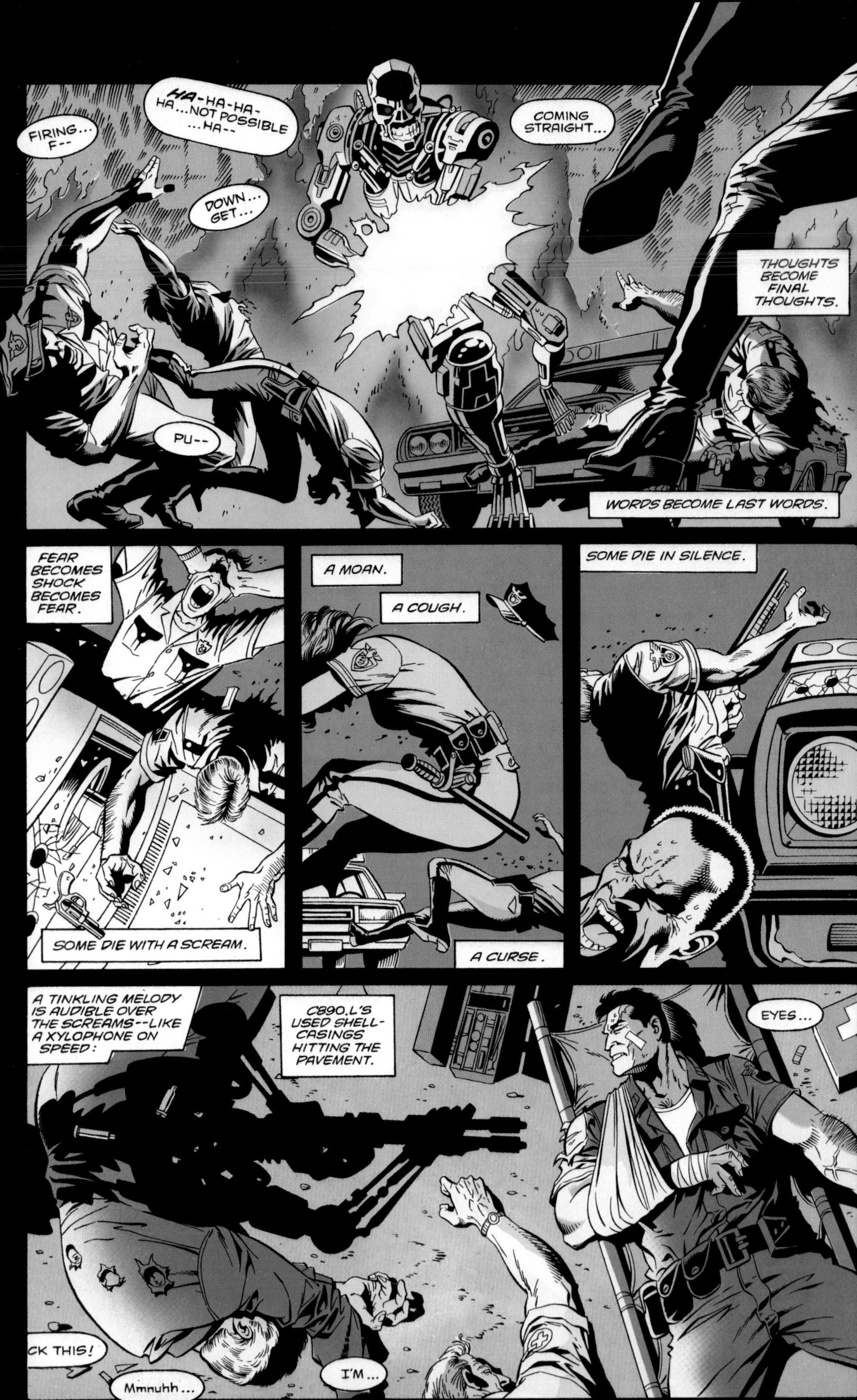
FIRING... F--
HA-HA-HA-HA...NOT POSSIBLE ...HA--
DOWN... GET...
COMING STRAIGHT...
THOUGHTS BECOME FINAL THOUGHTS.
PU--
WORDS BECOME LAST WORDS.
FEAR BECOMES SHOCK BECOMES FEAR.
SOME DIE WITH A SCREAM.
A MOAN.
A COUGH.
A CURSE.
SOME DIE IN SILENCE.
A TINKLING MELODY IS AUDIBLE OVER THE SCREAMS--LIKE A XYLOPHONE ON SPEED:
C890.L'S USED SHELL-CASINGS HITTING THE PAVEMENT.
EYES...
CK THIS!
Mmnuhh...
I'M...

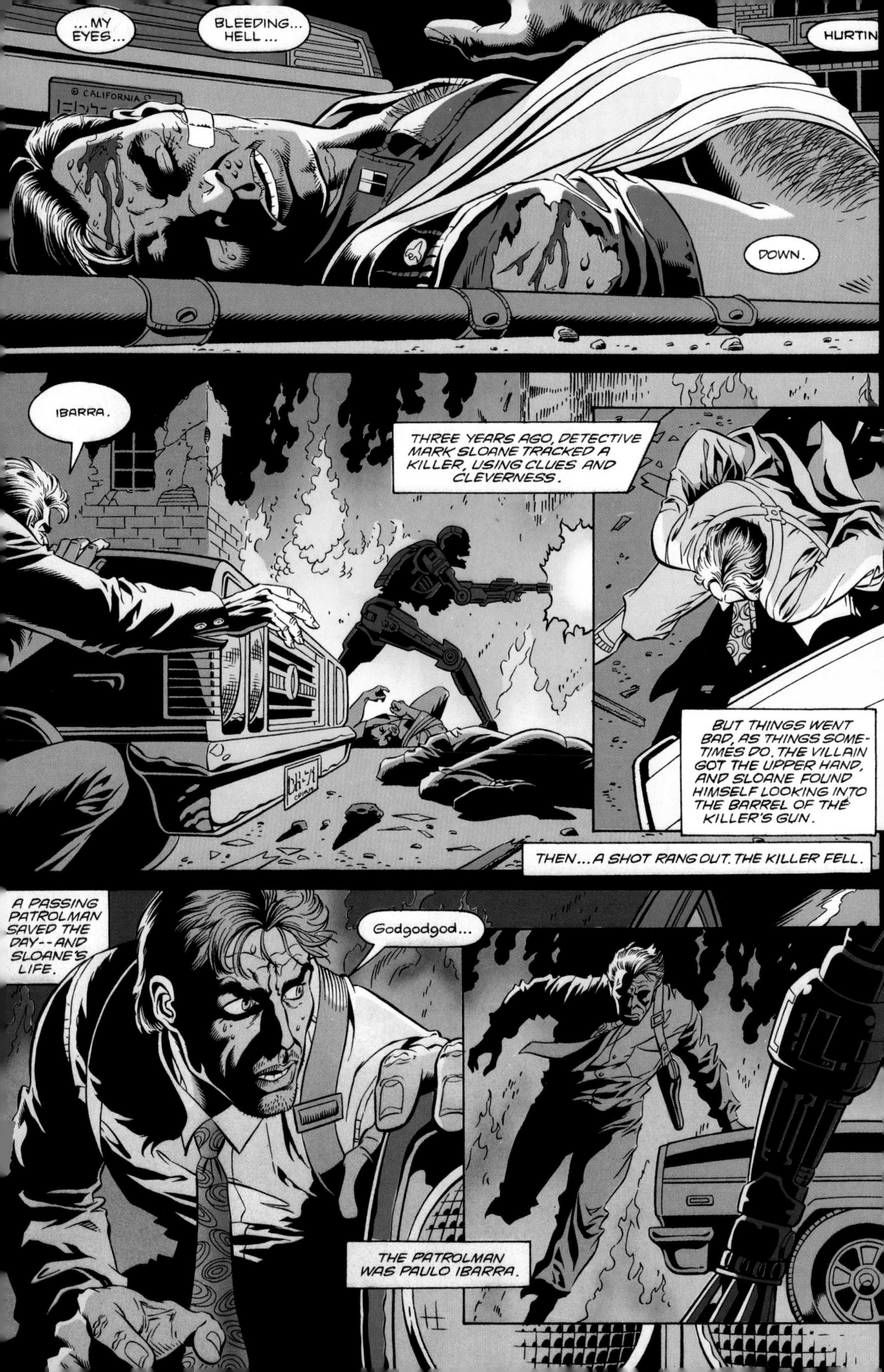
...MY EYES...
BLEEDING... HELL...
HURTIN
DOWN.
IBARRA.
THREE YEARS AGO, DETECTIVE MARK SLOANE TRACKED A KILLER, USING CLUES AND CLEVERNESS.
BUT THINGS WENT BAD, AS THINGS SOMETIMES DO. THE VILLAIN GOT THE UPPER HAND, AND SLOANE FOUND HIMSELF LOOKING INTO THE BARREL OF THE KILLER'S GUN.
THEN... A SHOT RANG OUT. THE KILLER FELL.
A PASSING PATROLMAN SAVED THE DAY--AND SLOANE'S LIFE.
Godgodgod...
THE PATROLMAN WAS PAULO IBARRA.

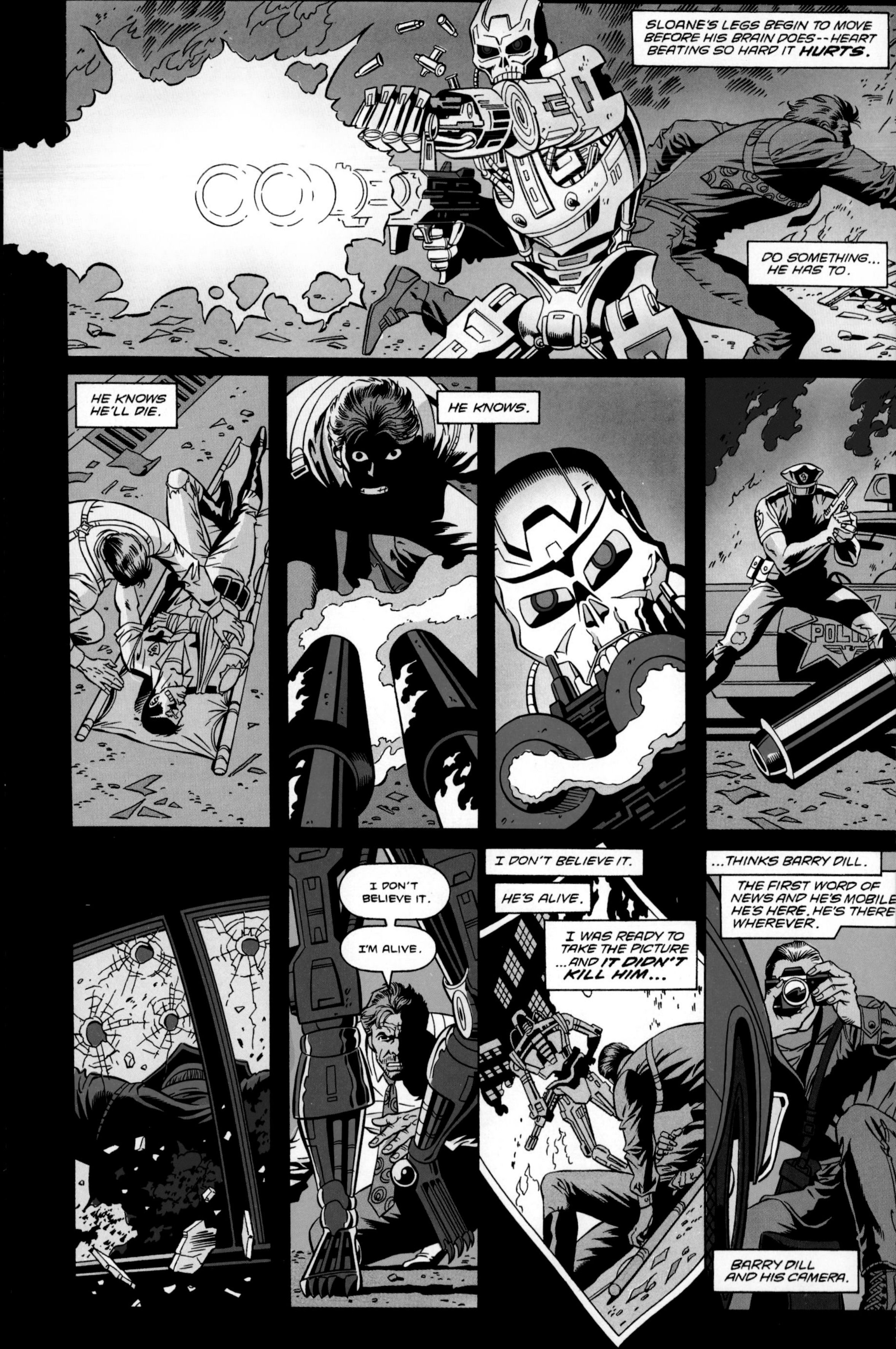
SLOANE'S LEGS BEGIN TO MOVE BEFORE HIS BRAIN DOES--HEART BEATING SO HARD IT **HURTS.**
DO SOMETHING... HE HAS TO.
HE KNOWS HE'LL DIE.
HE KNOWS.
POLI
I DON'T BELIEVE IT.
I'M ALIVE.
I DON'T BELIEVE IT.
HE'S ALIVE.
I WAS READY TO TAKE THE PICTURE ...AND *IT DIDN'T KILL HIM...*
...THINKS BARRY DILL.
THE FIRST WORD OF NEWS AND HE'S MOBILE HE'S HERE. HE'S THERE WHEREVER.
BARRY DILL AND HIS CAMERA.

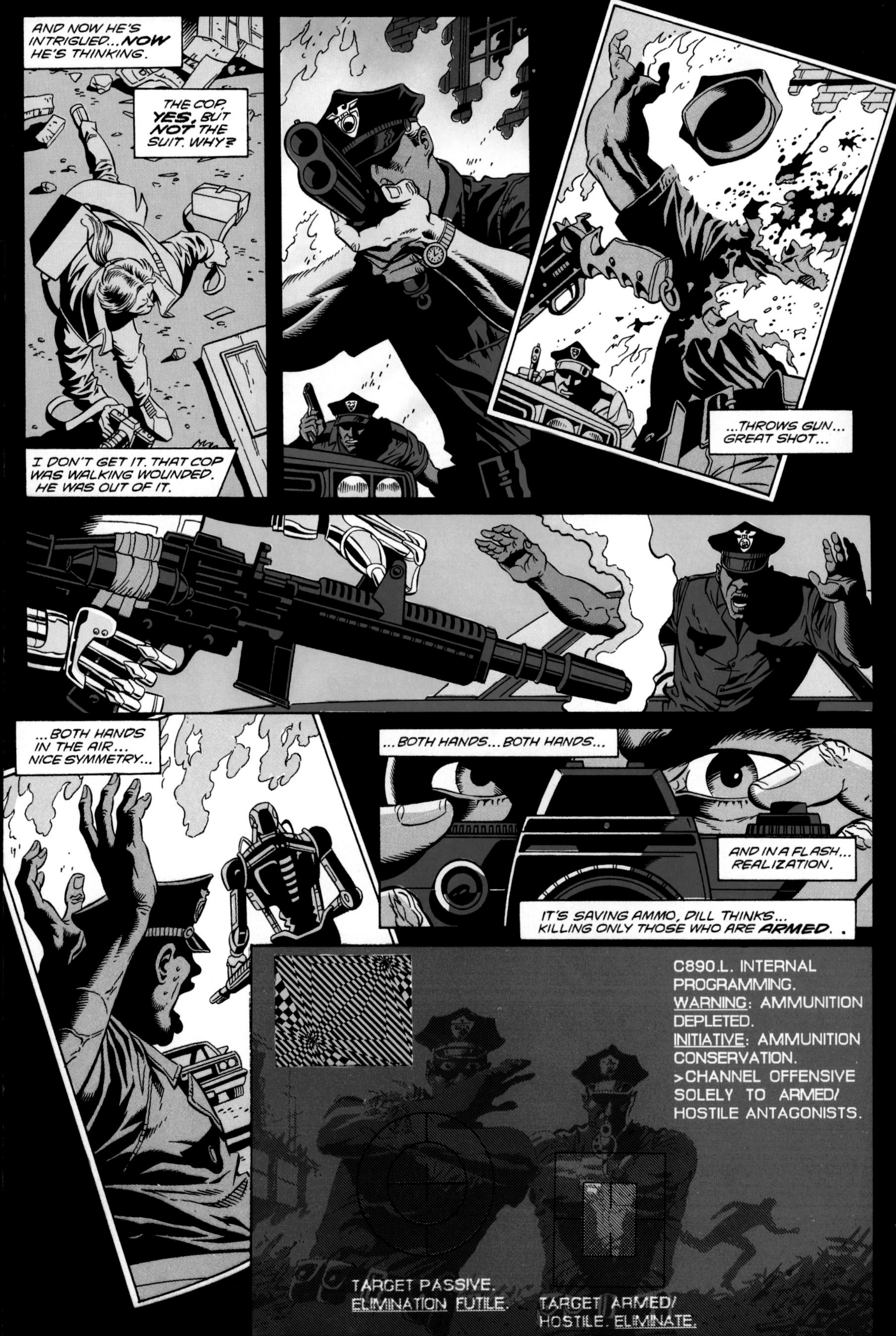
AND NOW HE'S INTRIGUED... NOW HE'S THINKING.
THE COP, YES, BUT NOT THE SUIT. WHY?
I DON'T GET IT. THAT COP WAS WALKING WOUNDED. HE WAS OUT OF IT.
...THROWS GUN... GREAT SHOT...
...BOTH HANDS IN THE AIR... NICE SYMMETRY...
...BOTH HANDS... BOTH HANDS...
AND IN A FLASH... REALIZATION.
IT'S SAVING AMMO, DILL THINKS... KILLING ONLY THOSE WHO ARE ARMED. .
C890.L. INTERNAL PROGRAMMING.
WARNING: AMMUNITION DEPLETED.
INITIATIVE: AMMUNITION CONSERVATION.
>CHANNEL OFFENSIVE SOLELY TO ARMED/ HOSTILE ANTAGONISTS.
TARGET PASSIVE. ELIMINATION FUTILE.
TARGET ARMED/ HOSTILE. ELIMINATE.

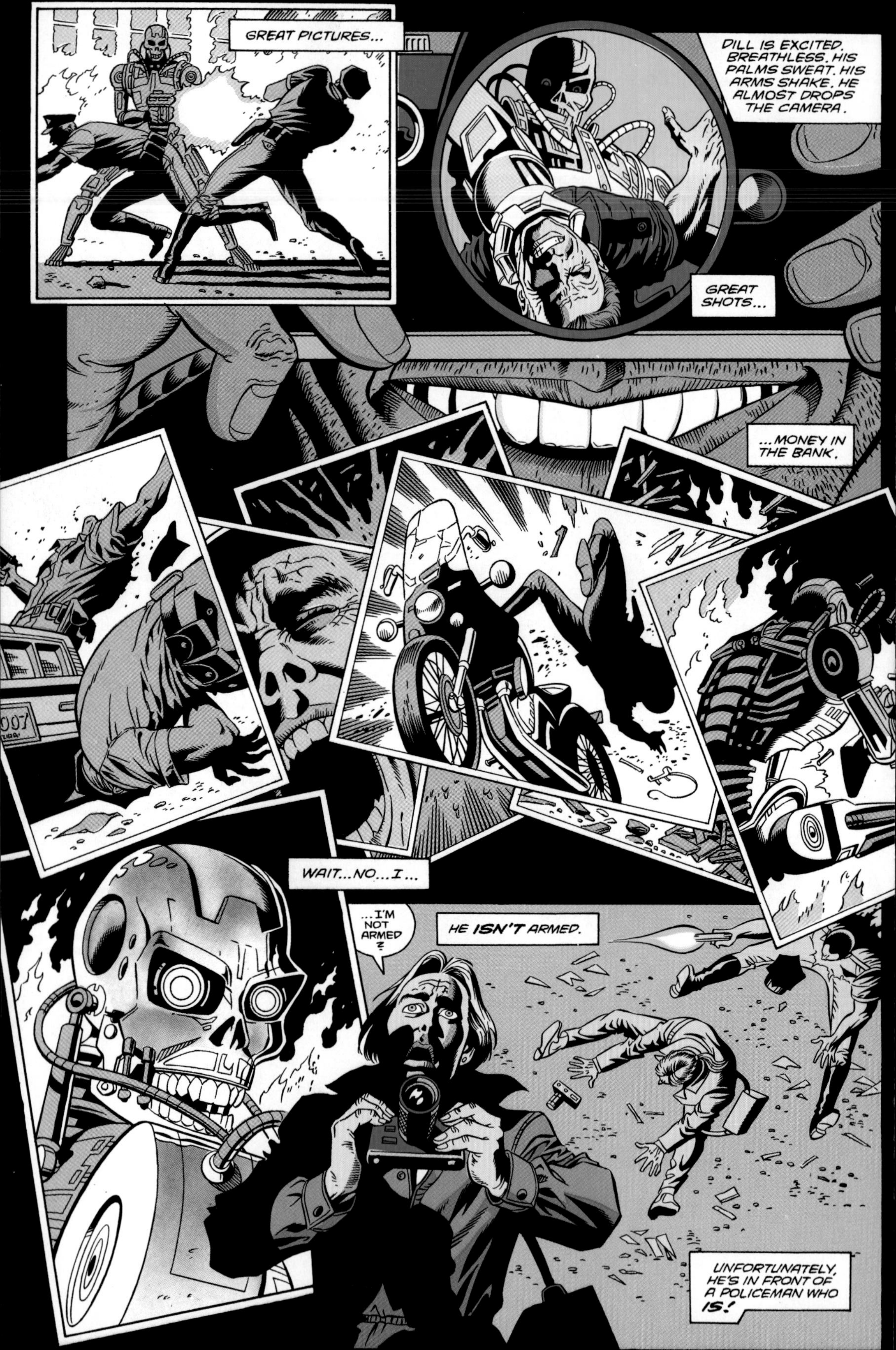

GREAT PICTURES...
DILL IS EXCITED. BREATHLESS. HIS PALMS SWEAT. HIS ARMS SHAKE. HE ALMOST DROPS THE CAMERA.
GREAT SHOTS...
...MONEY IN THE BANK.
WAIT...NO...I...
...I'M NOT ARMED
HE ISN'T ARMED.
UNFORTUNATELY, HE'S IN FRONT OF A POLICEMAN WHO IS!

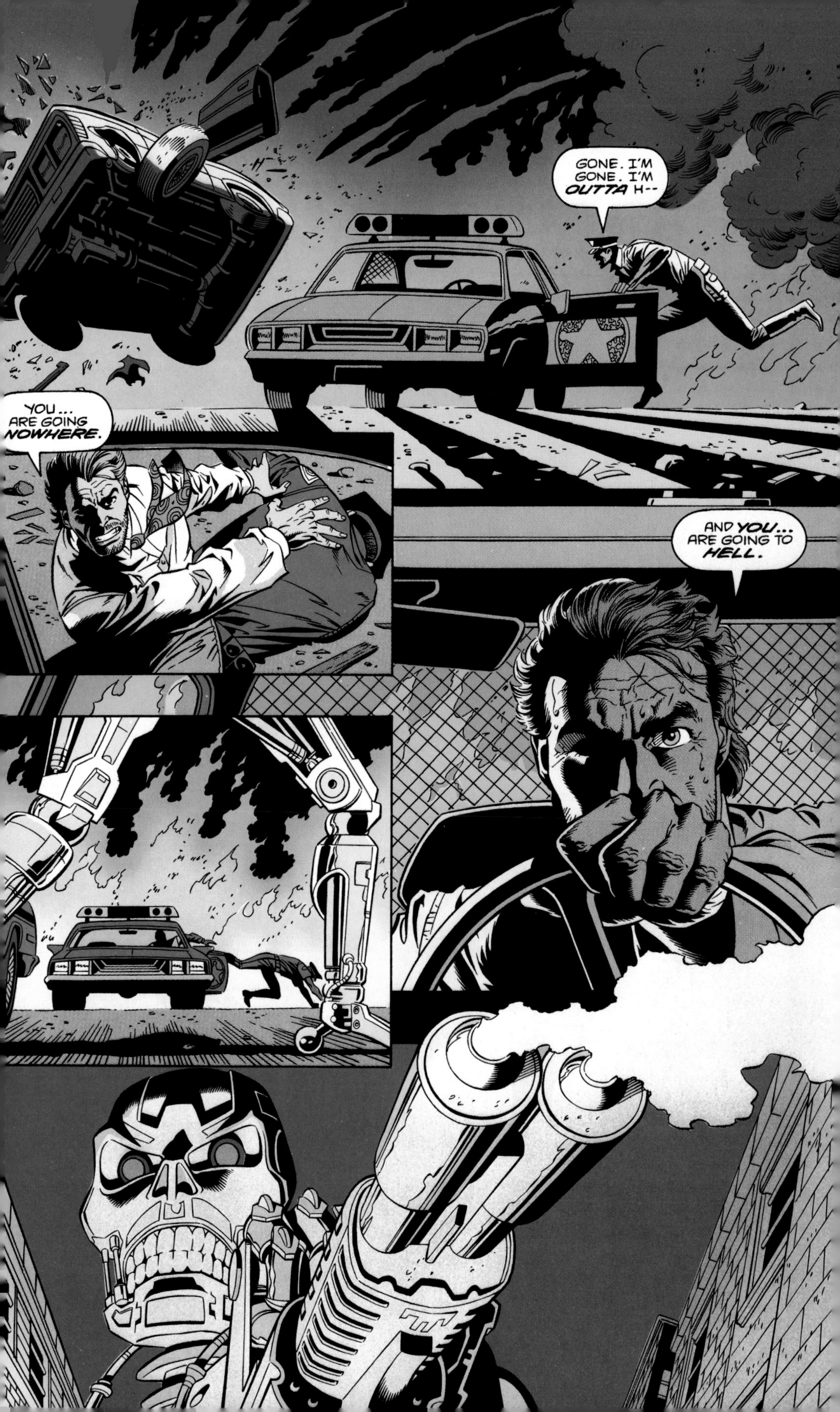
GONE. I'M GONE. I'M OUTTA H--
YOU... ARE GOING NOWHERE.
AND YOU... ARE GOING TO HELL.

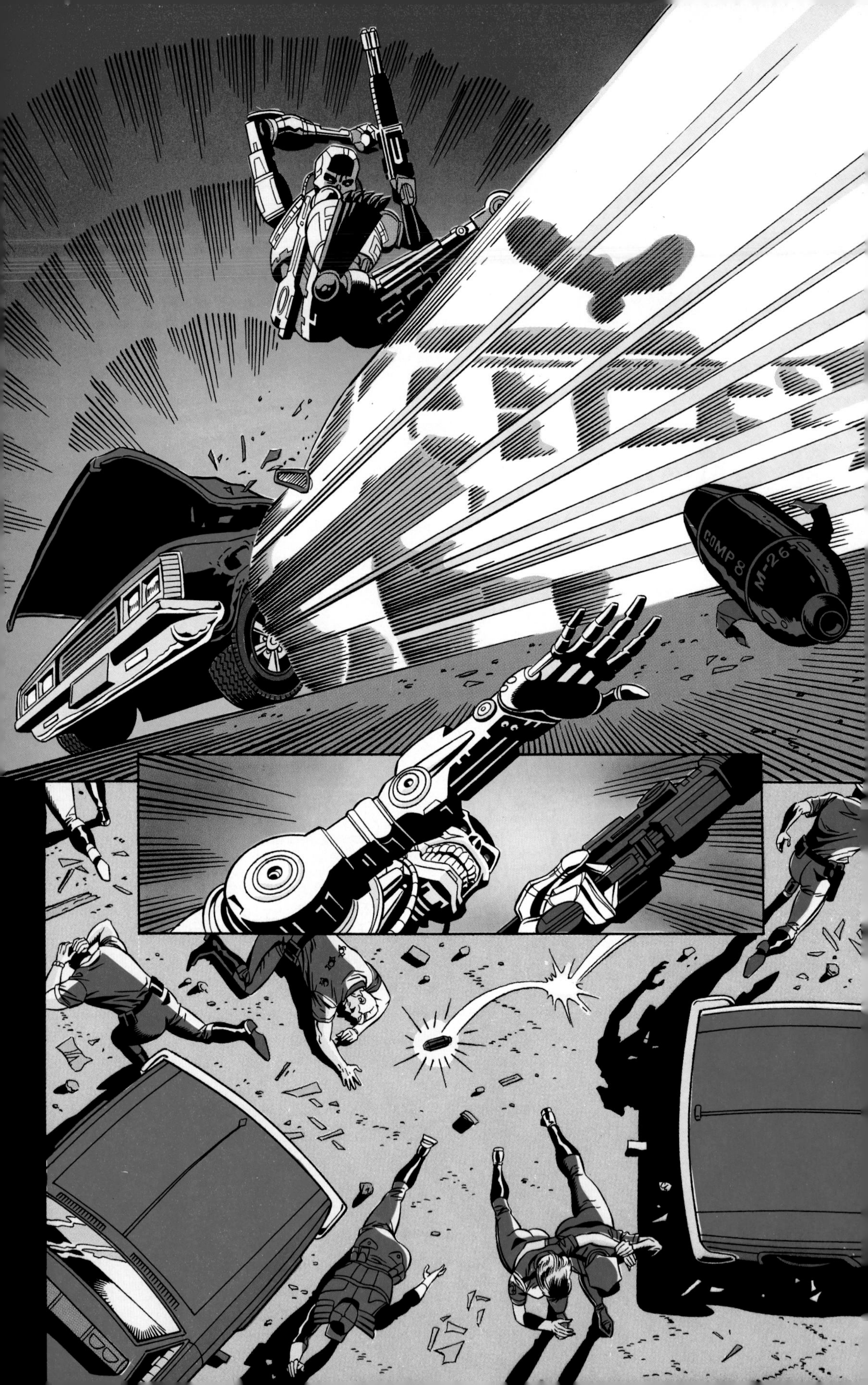
COMP 8
M-26-

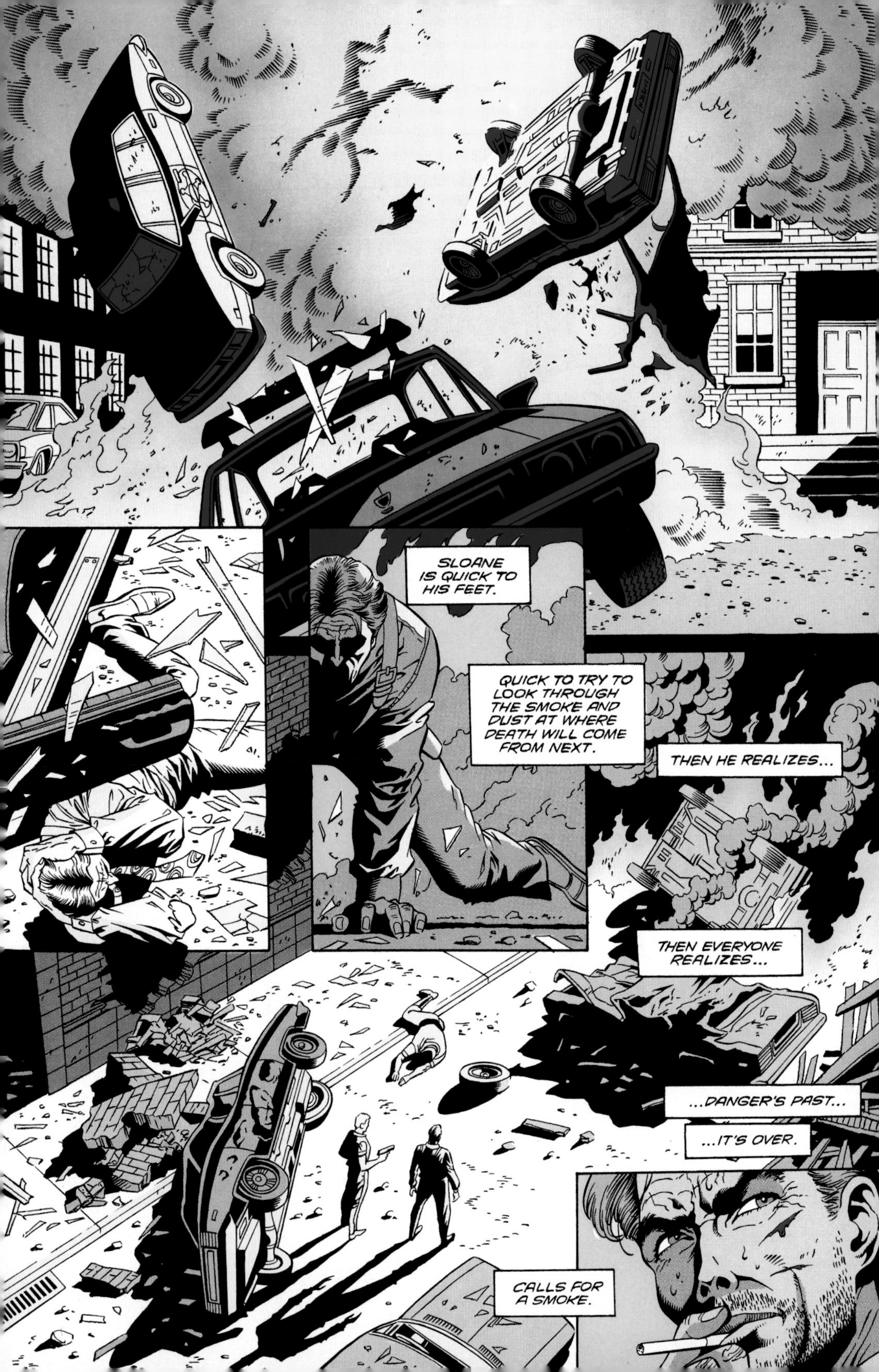
SLOANE IS QUICK TO HIS FEET.
QUICK TO TRY TO LOOK THROUGH THE SMOKE AND DUST AT WHERE DEATH WILL COME FROM NEXT.
THEN HE REALIZES...
THEN EVERYONE REALIZES...
...DANGER'S PAST...
...IT'S OVER.
CALLS FOR A SMOKE.

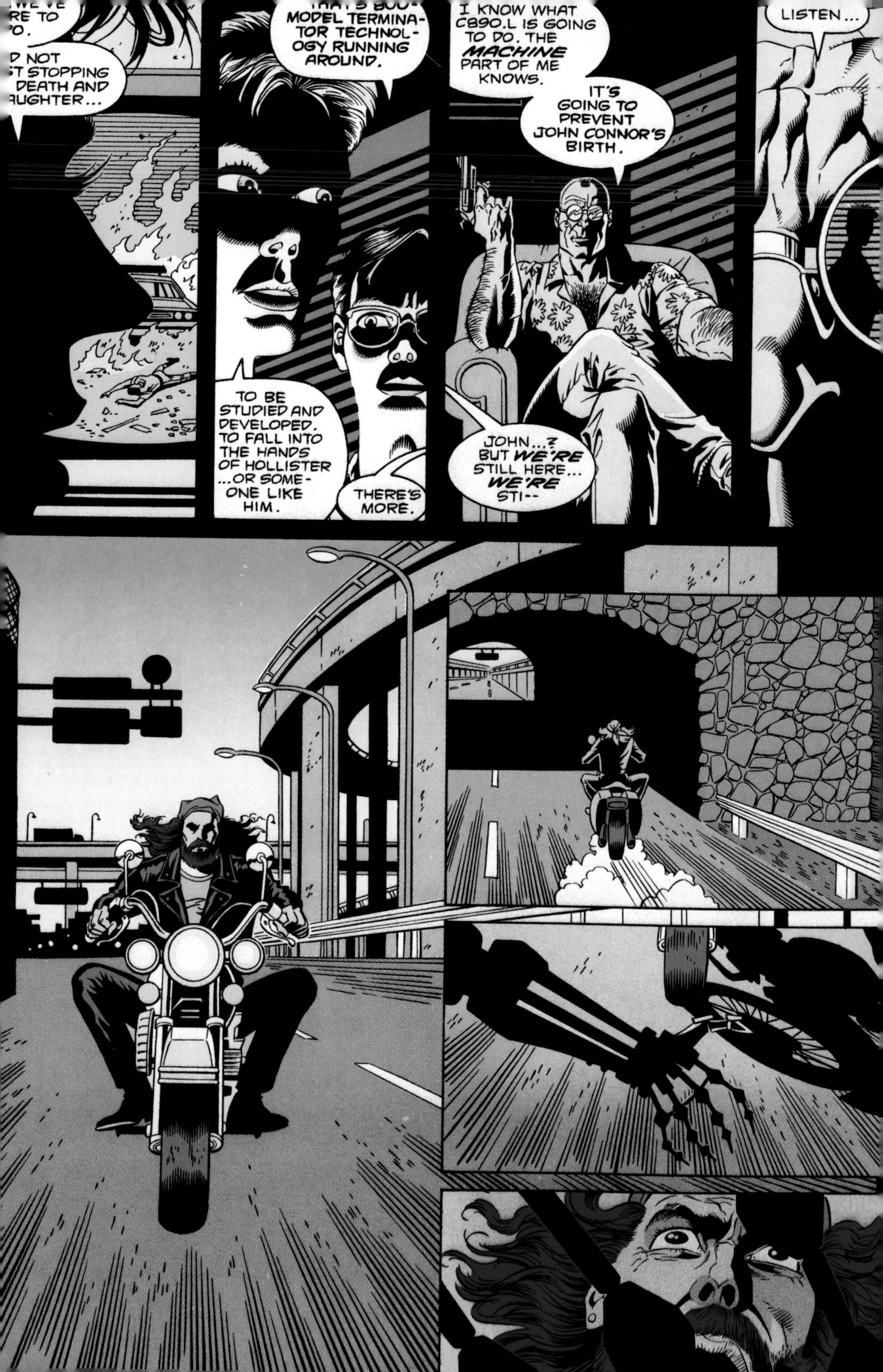

RE TO
D NOT
ST STOPPING
DEATH AND
AUGHTER...
MODEL TERMINATOR TECHNOLOGY RUNNING AROUND.
TO BE STUDIED AND DEVELOPED. TO FALL INTO THE HANDS OF HOLLISTER ...OR SOMEONE LIKE HIM.
THERE'S MORE.
I KNOW WHAT C890.L IS GOING TO DO. THE MACHINE PART OF ME KNOWS.
IT'S GOING TO PREVENT JOHN CONNOR'S BIRTH.
JOHN...? BUT WE'RE STILL HERE... WE'RE STI--
LISTEN...

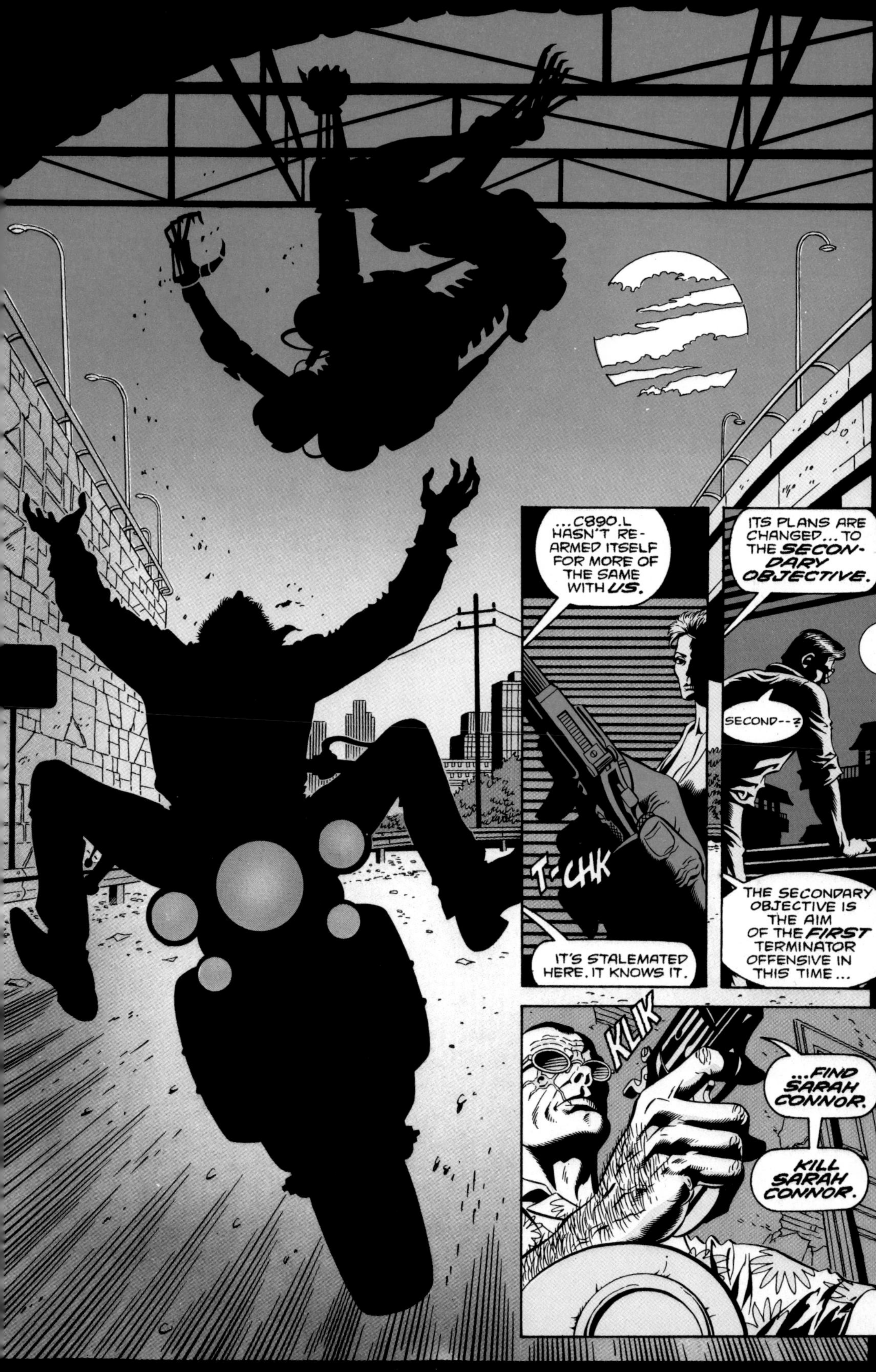

...C890.L HASN'T RE-ARMED ITSELF FOR MORE OF THE SAME WITH US.
T-CHK
IT'S STALEMATED HERE. IT KNOWS IT.
ITS PLANS ARE CHANGED... TO THE SECONDARY OBJECTIVE.
SECOND--?
THE SECONDARY OBJECTIVE IS THE AIM OF THE FIRST TERMINATOR OFFENSIVE IN THIS TIME...
KLIK
...FIND SARAH CONNOR.
KILL SARAH CONNOR.

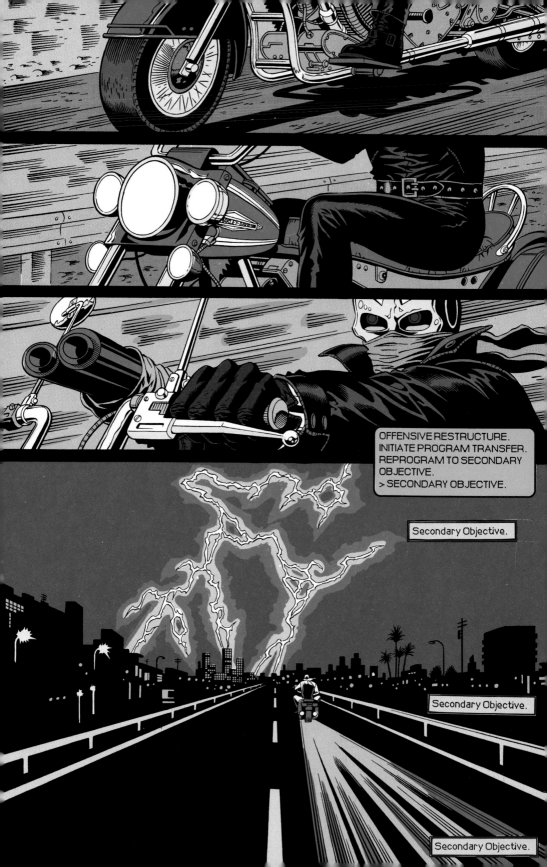

OFFENSIVE RESTRUCTURE.
INITIATE PROGRAM TRANSFER.
REPROGRAM TO SECONDARY
OBJECTIVE.
> SECONDARY OBJECTIVE.

Secondary Objective.

Secondary Objective.

Secondary Objective.

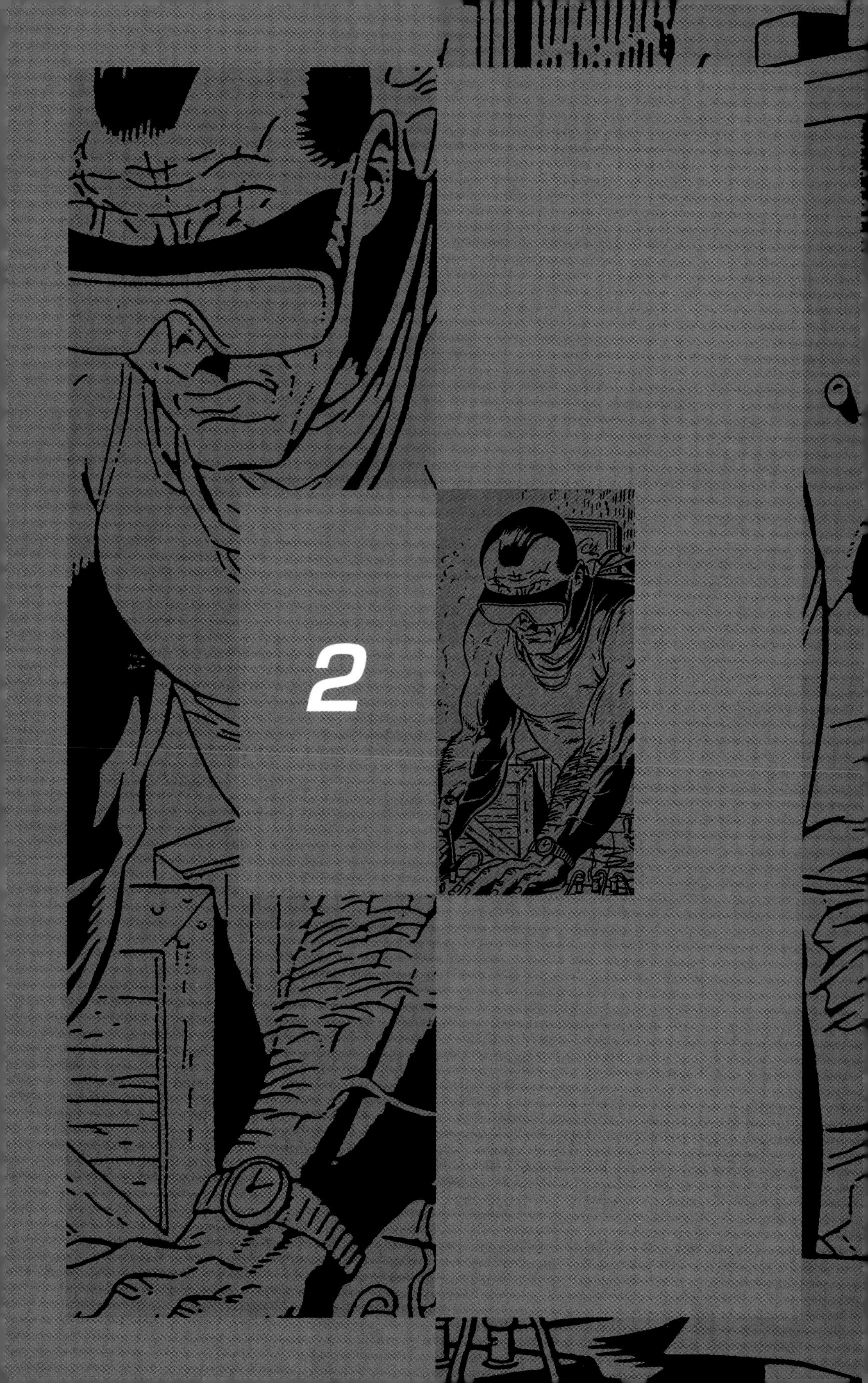

2

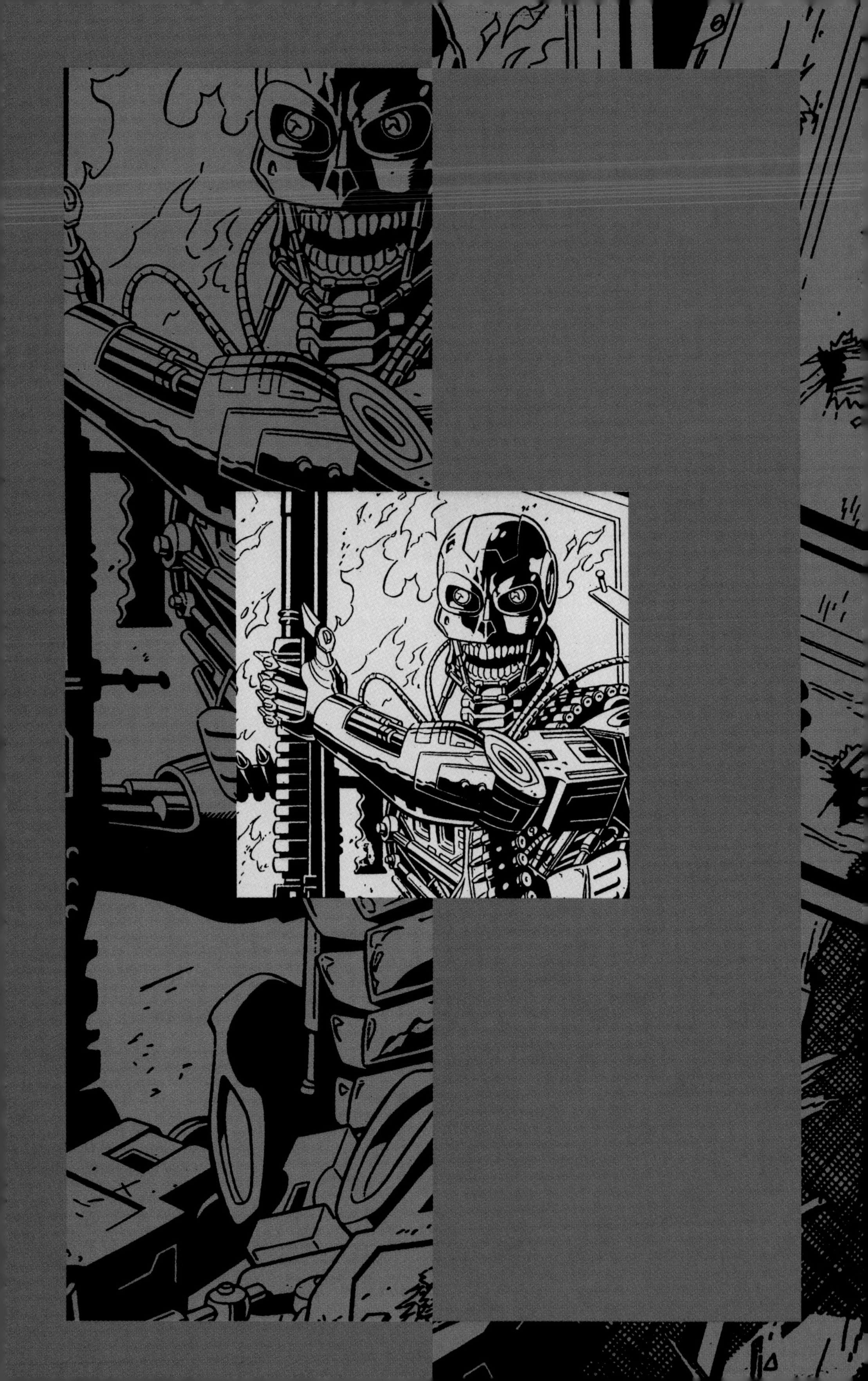

MONDAY.

A DAY FOR PUTTING ASIDE THE GOOD TIMES-- RETURNING TO THE RUSH-HOUR CRUSH OF THE FREEWAY.

TO THE DESKS AND COUNTERS OF WORK--TO JOYLESS TIMES.

BUT NOT FOR *LINDA PAUL*. SHE LOVES MONDAYS.

SHE'S A HAIR STYLIST, AND THE HAIR STYLIST'S WEEK IS FROM TUESDAY TO SATURDAY.

MONDAY IS TO RELAX, AND GLOAT AT A WORLD BECOMING WOUND TIGHT AGAIN.

ALMOST HABITUALLY LINDA VISITS THE BEACHES OF SANTA MONICA. SHE'S FOUND A FAVORITE SPOT, AWAY FROM THE PIER. EVEN ON BUSY DAYS IT'S SECLUDED. ON *MONDAY* IT'S ALL BUT DESERTED.

"HER OWN *PRIVATE* BEACH," OR SO LINDA LIKES TO THINK OF IT.

HER BOYFRIEND KNOWS THIS... AND USES IT TO HIS ADVANTAGE.

COME ON, HONEY. THERE'S NO ONE AROUND.

DWAYNE'S A ROCK GOD. WITHOUT MUSICAL ABILITY, WITHOUT A RECORD DEAL.

NO! THINK WITH YOUR *HEAD* FOR ONCE.

BUT WE DID IT HERE BEFORE.

AND *ONE* OF US ENJOYED HIMSELF.

I WAS TOO SCARED SOMEONE WOULD...

LINDA... *BABY...*

Ah... ohh...

YOU SEE...

...IT'S *GOOD.*

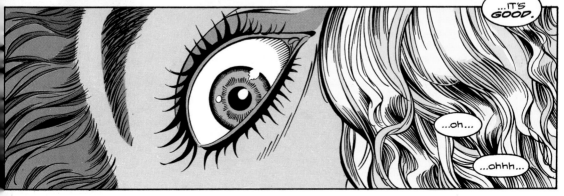

...oh...

...ohhh...

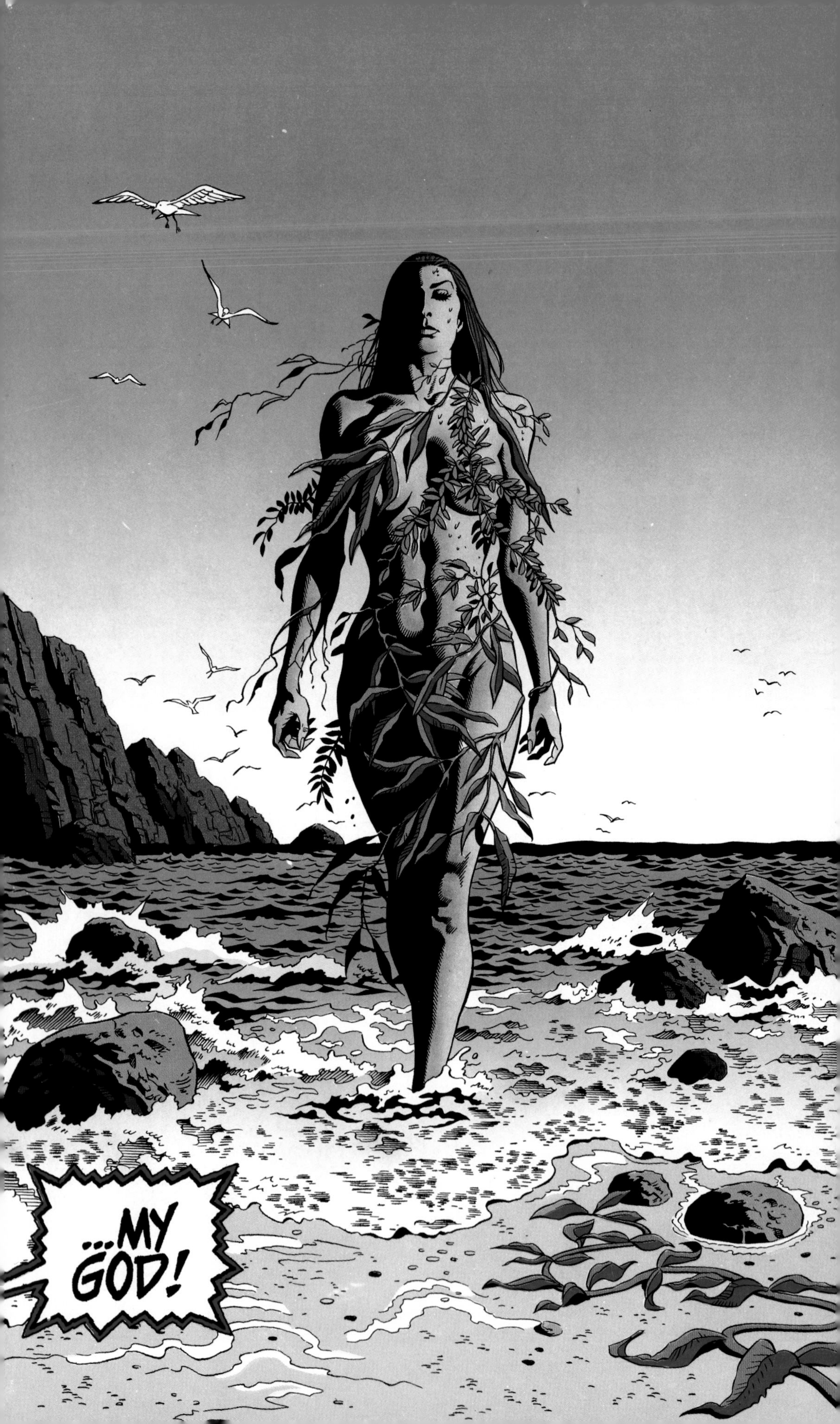
...MY GOD!

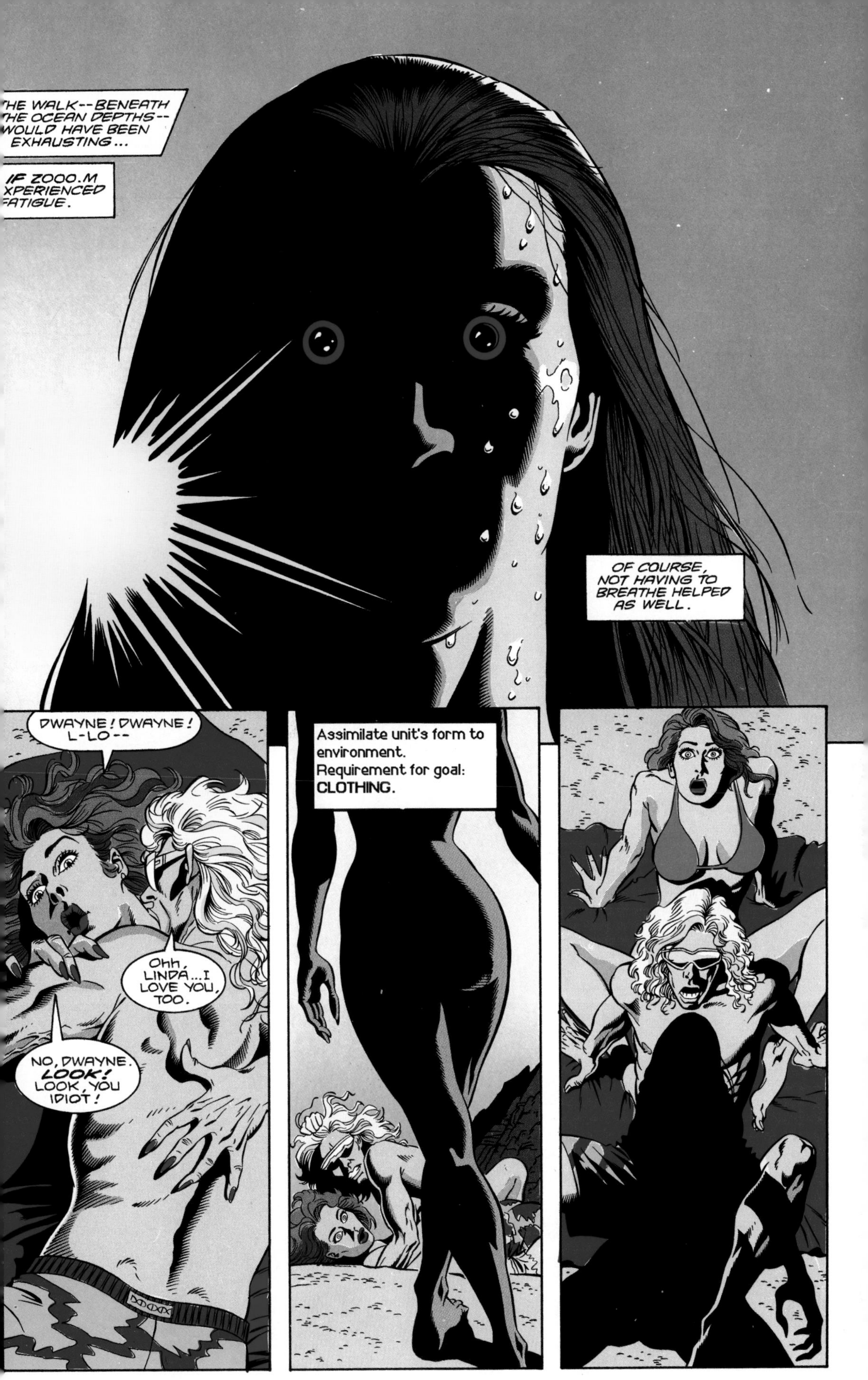
THE WALK--BENEATH THE OCEAN DEPTHS--WOULD HAVE BEEN EXHAUSTING...
IF ZOOO.M XPERIENCED FATIGUE.
OF COURSE, NOT HAVING TO BREATHE HELPED AS WELL.
DWAYNE! DWAYNE! L-LO--
Ohh, LINDA...I LOVE YOU, TOO.
NO, DWAYNE. LOOK! LOOK, YOU IDIOT!
Assimilate unit's form to environment.
Requirement for goal:
CLOTHING.

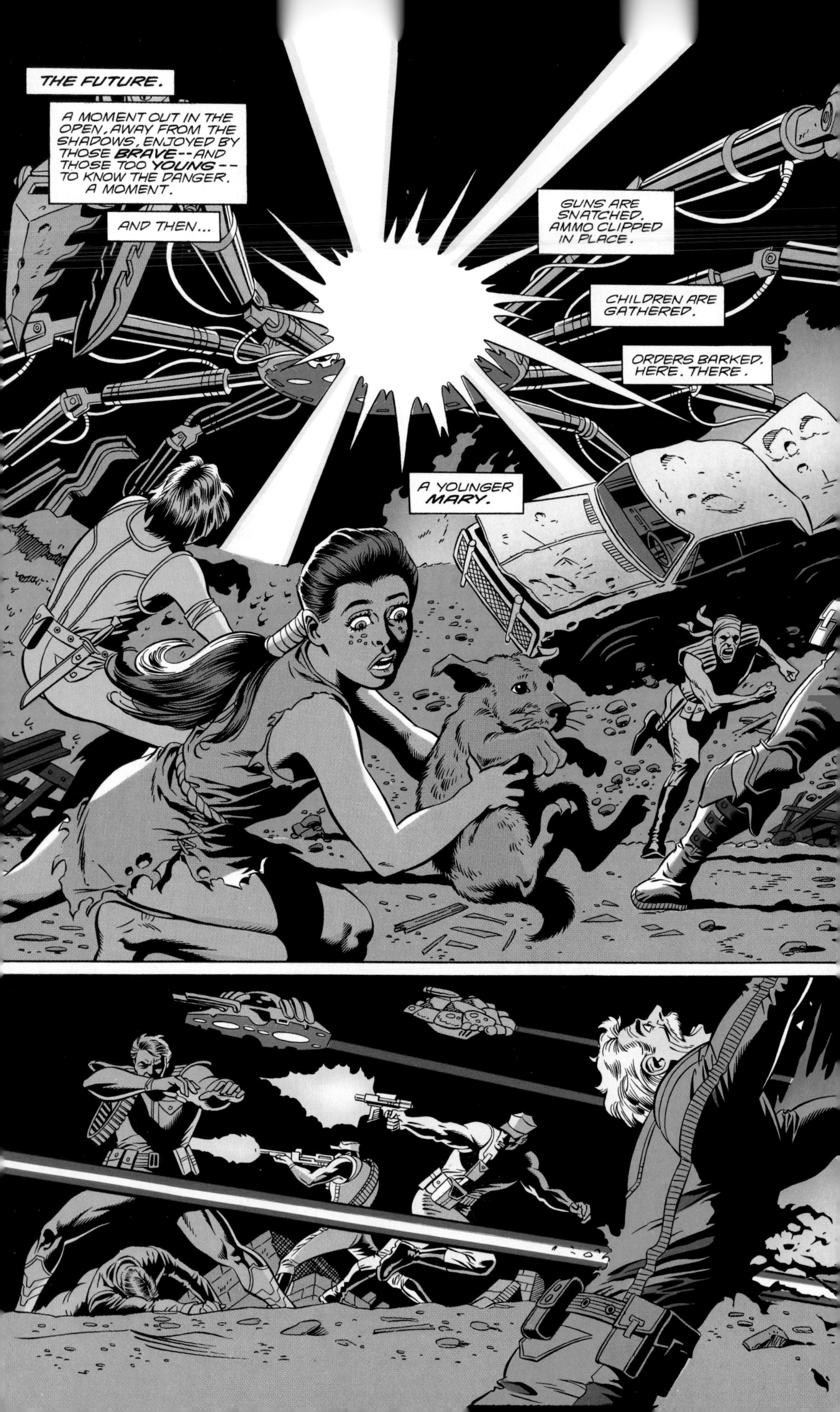

THE FUTURE.
A MOMENT OUT IN THE OPEN, AWAY FROM THE SHADOWS, ENJOYED BY THOSE BRAVE--AND THOSE TOO YOUNG--TO KNOW THE DANGER. A MOMENT.
AND THEN...
GUNS ARE SNATCHED. AMMO CLIPPED IN PLACE.
CHILDREN ARE GATHERED.
ORDERS BARKED. HERE. THERE.
A YOUNGER MARY.

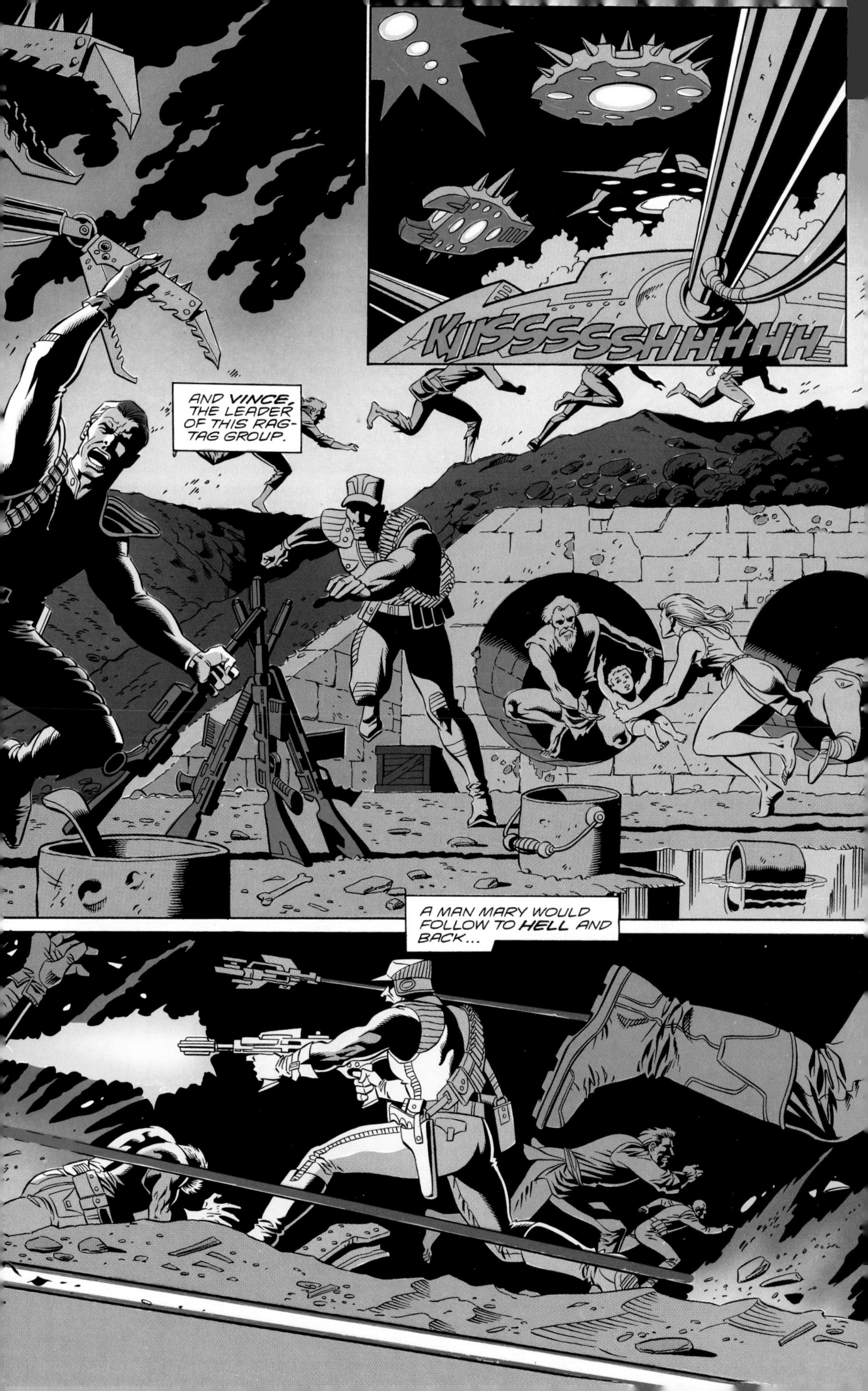
KKISSSSSSHHHHHH
AND VINCE, THE LEADER OF THIS RAG-TAG GROUP.
A MAN MARY WOULD FOLLOW TO HELL AND BACK...

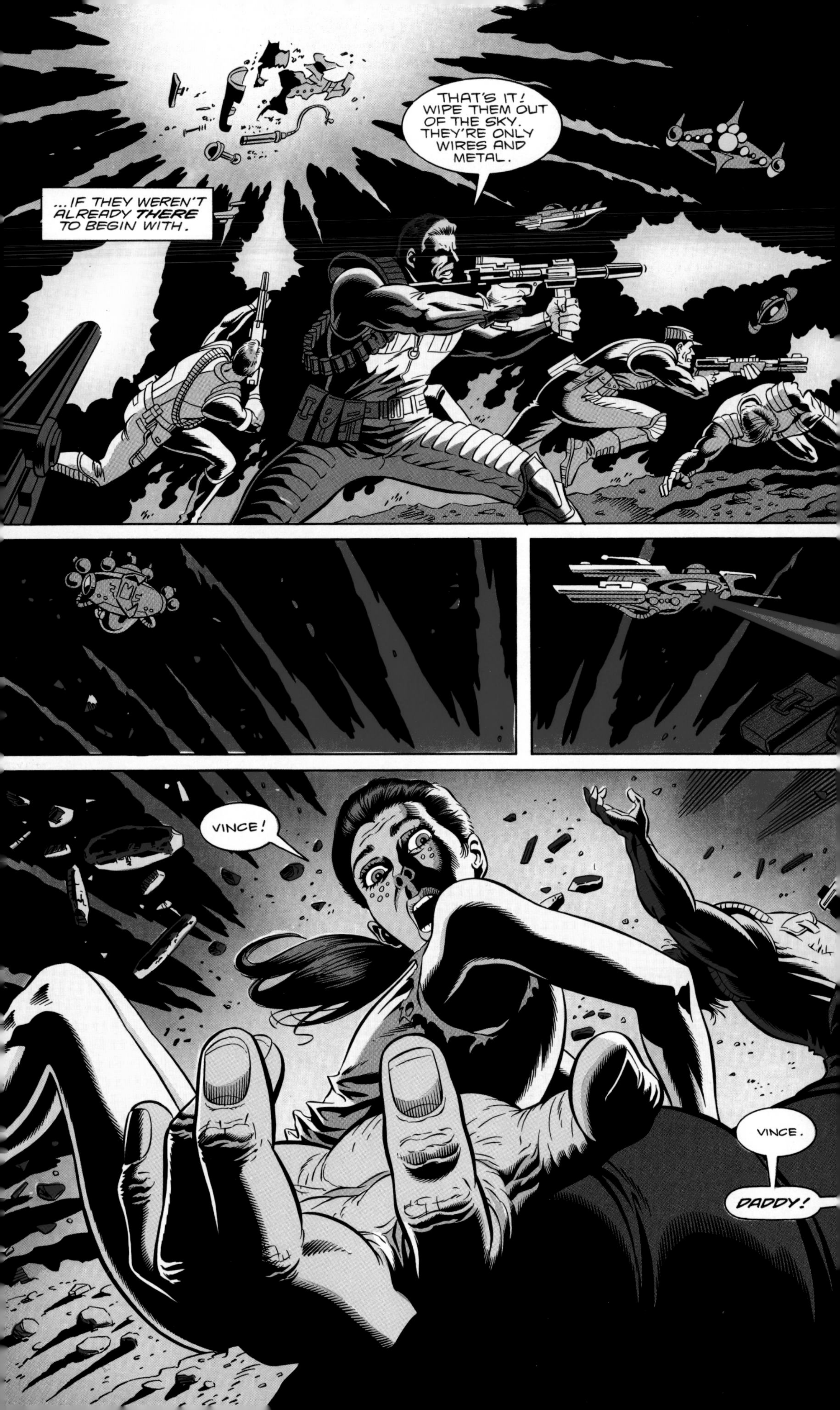
...IF THEY WEREN'T ALREADY THERE TO BEGIN WITH.
THAT'S IT! WIPE THEM OUT OF THE SKY. THEY'RE ONLY WIRES AND METAL.
VINCE!
VINCE.
DADDY!

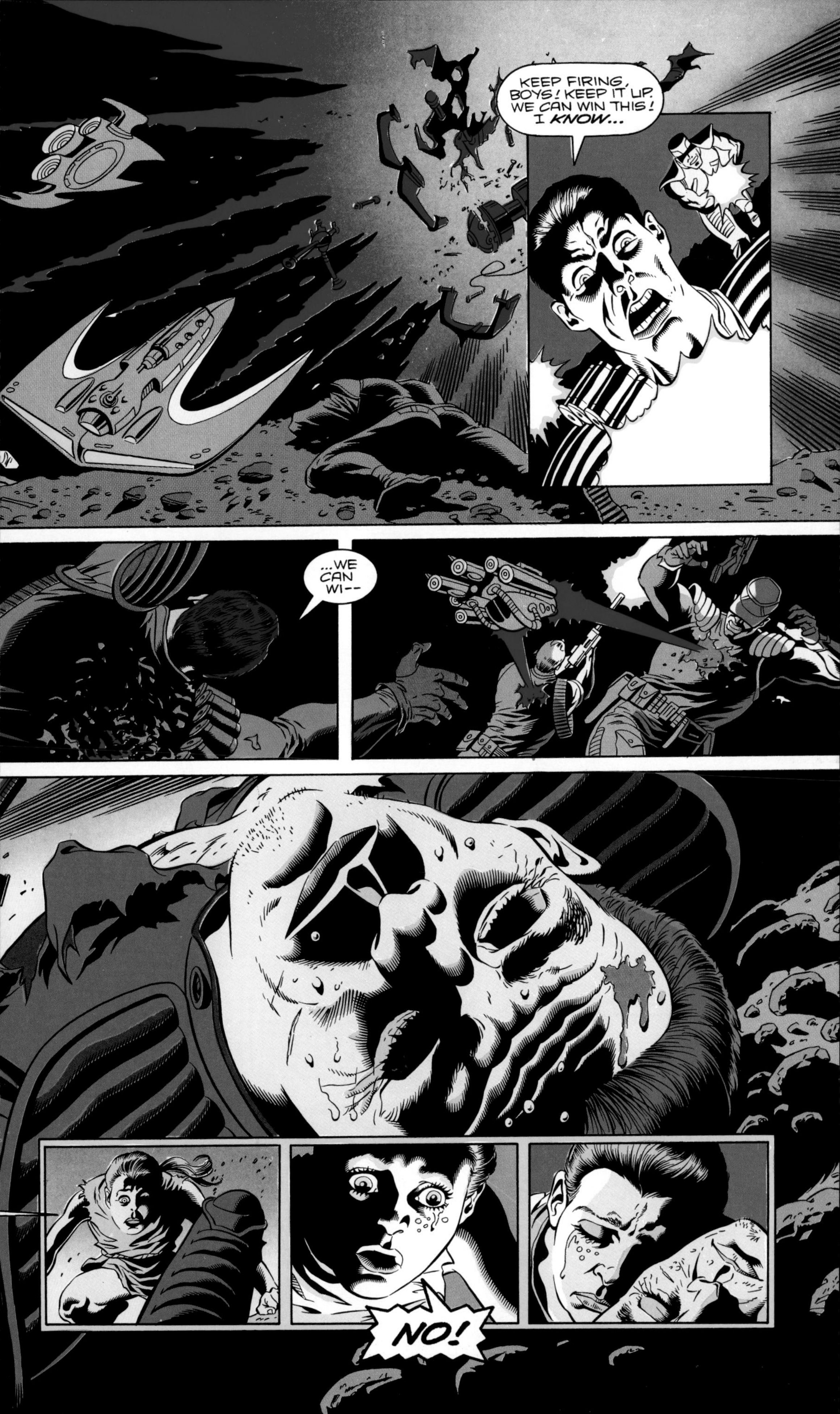
KEEP FIRING, BOYS! KEEP IT UP. WE CAN WIN THIS! I KNOW...
...WE CAN WI--
NO!

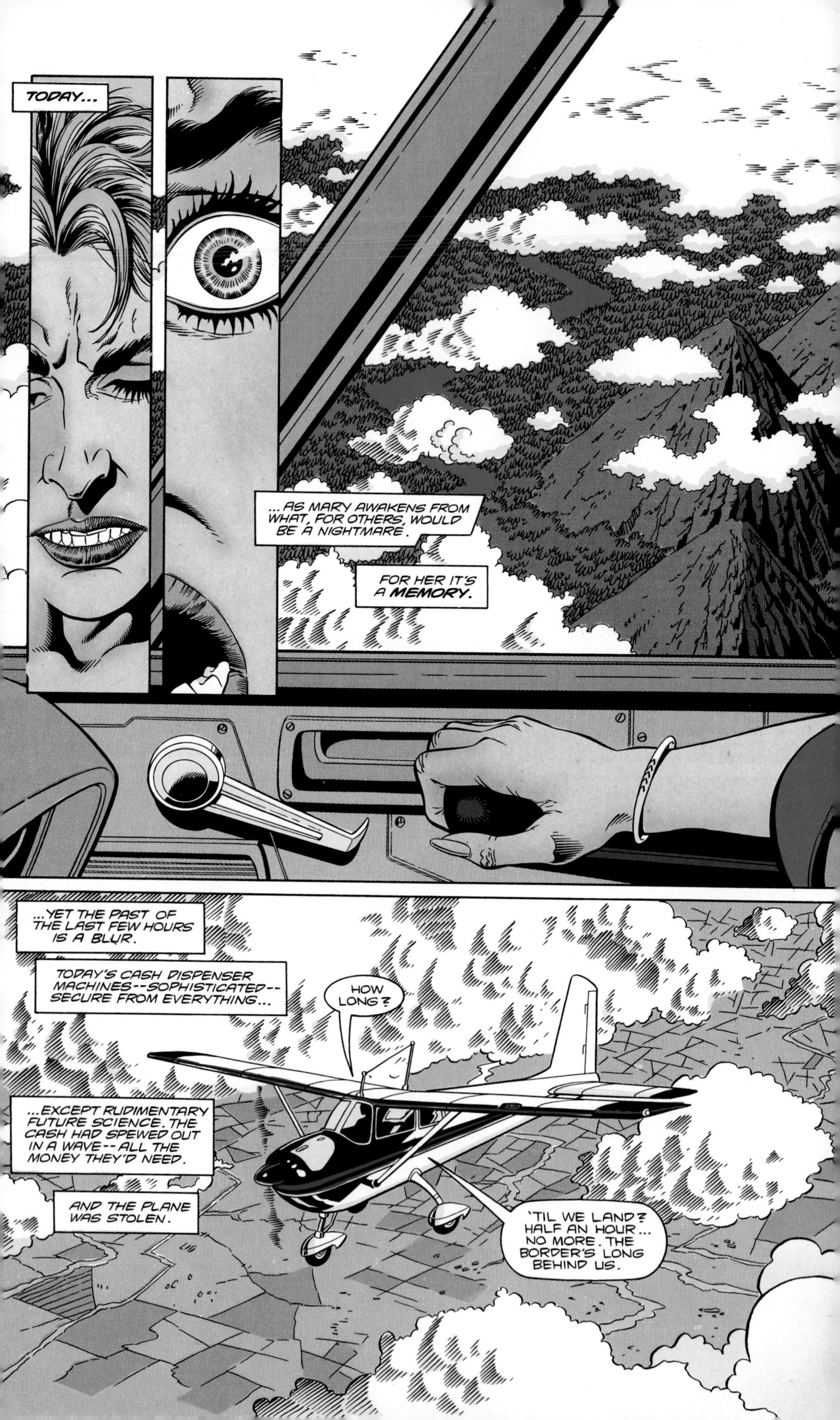
TODAY...
...AS MARY AWAKENS FROM WHAT, FOR OTHERS, WOULD BE A NIGHTMARE.
FOR HER IT'S A **MEMORY**.
...YET THE PAST OF THE LAST FEW HOURS IS A BLUR.
TODAY'S CASH DISPENSER MACHINES--SOPHISTICATED--SECURE FROM EVERYTHING...
HOW LONG?
...EXCEPT RUDIMENTARY FUTURE SCIENCE. THE CASH HAD SPEWED OUT IN A WAVE--ALL THE MONEY THEY'D NEED.
AND THE PLANE WAS STOLEN.
'TIL WE LAND? HALF AN HOUR... NO MORE. THE BORDER'S LONG BEHIND US.

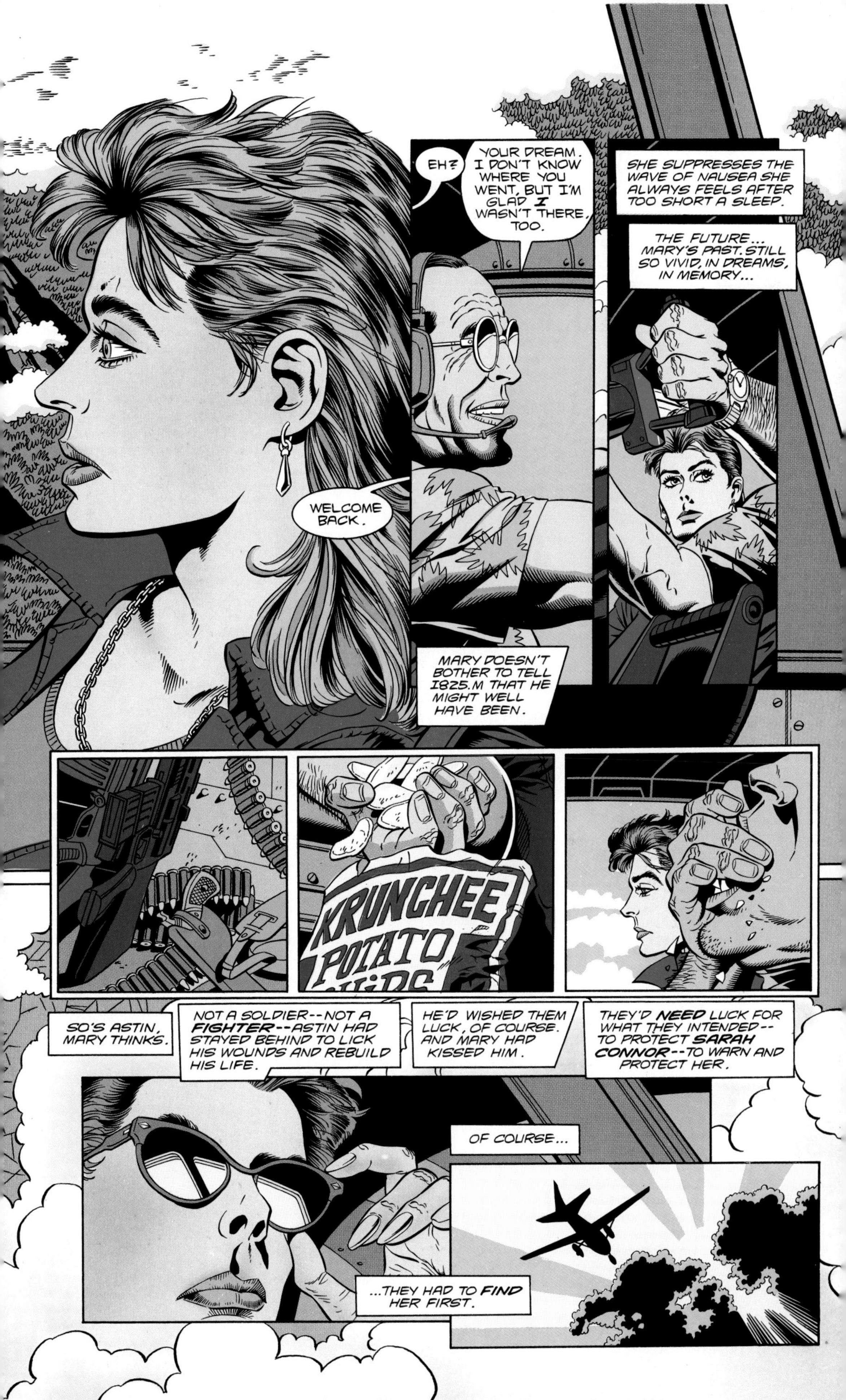

WELCOME BACK.
EH?
YOUR DREAM. I DON'T KNOW WHERE YOU WENT, BUT I'M GLAD I WASN'T THERE, TOO.
MARY DOESN'T BOTHER TO TELL I825.M THAT HE MIGHT WELL HAVE BEEN.
SHE SUPPRESSES THE WAVE OF NAUSEA SHE ALWAYS FEELS AFTER TOO SHORT A SLEEP.
THE FUTURE... MARY'S PAST. STILL SO VIVID, IN DREAMS, IN MEMORY...
KRUNCHEE POTATO
SO'S ASTIN, MARY THINKS.
NOT A SOLDIER--NOT A FIGHTER--ASTIN HAD STAYED BEHIND TO LICK HIS WOUNDS AND REBUILD HIS LIFE.
HE'D WISHED THEM LUCK, OF COURSE. AND MARY HAD KISSED HIM.
THEY'D NEED LUCK FOR WHAT THEY INTENDED--TO PROTECT SARAH CONNOR--TO WARN AND PROTECT HER.
OF COURSE...
...THEY HAD TO FIND HER FIRST.

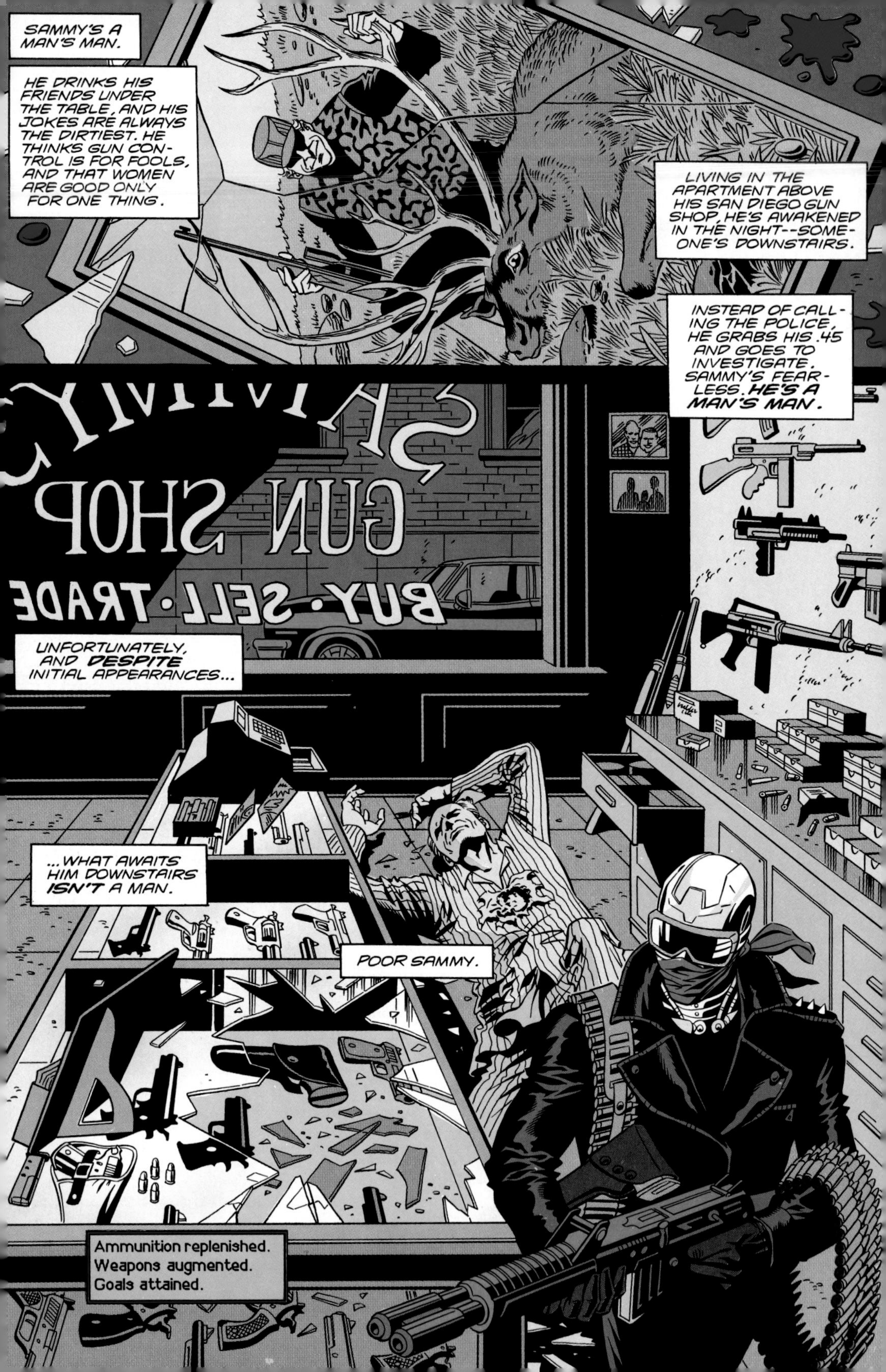
SAMMY'S A MAN'S MAN.
HE DRINKS HIS FRIENDS UNDER THE TABLE, AND HIS JOKES ARE ALWAYS THE DIRTIEST. HE THINKS GUN CONTROL IS FOR FOOLS, AND THAT WOMEN ARE GOOD ONLY FOR ONE THING.
LIVING IN THE APARTMENT ABOVE HIS SAN DIEGO GUN SHOP, HE'S AWAKENED IN THE NIGHT--SOMEONE'S DOWNSTAIRS.
INSTEAD OF CALLING THE POLICE, HE GRABS HIS .45 AND GOES TO INVESTIGATE. SAMMY'S FEARLESS. **HE'S A MAN'S MAN**.
SAMMY'S GUN SHOP
BUY · SELL · TRADE
UNFORTUNATELY, AND **DESPITE** INITIAL APPEARANCES...
...WHAT AWAITS HIM DOWNSTAIRS ***ISN'T*** A MAN.
POOR SAMMY.
Ammunition replenished.
Weapons augmented.
Goals attained.

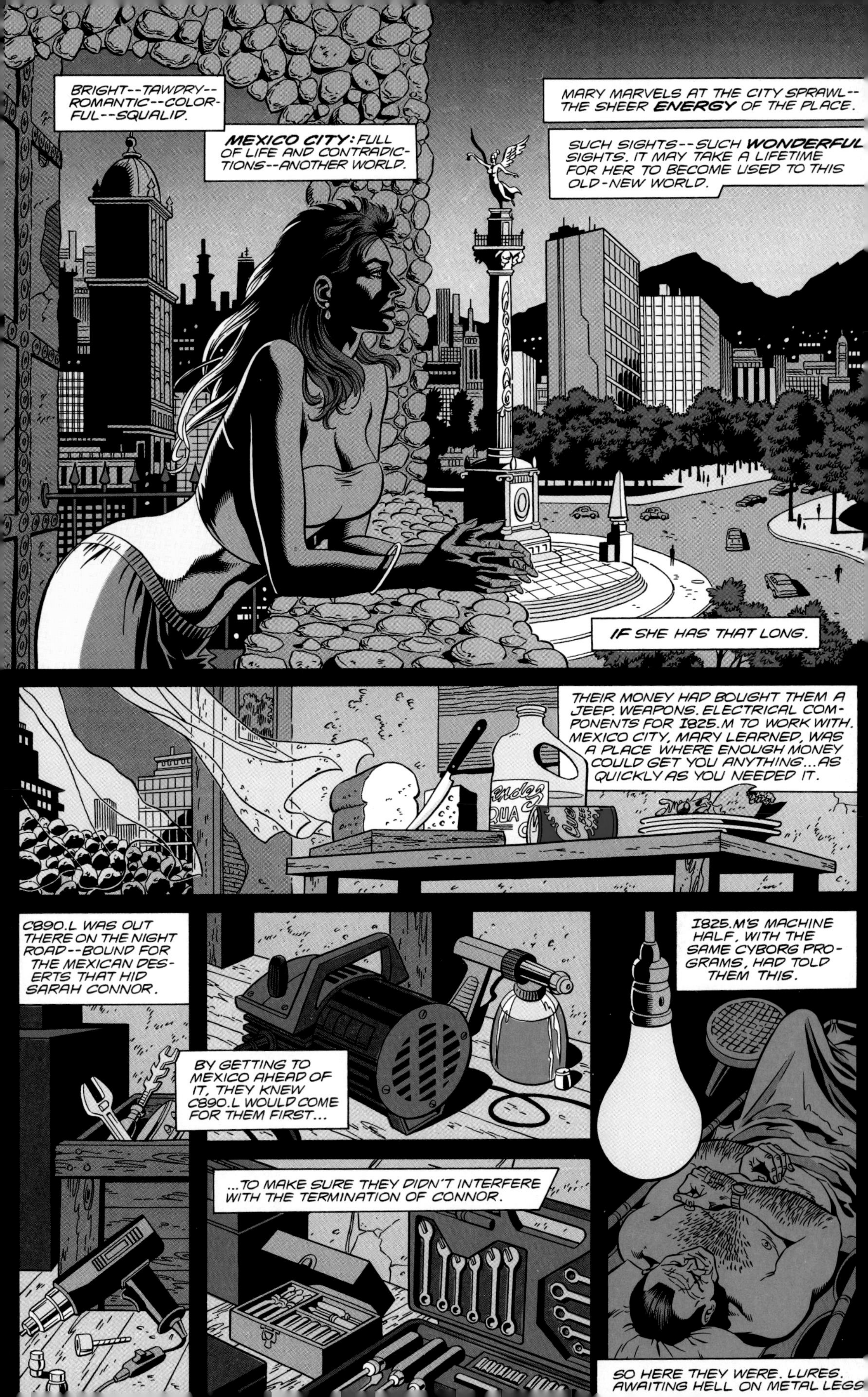

BRIGHT--TAWDRY--ROMANTIC--COLORFUL--SQUALID.
MEXICO CITY: FULL OF LIFE AND CONTRADICTIONS--ANOTHER WORLD.
MARY MARVELS AT THE CITY SPRAWL--THE SHEER ENERGY OF THE PLACE.
SUCH SIGHTS--SUCH WONDERFUL SIGHTS. IT MAY TAKE A LIFETIME FOR HER TO BECOME USED TO THIS OLD-NEW WORLD.
IF SHE HAS THAT LONG.
THEIR MONEY HAD BOUGHT THEM A JEEP. WEAPONS. ELECTRICAL COMPONENTS FOR I825.M TO WORK WITH. MEXICO CITY, MARY LEARNED, WAS A PLACE WHERE ENOUGH MONEY COULD GET YOU ANYTHING...AS QUICKLY AS YOU NEEDED IT.
C890.L WAS OUT THERE ON THE NIGHT ROAD--BOUND FOR THE MEXICAN DESERTS THAT HID SARAH CONNOR.
BY GETTING TO MEXICO AHEAD OF IT, THEY KNEW C890.L WOULD COME FOR THEM FIRST...
...TO MAKE SURE THEY DIDN'T INTERFERE WITH THE TERMINATION OF CONNOR.
I825.M'S MACHINE HALF, WITH THE SAME CYBORG PROGRAMS, HAD TOLD THEM THIS.
SO HERE THEY WERE. LURES. AWAITING HELL ON METAL LEGS.

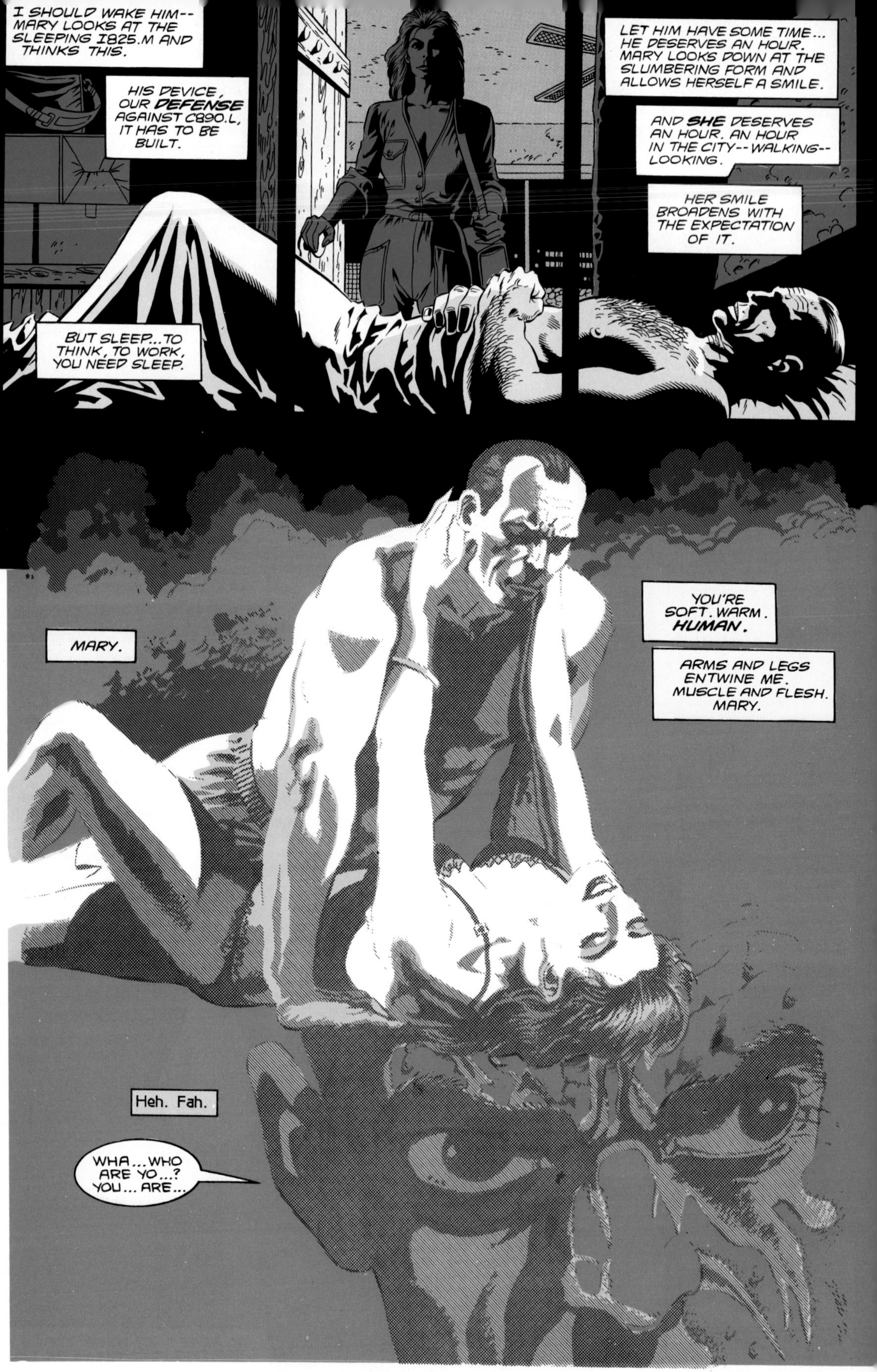
I SHOULD WAKE HIM-- MARY LOOKS AT THE SLEEPING I825.M AND THINKS THIS.
HIS DEVICE, OUR DEFENSE AGAINST C890.L, IT HAS TO BE BUILT.
LET HIM HAVE SOME TIME... HE DESERVES AN HOUR. MARY LOOKS DOWN AT THE SLUMBERING FORM AND ALLOWS HERSELF A SMILE.
AND SHE DESERVES AN HOUR. AN HOUR IN THE CITY--WALKING-- LOOKING.
HER SMILE BROADENS WITH THE EXPECTATION OF IT.
BUT SLEEP...TO THINK, TO WORK, YOU NEED SLEEP.
MARY.
YOU'RE SOFT. WARM. HUMAN.
ARMS AND LEGS ENTWINE ME. MUSCLE AND FLESH. MARY.
Heh. Fah.
WHA...WHO ARE YO...? YOU... ARE...

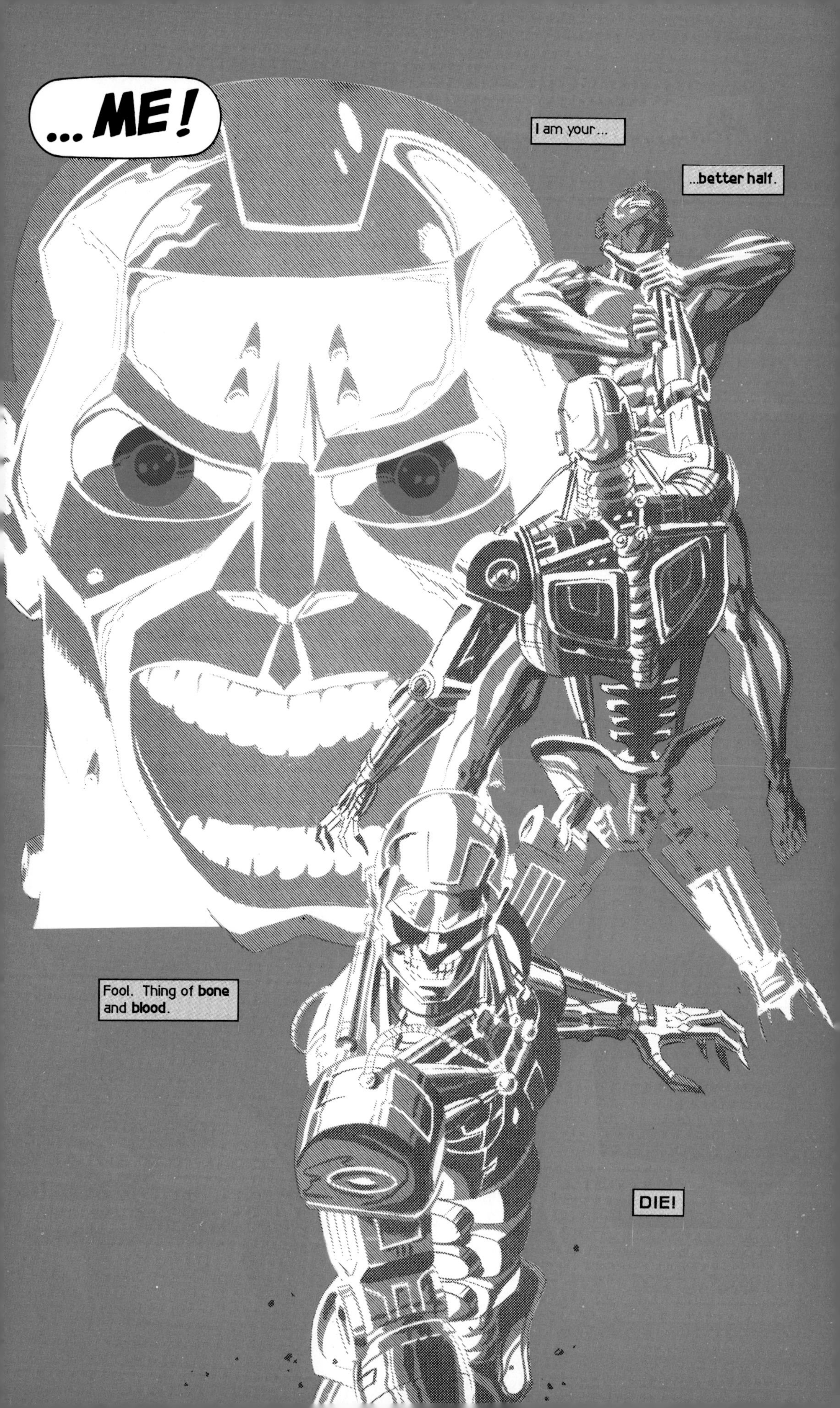
...ME!
I am your...
...better half.
Fool. Thing of bone and blood.
DIE!

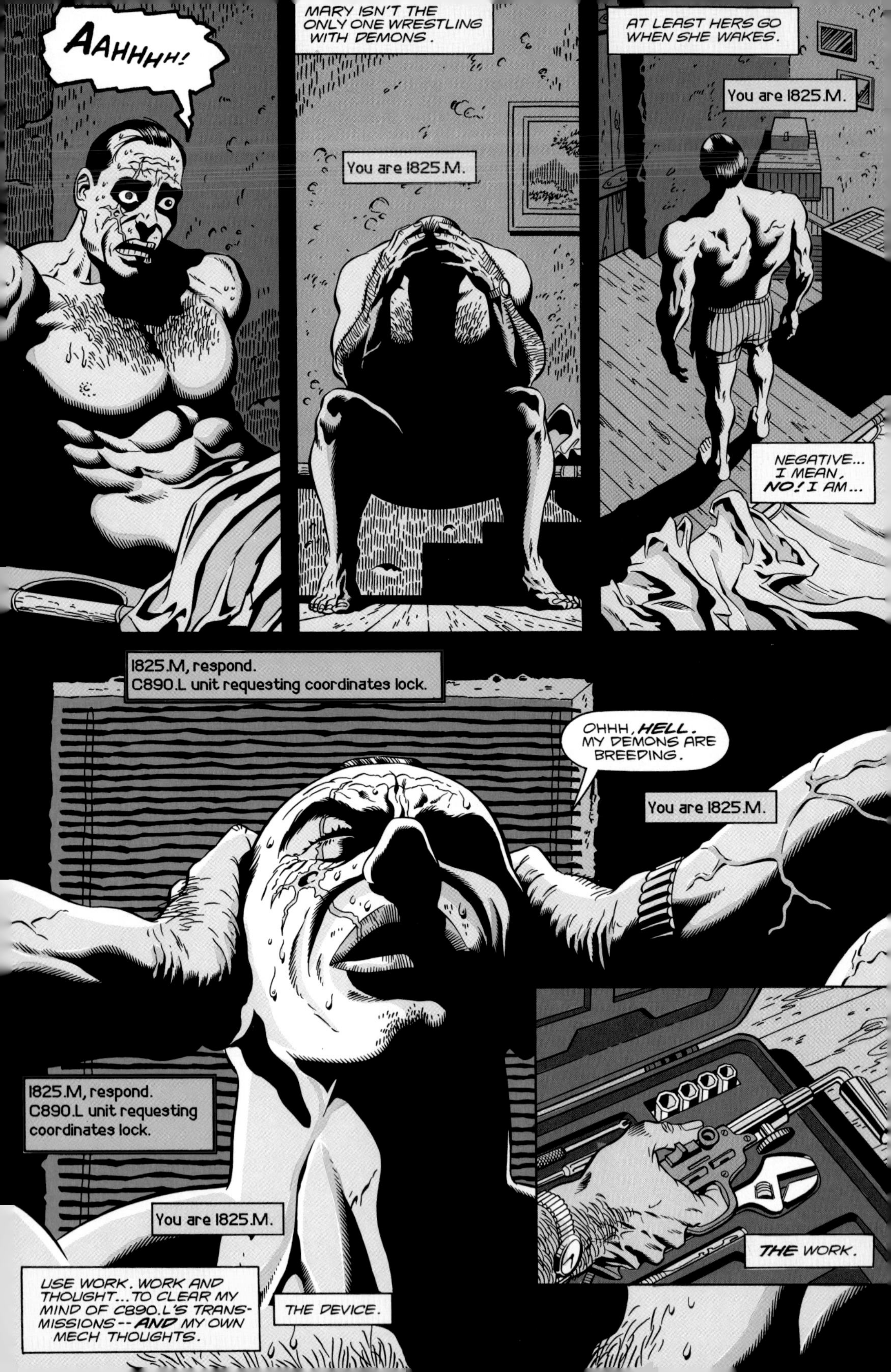
AAHHHH!
MARY ISN'T THE ONLY ONE WRESTLING WITH DEMONS.
You are 1825.M.
AT LEAST HERS GO WHEN SHE WAKES.
You are 1825.M.
NEGATIVE... I MEAN, NO! I AM...
1825.M, respond.
C890.L unit requesting coordinates lock.
OHHH, HELL. MY DEMONS ARE BREEDING.
You are 1825.M.
1825.M, respond.
C890.L unit requesting coordinates lock.
You are 1825.M.
USE WORK. WORK AND THOUGHT... TO CLEAR MY MIND OF C890.L'S TRANSMISSIONS-- AND MY OWN MECH THOUGHTS.
THE DEVICE.
THE WORK.

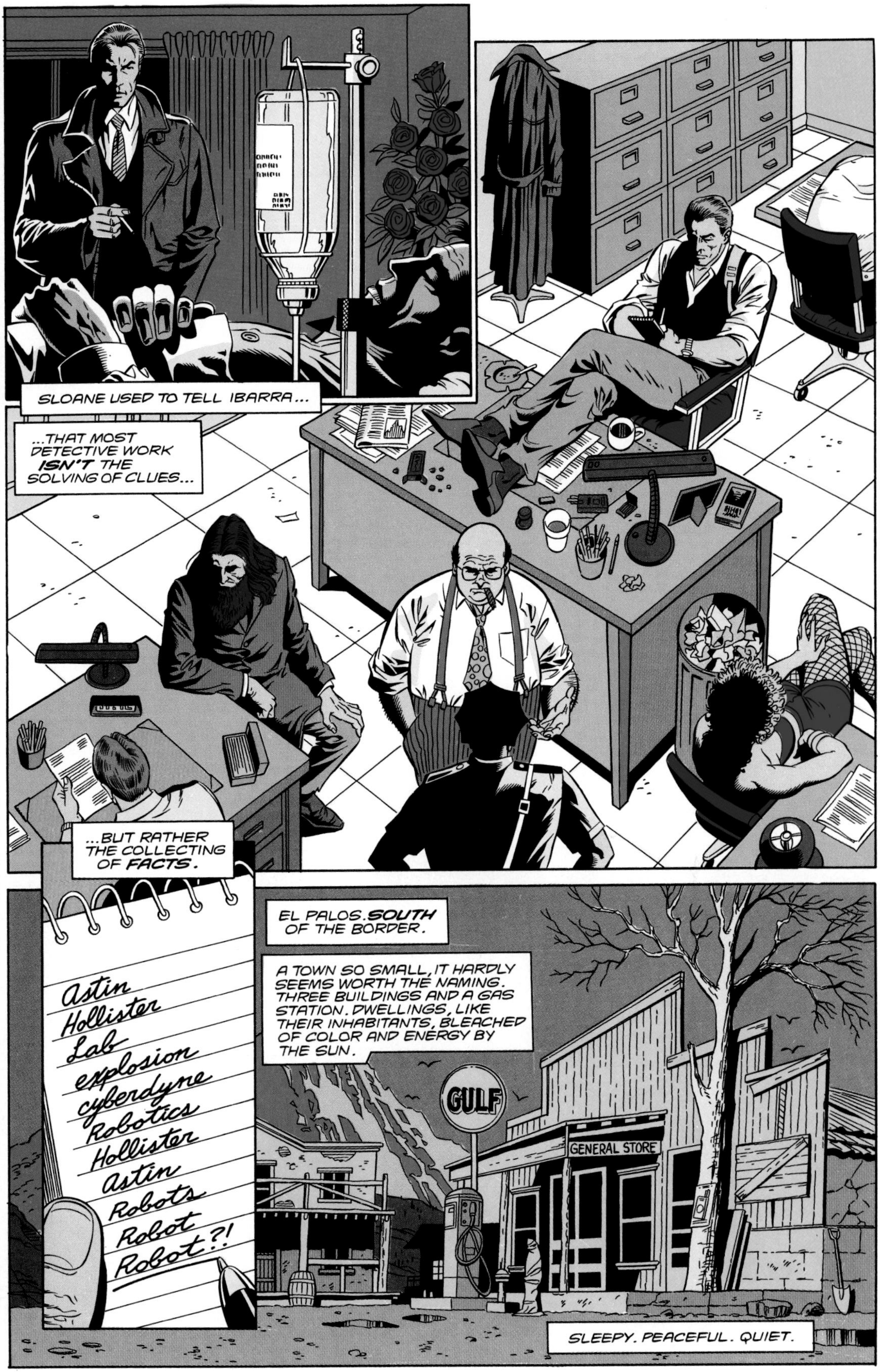
SLOANE USED TO TELL IBARRA...
...THAT MOST DETECTIVE WORK ISN'T THE SOLVING OF CLUES...
...BUT RATHER THE COLLECTING OF FACTS.
Astin
Hollister
Lab
explosion
cyberdyne
Robotics
Hollister
Astin
Robots
Robot
Robot?!
EL PALOS. SOUTH OF THE BORDER.
A TOWN SO SMALL, IT HARDLY SEEMS WORTH THE NAMING. THREE BUILDINGS AND A GAS STATION. DWELLINGS, LIKE THEIR INHABITANTS, BLEACHED OF COLOR AND ENERGY BY THE SUN.
GULF
GENERAL STORE
SLEEPY. PEACEFUL. QUIET.

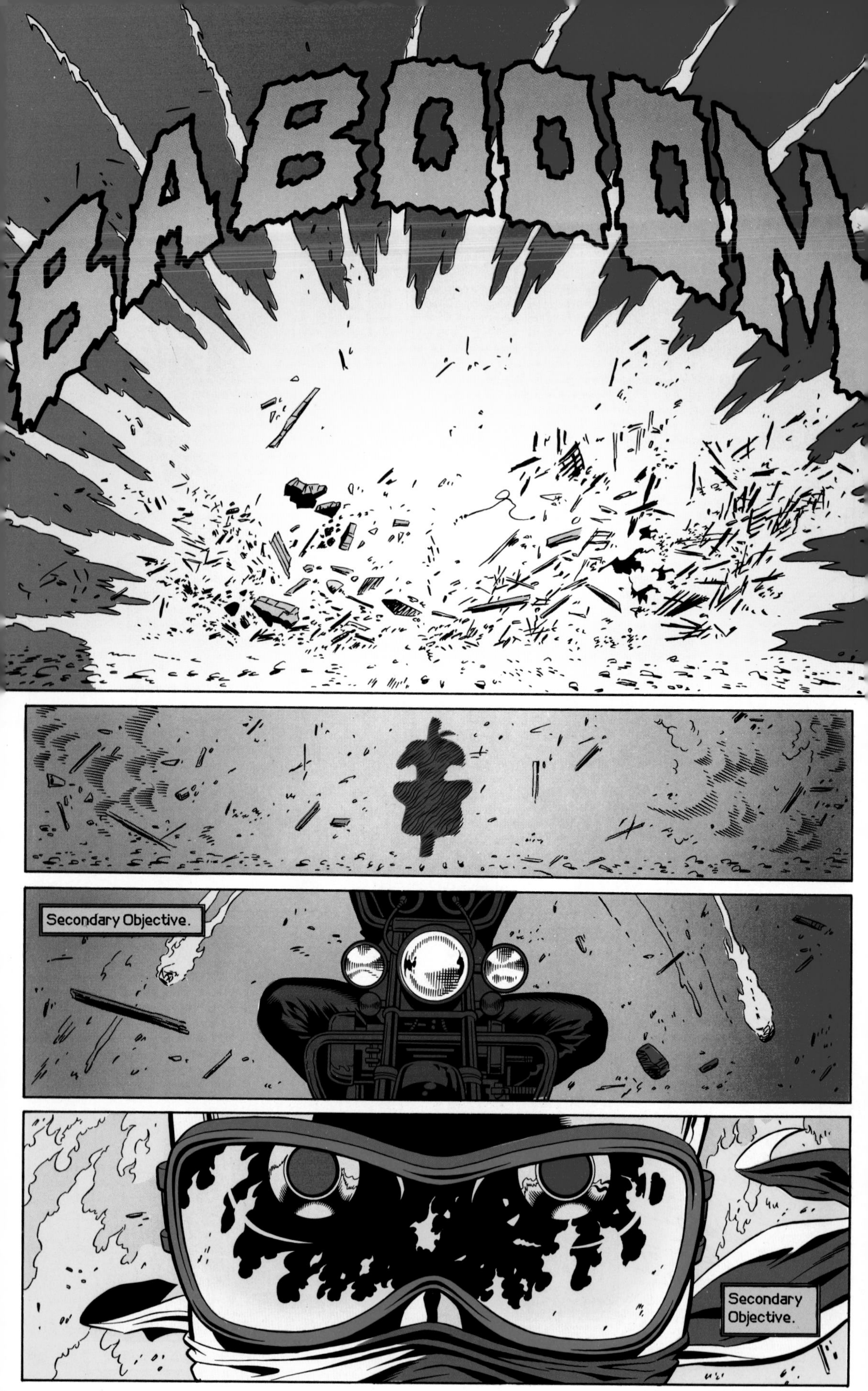
BABOOM
Secondary Objective.
Secondary Objective.

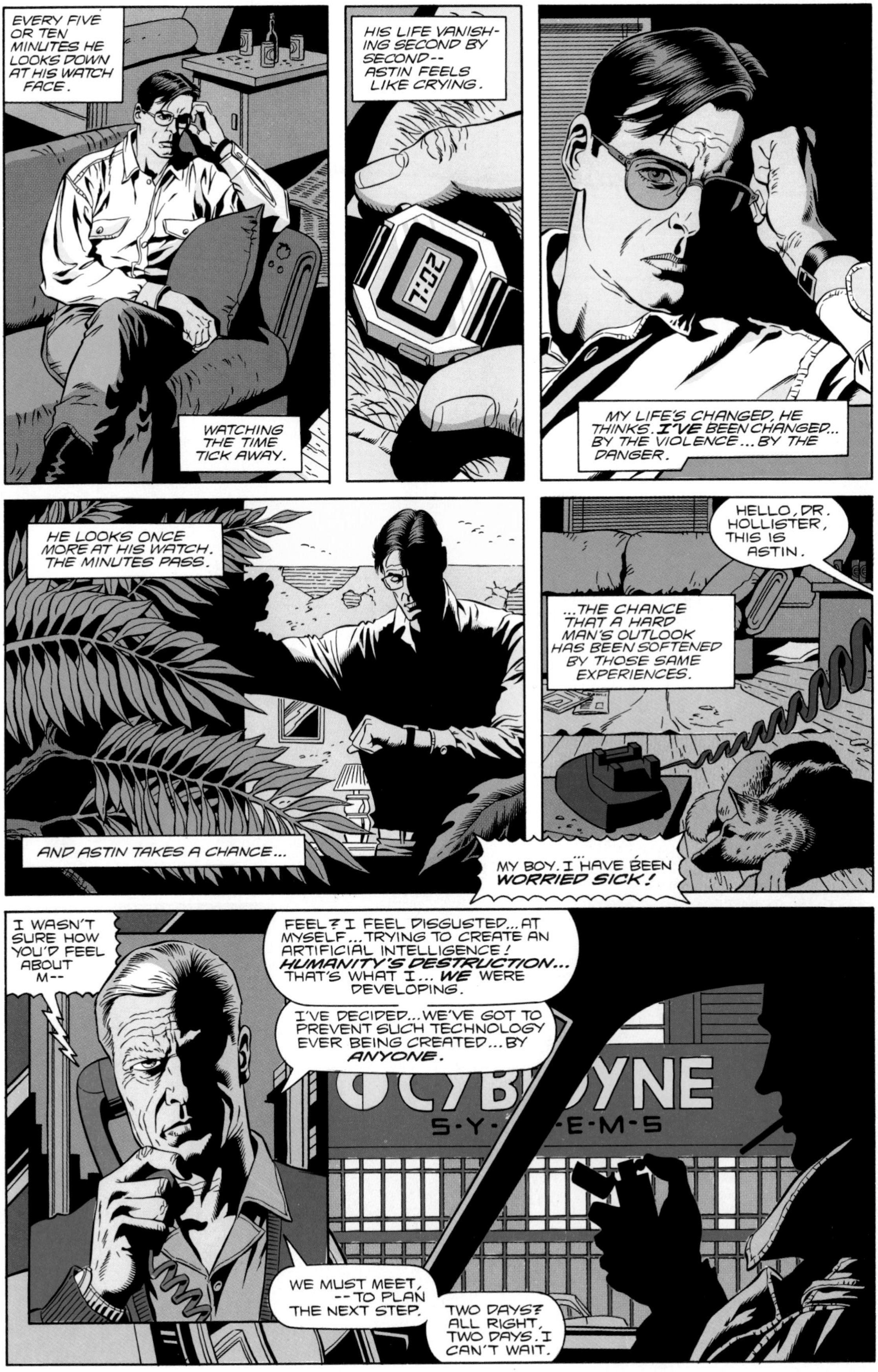

EVERY FIVE OR TEN MINUTES HE LOOKS DOWN AT HIS WATCH FACE.
WATCHING THE TIME TICK AWAY.
HIS LIFE VANISHING SECOND BY SECOND -- ASTIN FEELS LIKE CRYING.
7:02
MY LIFE'S CHANGED, HE THINKS. I'VE BEEN CHANGED... BY THE VIOLENCE... BY THE DANGER.
HE LOOKS ONCE MORE AT HIS WATCH. THE MINUTES PASS.
AND ASTIN TAKES A CHANCE...
...THE CHANCE THAT A HARD MAN'S OUTLOOK HAS BEEN SOFTENED BY THOSE SAME EXPERIENCES.
HELLO, DR. HOLLISTER, THIS IS ASTIN.
...MY BOY. I HAVE BEEN WORRIED SICK!
I WASN'T SURE HOW YOU'D FEEL ABOUT M--
FEEL? I FEEL DISGUSTED... AT MYSELF... TRYING TO CREATE AN ARTIFICIAL INTELLIGENCE! HUMANITY'S DESTRUCTION... THAT'S WHAT I... WE WERE DEVELOPING.
I'VE DECIDED... WE'VE GOT TO PREVENT SUCH TECHNOLOGY EVER BEING CREATED... BY ANYONE.
WE MUST MEET, -- TO PLAN THE NEXT STEP.
TWO DAYS? ALL RIGHT, TWO DAYS. I CAN'T WAIT.

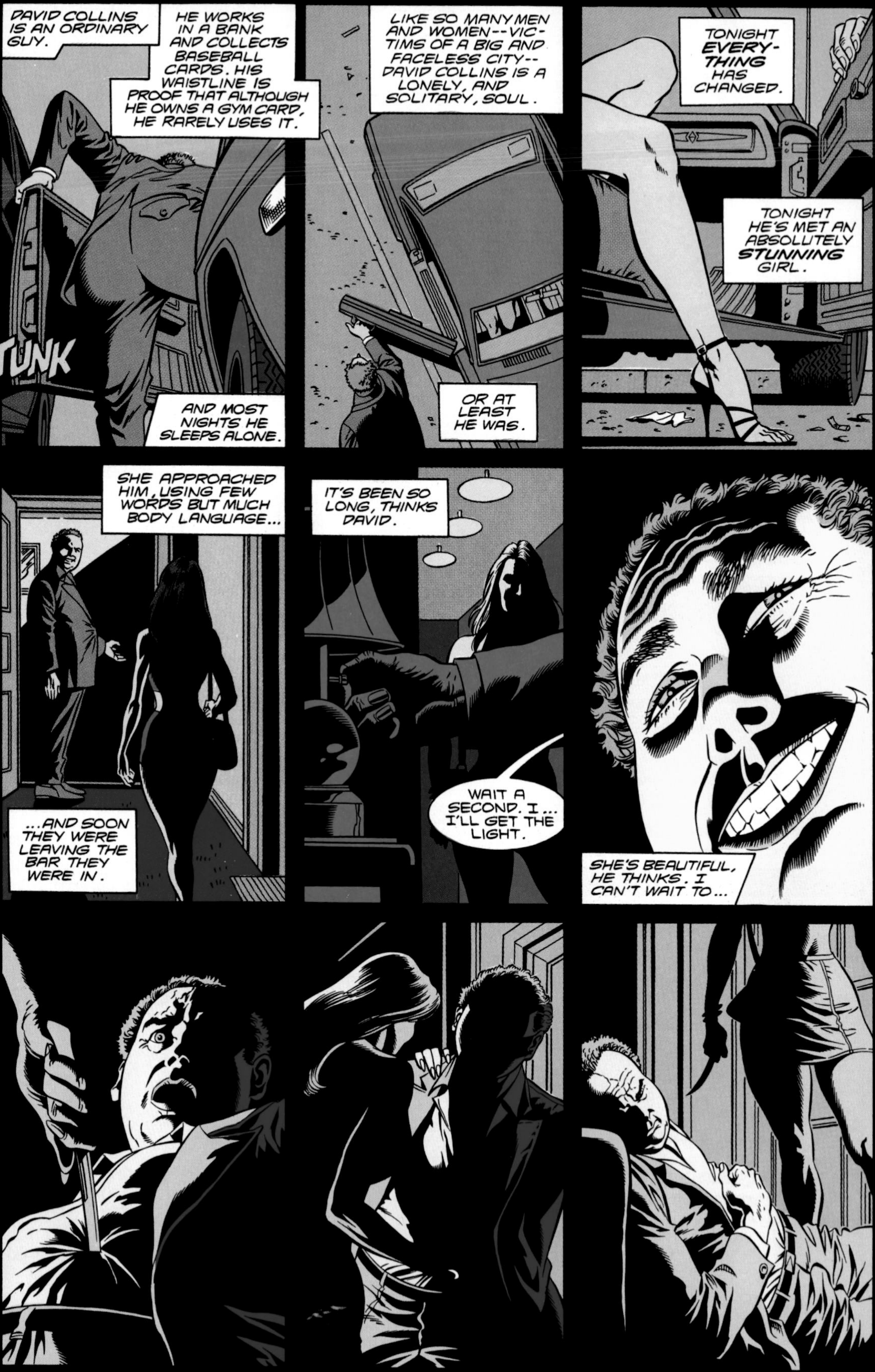
DAVID COLLINS IS AN ORDINARY GUY.
HE WORKS IN A BANK AND COLLECTS BASEBALL CARDS. HIS WAISTLINE IS PROOF THAT ALTHOUGH HE OWNS A GYM CARD, HE RARELY USES IT.
TUNK
AND MOST NIGHTS HE SLEEPS ALONE.
LIKE SO MANY MEN AND WOMEN--VICTIMS OF A BIG AND FACELESS CITY--DAVID COLLINS IS A LONELY, AND SOLITARY, SOUL.
OR AT LEAST HE WAS.
TONIGHT EVERYTHING HAS CHANGED.
TONIGHT HE'S MET AN ABSOLUTELY STUNNING GIRL.
SHE APPROACHED HIM, USING FEW WORDS BUT MUCH BODY LANGUAGE...
...AND SOON THEY WERE LEAVING THE BAR THEY WERE IN.
IT'S BEEN SO LONG, THINKS DAVID.
WAIT A SECOND. I... I'LL GET THE LIGHT.
SHE'S BEAUTIFUL, HE THINKS. I CAN'T WAIT TO...

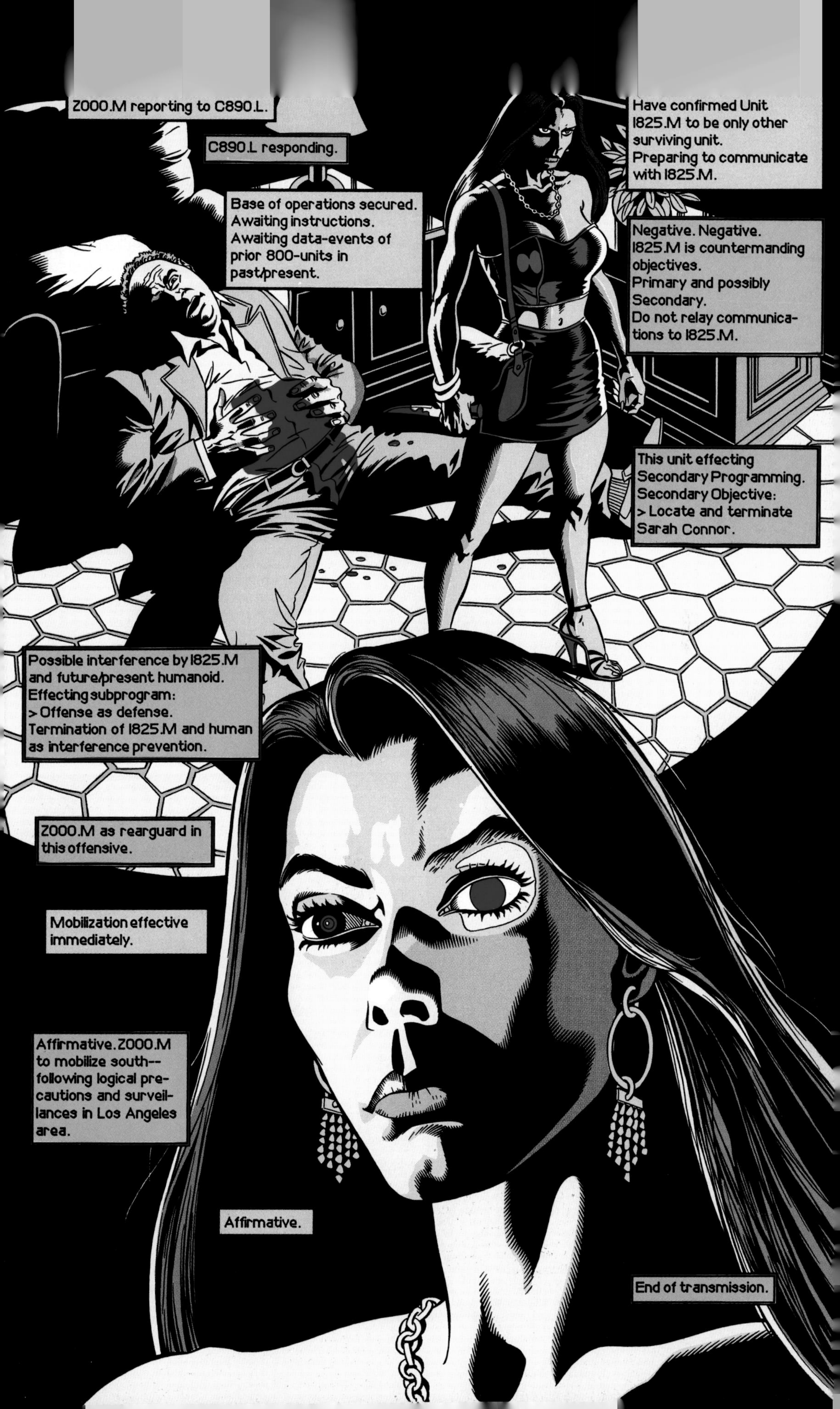
Z000.M reporting to C890.L.
C890.L responding.
Base of operations secured. Awaiting instructions. Awaiting data-events of prior 800-units in past/present.
Have confirmed Unit 1825.M to be only other surviving unit. Preparing to communicate with 1825.M.
Negative. Negative. 1825.M is countermanding objectives. Primary and possibly Secondary. Do not relay communica-tions to 1825.M.
This unit effecting Secondary Programming. Secondary Objective: > Locate and terminate Sarah Connor.
Possible interference by 1825.M and future/present humanoid. Effecting subprogram: > Offense as defense. Termination of 1825.M and human as interference prevention.
Z000.M as rearguard in this offensive.
Mobilization effective immediately.
Affirmative. Z000.M to mobilize south-- following logical pre-cautions and surveil-lances in Los Angeles area.
Affirmative.
End of transmission.

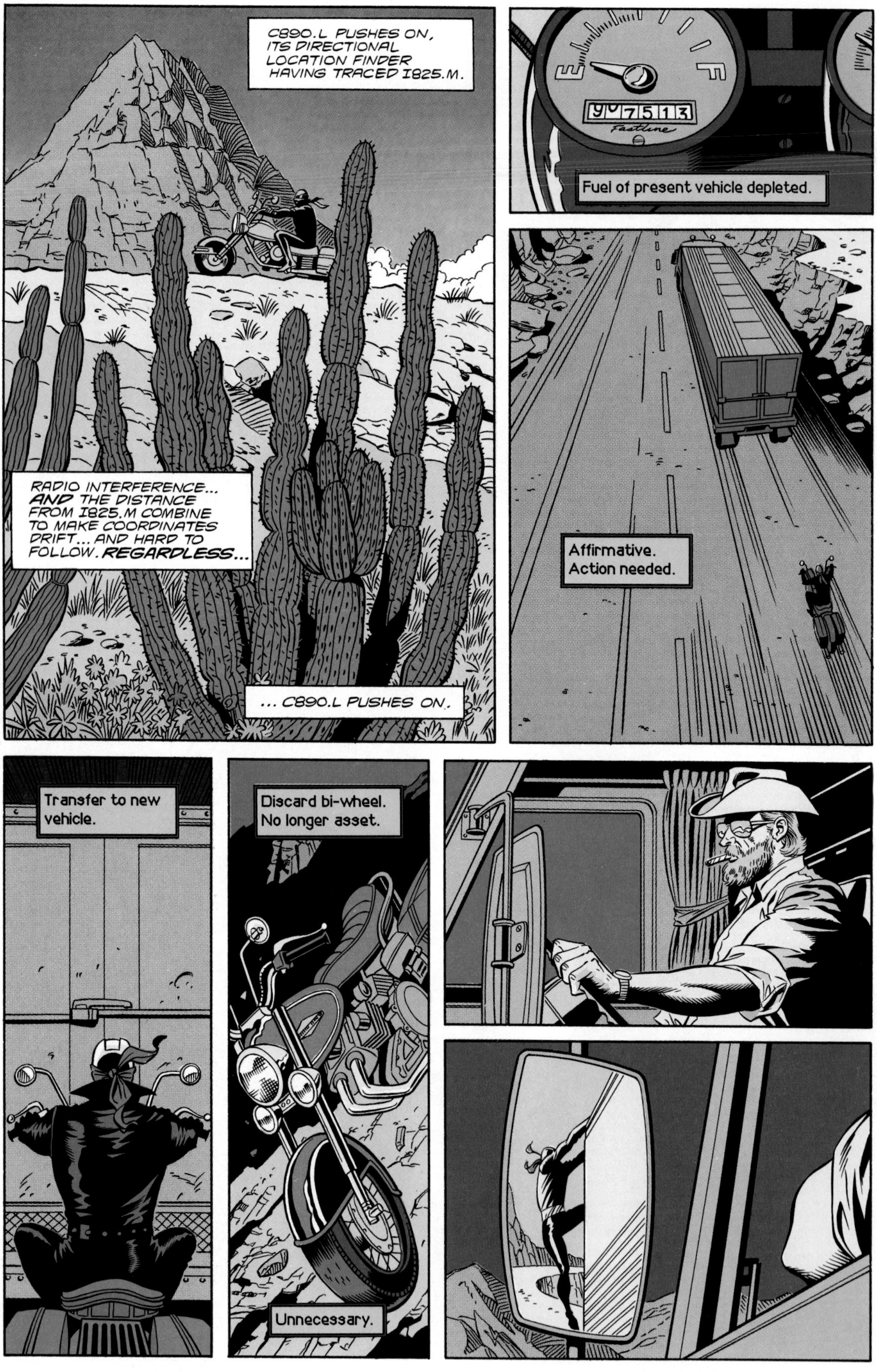
C890.L PUSHES ON, ITS DIRECTIONAL LOCATION FINDER HAVING TRACED I825.M.
RADIO INTERFERENCE... AND THE DISTANCE FROM I825.M COMBINE TO MAKE COORDINATES DRIFT... AND HARD TO FOLLOW. REGARDLESS...
... C890.L PUSHES ON.
Fastline
Fuel of present vehicle depleted.
Affirmative.
Action needed.
Transfer to new vehicle.
Discard bi-wheel.
No longer asset.
Unnecessary.

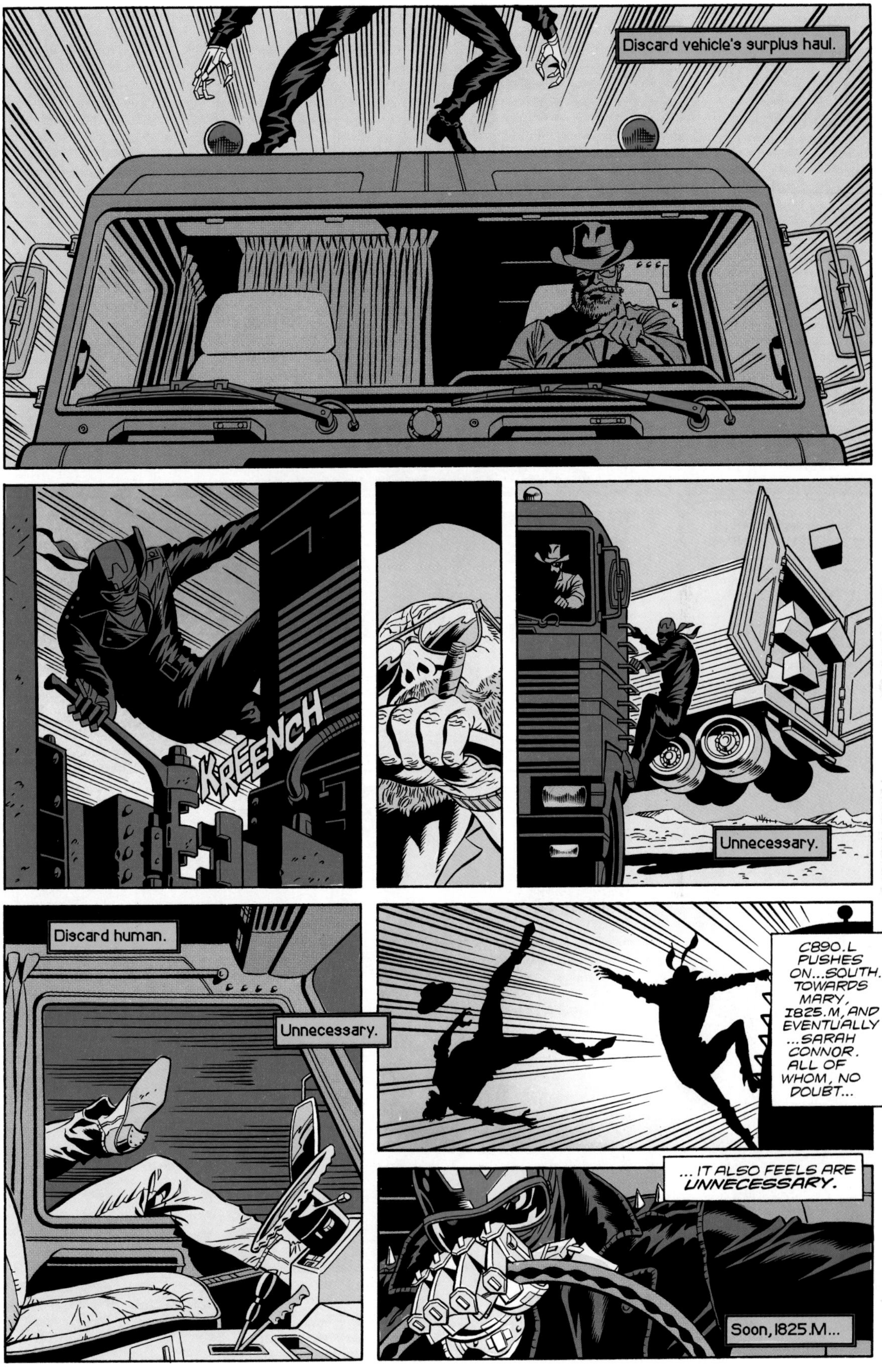
Discard vehicle's surplus haul.
KREENCH
Unnecessary.
Discard human.
Unnecessary.
C890.L PUSHES ON...SOUTH. TOWARDS MARY, 1825.M, AND EVENTUALLY ...SARAH CONNOR. ALL OF WHOM, NO DOUBT...
...IT ALSO FEELS ARE UNNECESSARY.
Soon, 1825.M...

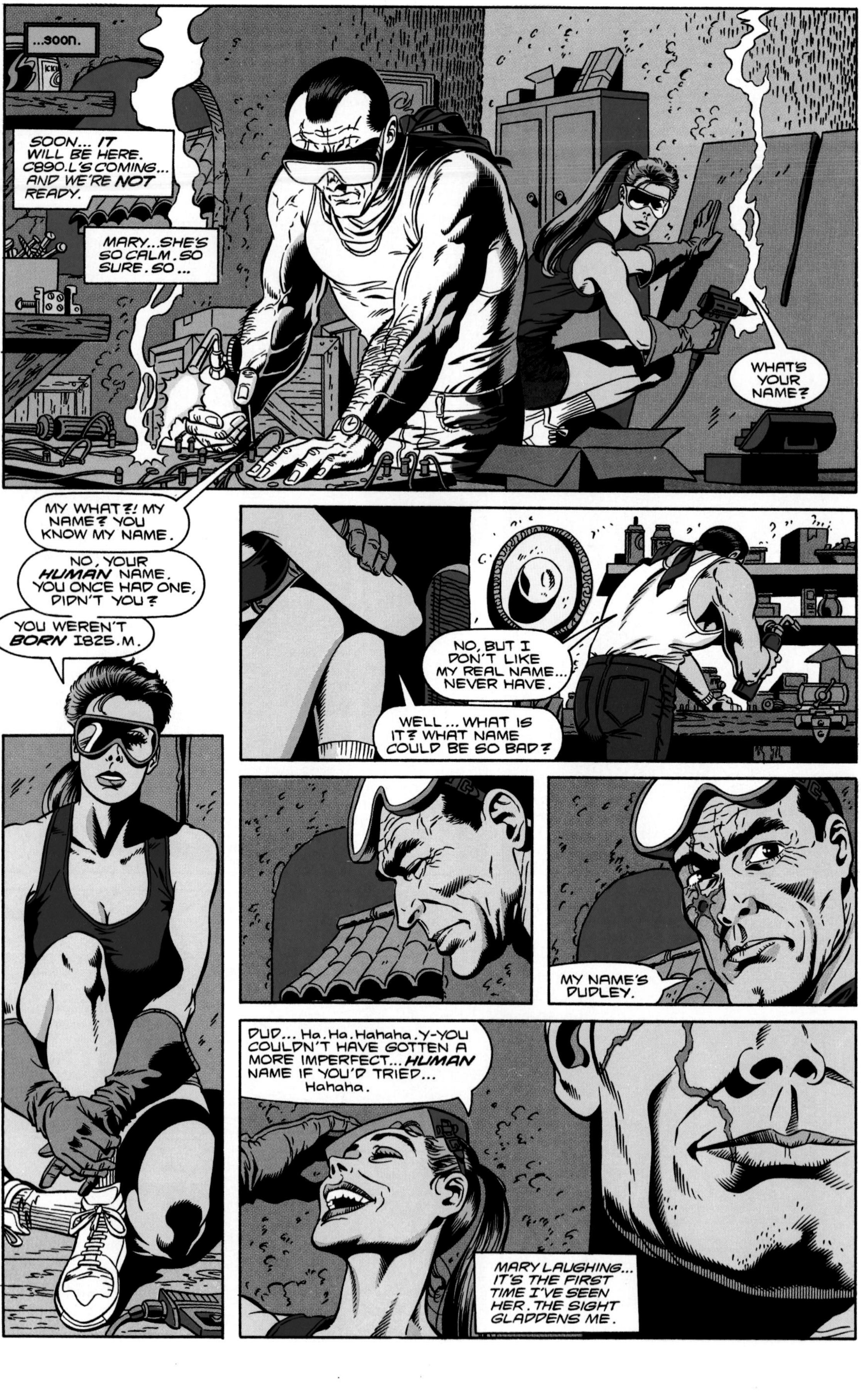
...soon.
SOON... IT WILL BE HERE. C890.L'S COMING... AND WE'RE NOT READY.
MARY...SHE'S SO CALM. SO SURE. SO...
WHAT'S YOUR NAME?
MY WHAT?! MY NAME? YOU KNOW MY NAME.
NO, YOUR HUMAN NAME. YOU ONCE HAD ONE, DIDN'T YOU?
YOU WEREN'T BORN I825.M.
NO, BUT I DON'T LIKE MY REAL NAME... NEVER HAVE.
WELL ... WHAT IS IT? WHAT NAME COULD BE SO BAD?
MY NAME'S DUDLEY.
DUD... Ha. Ha. Hahaha. Y-YOU COULDN'T HAVE GOTTEN A MORE IMPERFECT... HUMAN NAME IF YOU'D TRIED... Hahaha.
MARY LAUGHING... IT'S THE FIRST TIME I'VE SEEN HER. THE SIGHT GLADDENS ME.

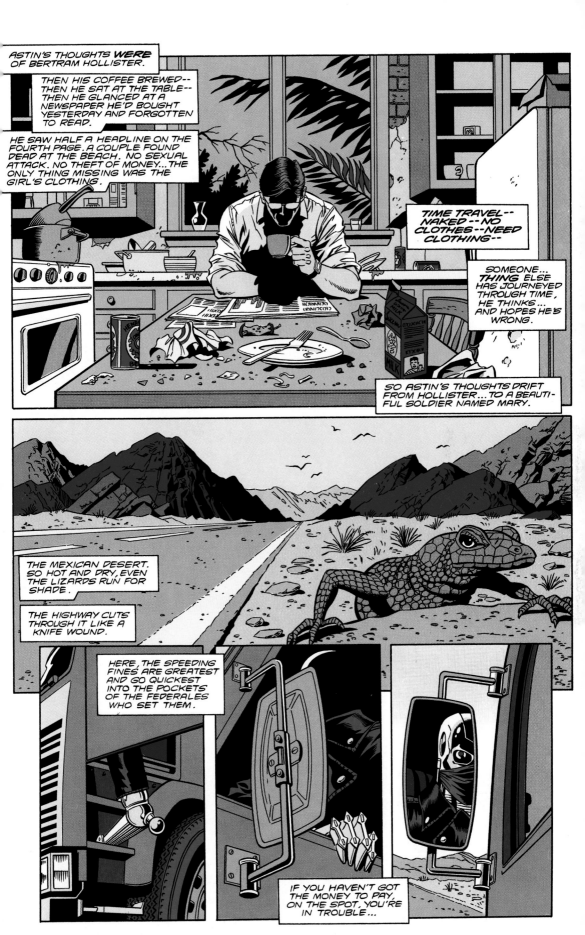

ASTIN'S THOUGHTS **WERE** OF BERTRAM HOLLISTER.

THEN HIS COFFEE BREWED-- THEN HE SAT AT THE TABLE-- THEN HE GLANCED AT A NEWSPAPER HE'D BOUGHT YESTERDAY AND FORGOTTEN TO READ.

HE SAW HALF A HEADLINE ON THE FOURTH PAGE. A COUPLE FOUND DEAD AT THE BEACH. NO SEXUAL ATTACK. NO THEFT OF MONEY...THE ONLY THING MISSING WAS THE GIRL'S CLOTHING.

TIME TRAVEL-- NAKED -- NO CLOTHES--NEED CLOTHING--

SOMEONE... *THING* ELSE HAS JOURNEYED THROUGH TIME, HE THINKS... AND HOPES HE'S WRONG.

SO ASTIN'S THOUGHTS DRIFT FROM HOLLISTER...TO A BEAUTIFUL SOLDIER NAMED MARY.

THE MEXICAN DESERT. SO HOT AND DRY, EVEN THE LIZARDS RUN FOR SHADE.

THE HIGHWAY CUTS THROUGH IT LIKE A KNIFE WOUND.

HERE, THE SPEEDING FINES ARE GREATEST AND GO QUICKEST INTO THE POCKETS OF THE FEDERALES WHO SET THEM.

IF YOU HAVEN'T GOT THE MONEY TO PAY, ON THE SPOT, YOU'RE IN TROUBLE...

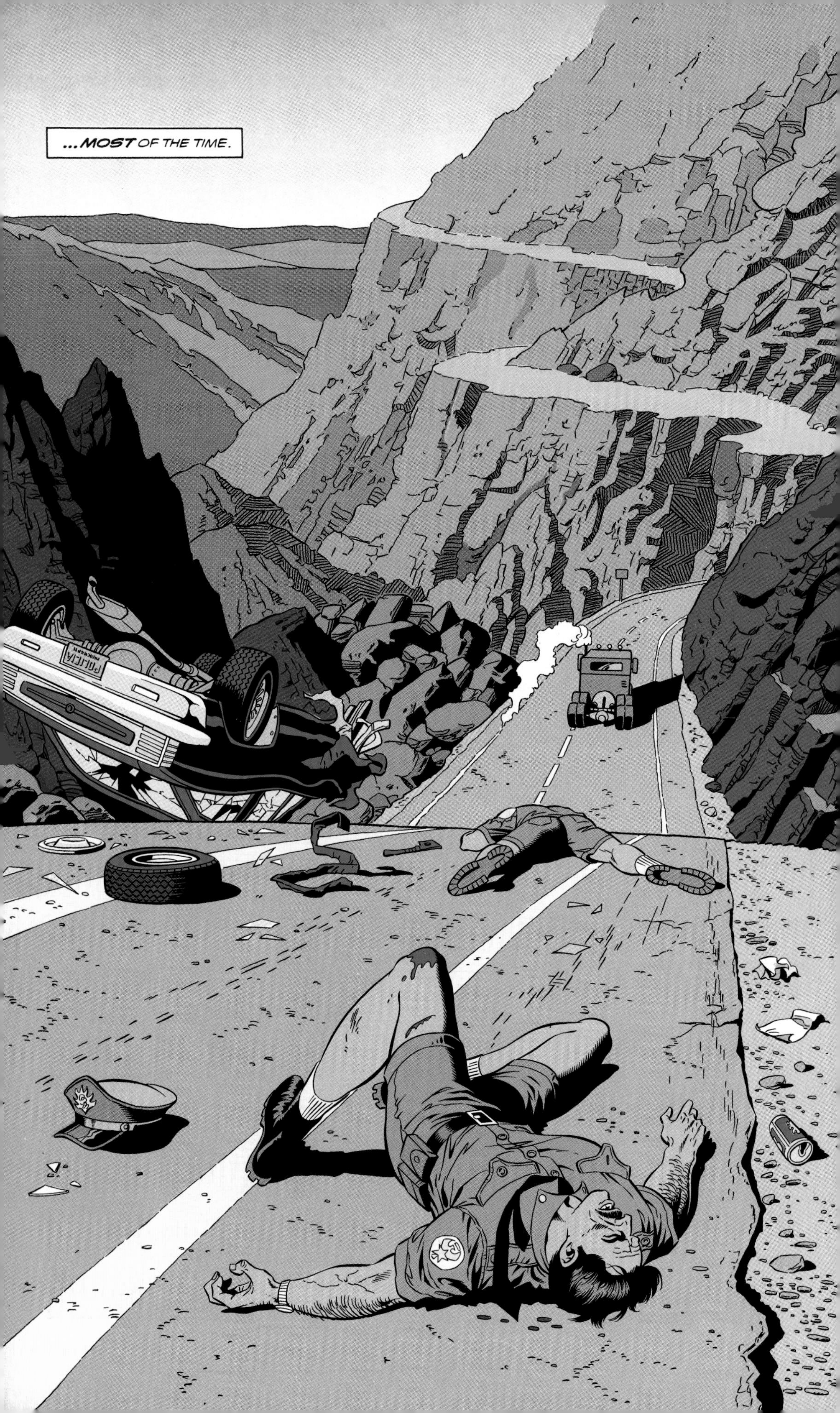
...MOST OF THE TIME.
POLICIA

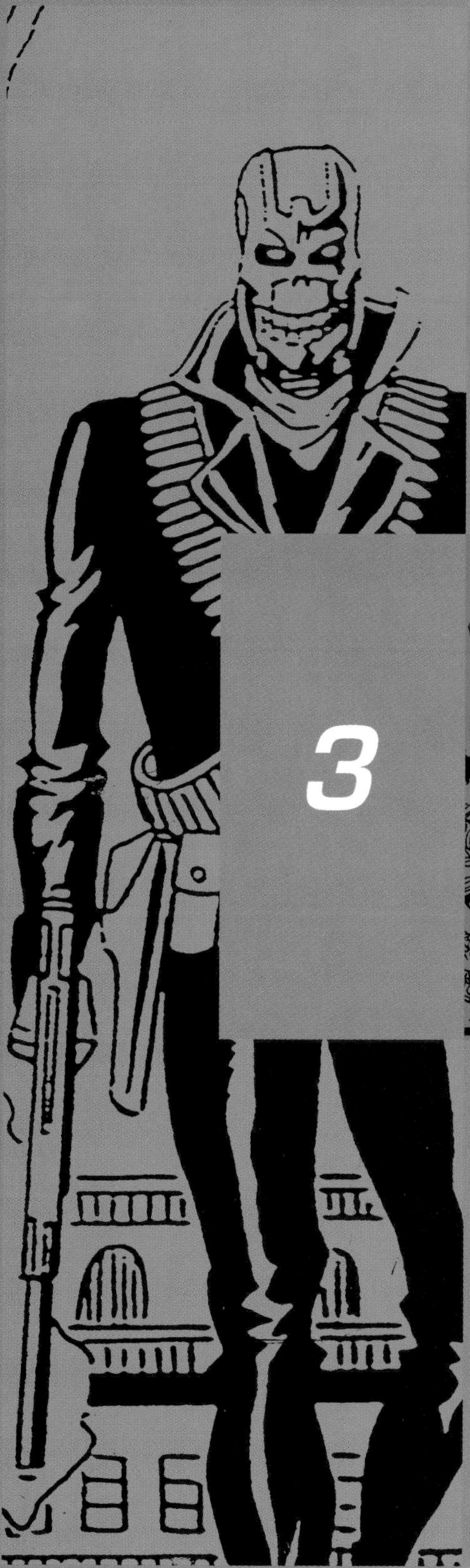

3

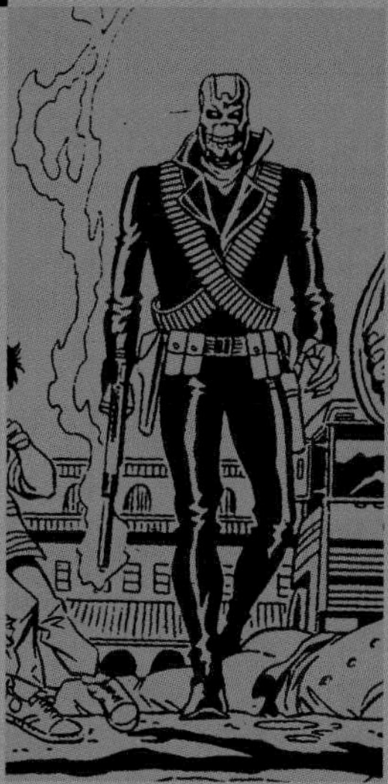

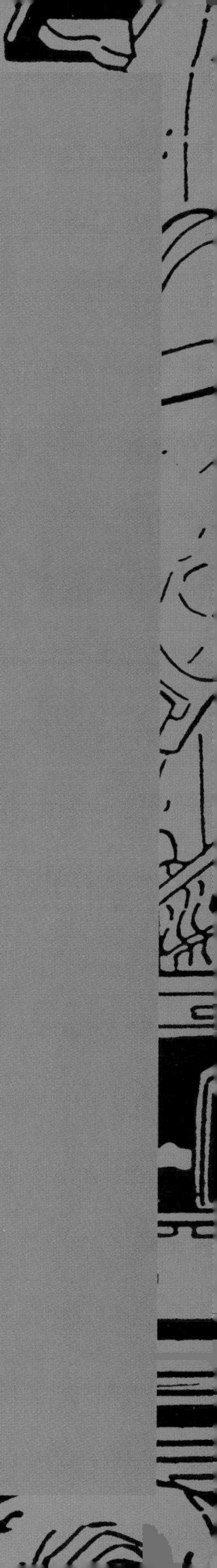

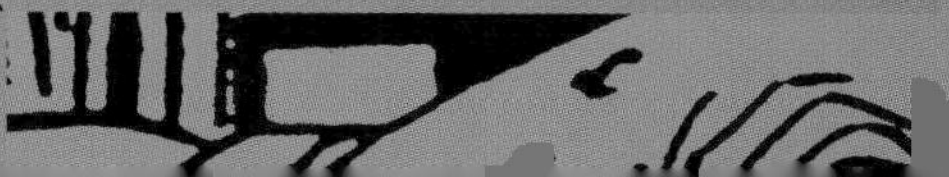

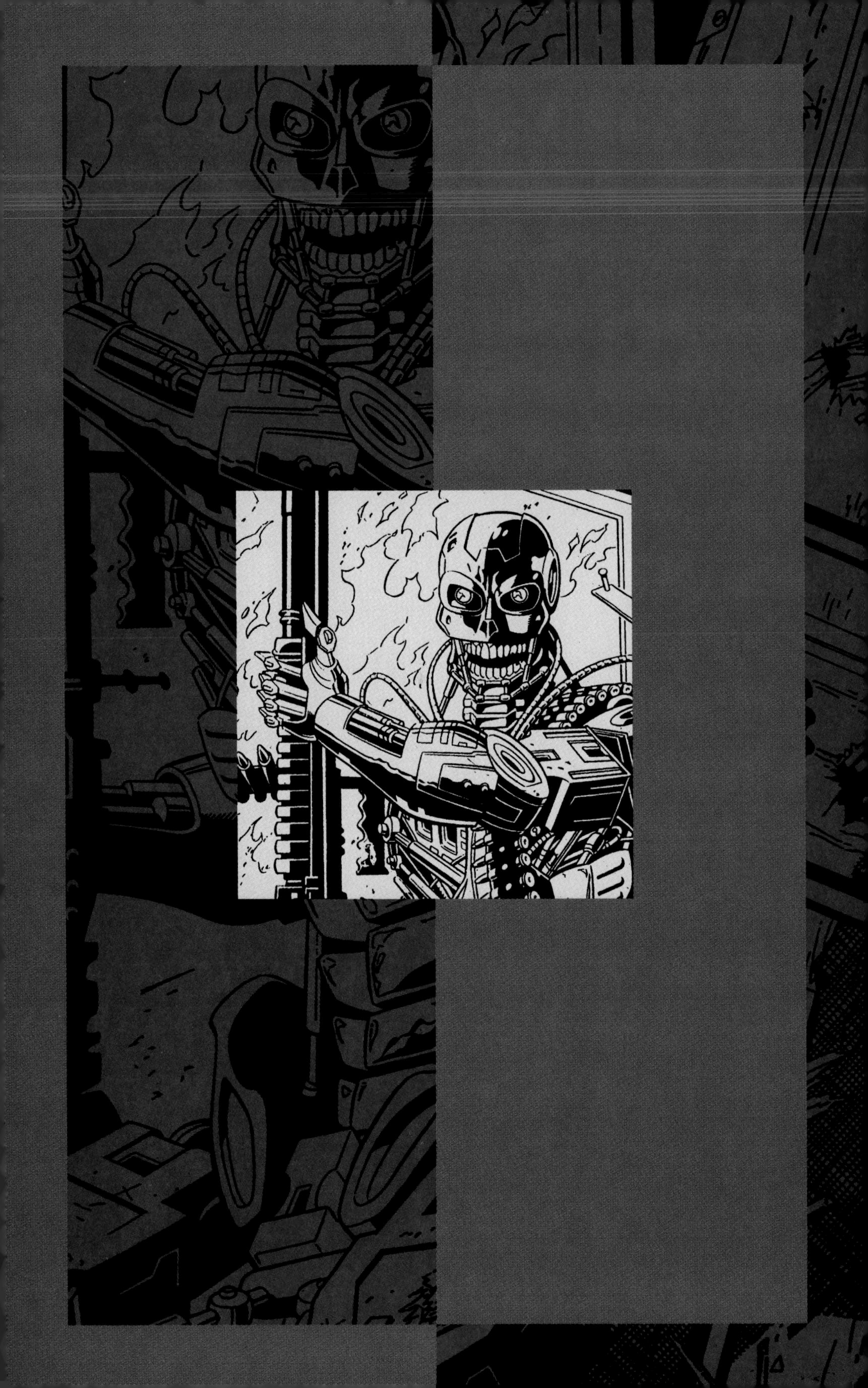

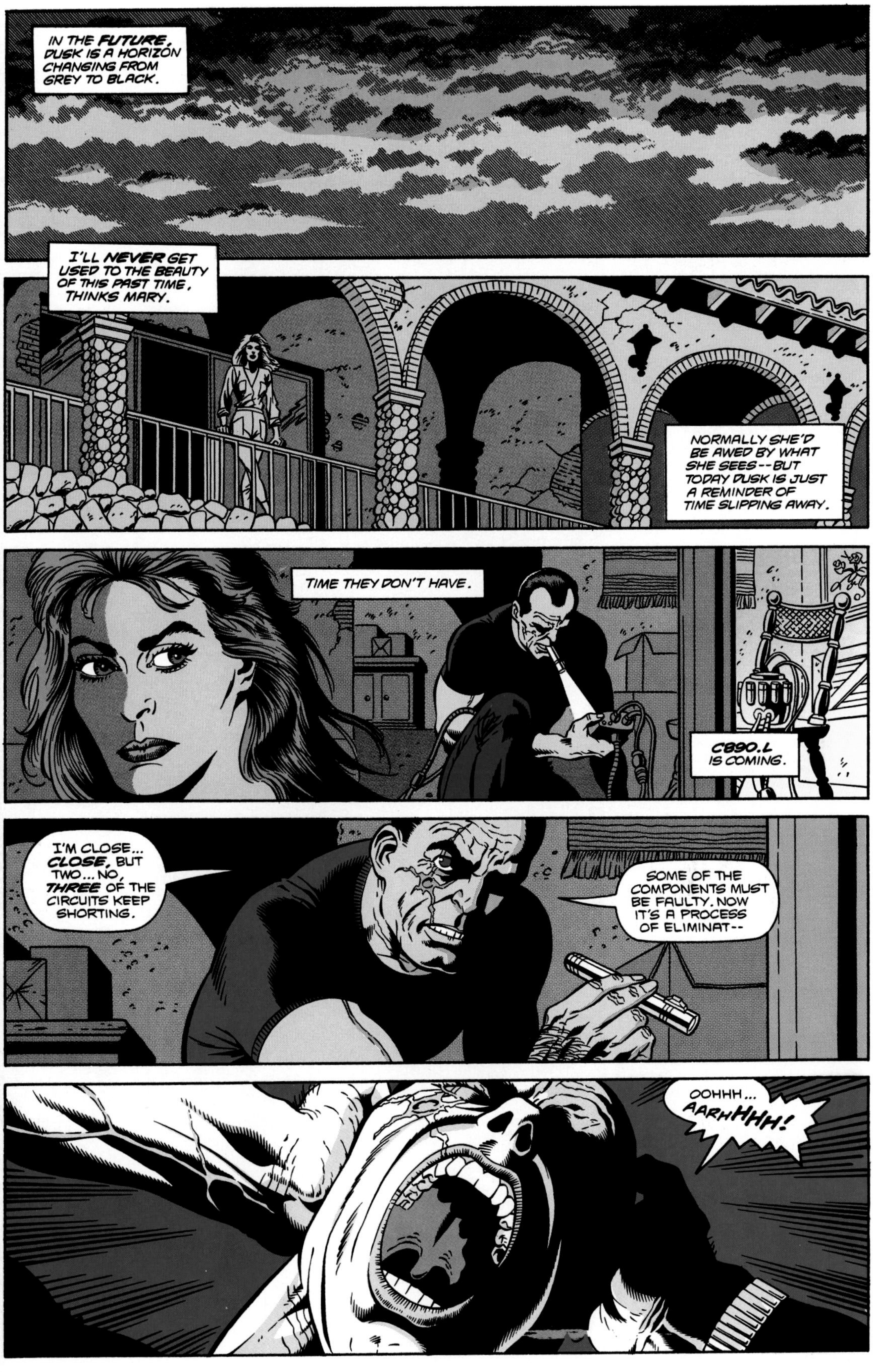

IN THE FUTURE, DUSK IS A HORIZON CHANGING FROM GREY TO BLACK.
I'LL NEVER GET USED TO THE BEAUTY OF THIS PAST TIME, THINKS MARY.
NORMALLY SHE'D BE AWED BY WHAT SHE SEES--BUT TODAY DUSK IS JUST A REMINDER OF TIME SLIPPING AWAY.
TIME THEY DON'T HAVE.
C890.L IS COMING.
I'M CLOSE... CLOSE, BUT TWO... NO, THREE OF THE CIRCUITS KEEP SHORTING.
SOME OF THE COMPONENTS MUST BE FAULTY. NOW IT'S A PROCESS OF ELIMINAT--
OOHHH... AARHHHH!

C890.L IS COMING.

TO KILL MARY.

TO KILL I825.M--THE HALF MAN, DUDLEY.

TO REMOVE **ANY** OBSTACLES TO ITS ULTIMATE AIM--THE DEATH OF SARAH CONNOR.

DUDLEY LABORED--TO COMPLETE A DEVICE THAT WOULD STOP THE TERMINATOR--USING TOOLS THAT, TO HIM, SEEMED TO COME FROM THE STONE AGE, AND WHICH TURNED THE WORK OF **HOURS** INTO THE WORK OF **DAYS**.

BUT THERE WAS **GOOD** NEWS.

TO TRACK DUDLEY, C890.L WAS NO DOUBT FOLLOWING THE IN-BUILT DIRECTIONAL COMPASS THAT ENABLES TERMINATORS TO LOCATE EACH OTHER. BUT WITHOUT DUDLEY RESPONDING TO C890.L, GIVING IT A COORDINATES-LOCK, THIS TRAIL TO THE FUTURE HUMANS WAS PROBABLY WEAK--SCATTERED--AND PRONE TO ERROR.

MARY **HOPED** THIS WAS THE CASE--AND THAT THE SPRAWL OF MEXICO CITY'S SLUMS, WHERE THEY'D MADE THEIR BASE, WOULD MAKE THEM EVEN HARDER TO FIND--AND BUY THEM YET MORE TIME.

NOT TO MENTION KEEPING THE TERMINATOR AWAY FROM THE DESERTS THAT HID SARAH CONNOR.

THAT WAS THE GOOD NEWS.

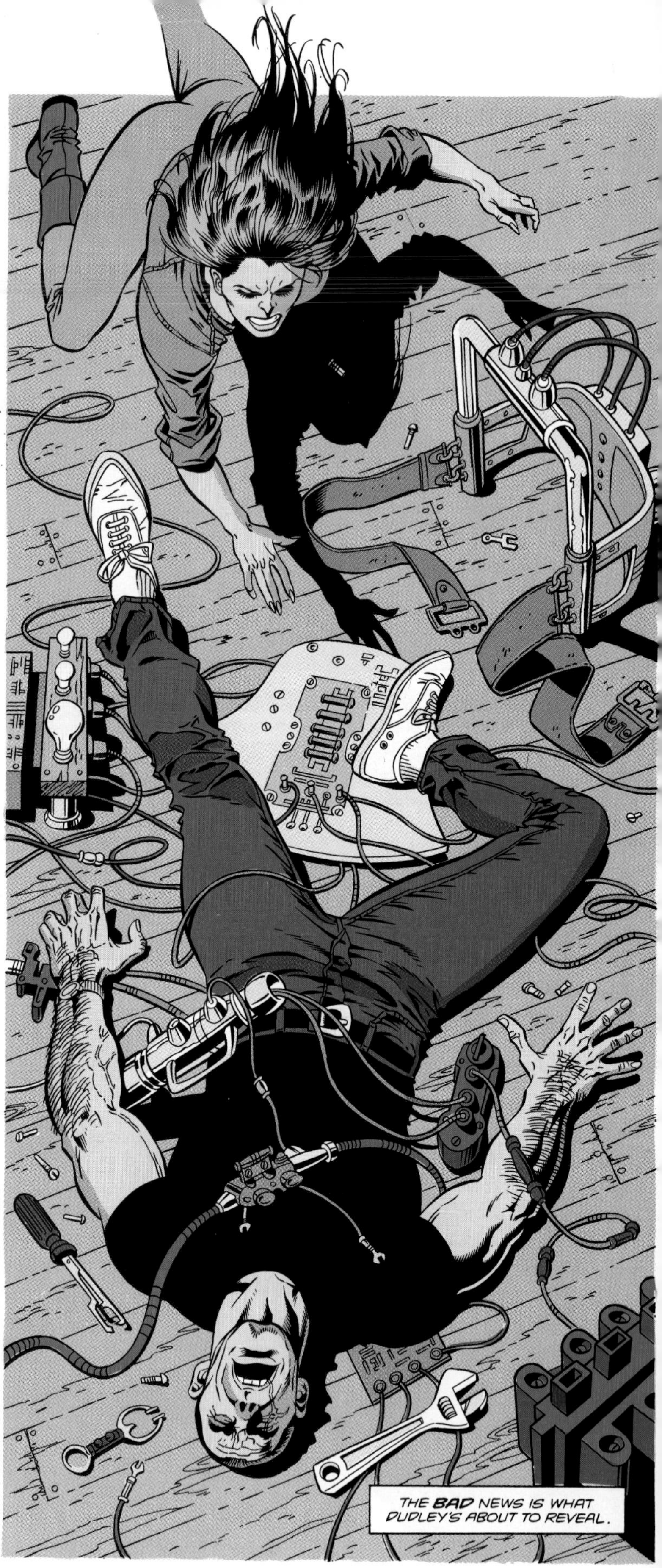
THE **BAD** NEWS IS WHAT DUDLEY'S ABOUT TO REVEAL.

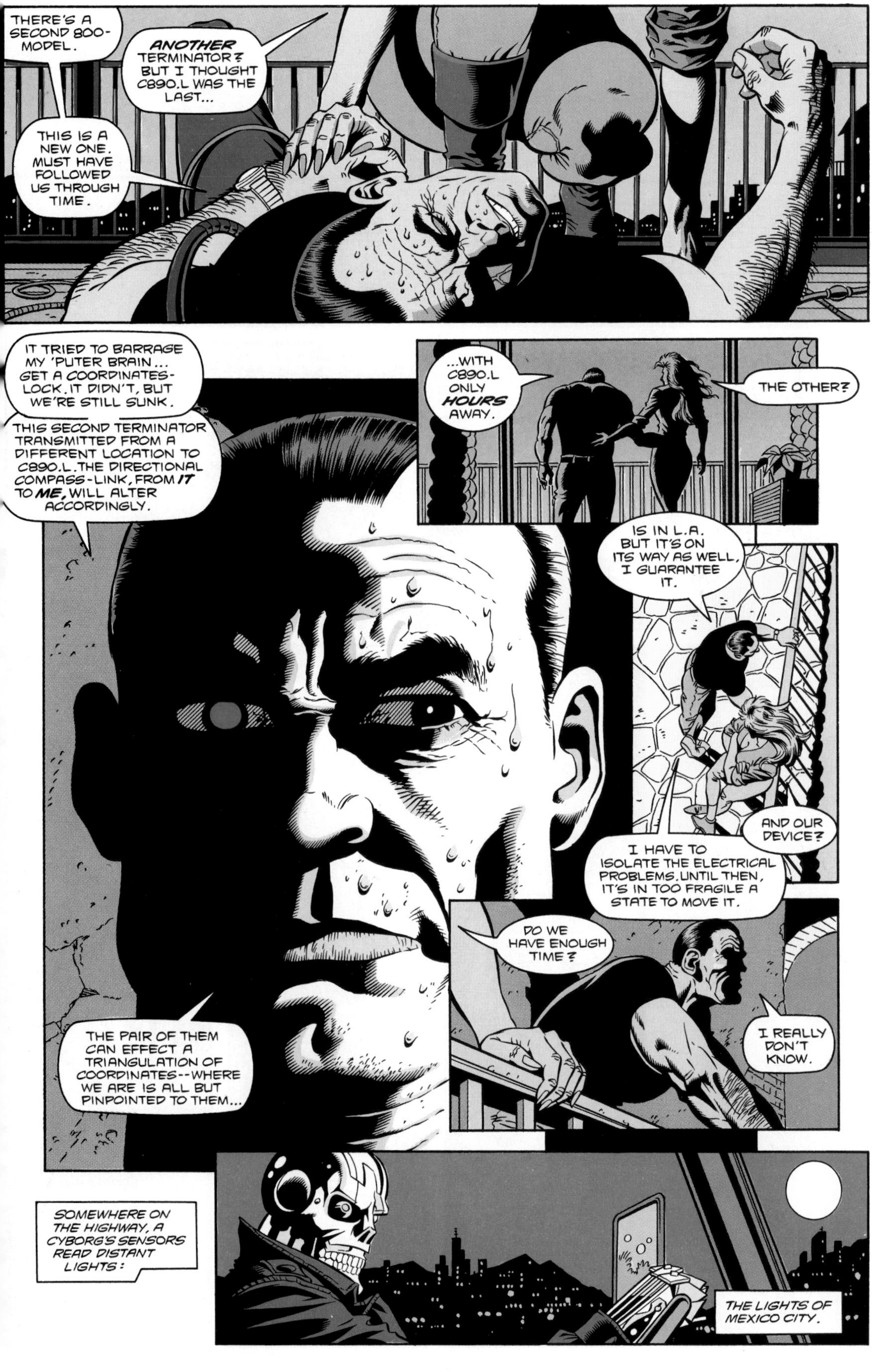

THERE'S A SECOND 800-MODEL.
ANOTHER TERMINATOR? BUT I THOUGHT C890.L WAS THE LAST...
THIS IS A NEW ONE. MUST HAVE FOLLOWED US THROUGH TIME.
IT TRIED TO BARRAGE MY 'PUTER BRAIN... GET A COORDINATES-LOCK. IT DIDN'T, BUT WE'RE STILL SUNK.
THIS SECOND TERMINATOR TRANSMITTED FROM A DIFFERENT LOCATION TO C890.L. THE DIRECTIONAL COMPASS-LINK, FROM IT TO ME, WILL ALTER ACCORDINGLY.
THE PAIR OF THEM CAN EFFECT A TRIANGULATION OF COORDINATES--WHERE WE ARE IS ALL BUT PINPOINTED TO THEM...
...WITH C890.L ONLY HOURS AWAY.
THE OTHER?
IS IN L.A. BUT IT'S ON ITS WAY AS WELL, I GUARANTEE IT.
AND OUR DEVICE?
I HAVE TO ISOLATE THE ELECTRICAL PROBLEMS. UNTIL THEN, IT'S IN TOO FRAGILE A STATE TO MOVE IT.
DO WE HAVE ENOUGH TIME?
I REALLY DON'T KNOW.
SOMEWHERE ON THE HIGHWAY, A CYBORG'S SENSORS READ DISTANT LIGHTS:
THE LIGHTS OF MEXICO CITY.

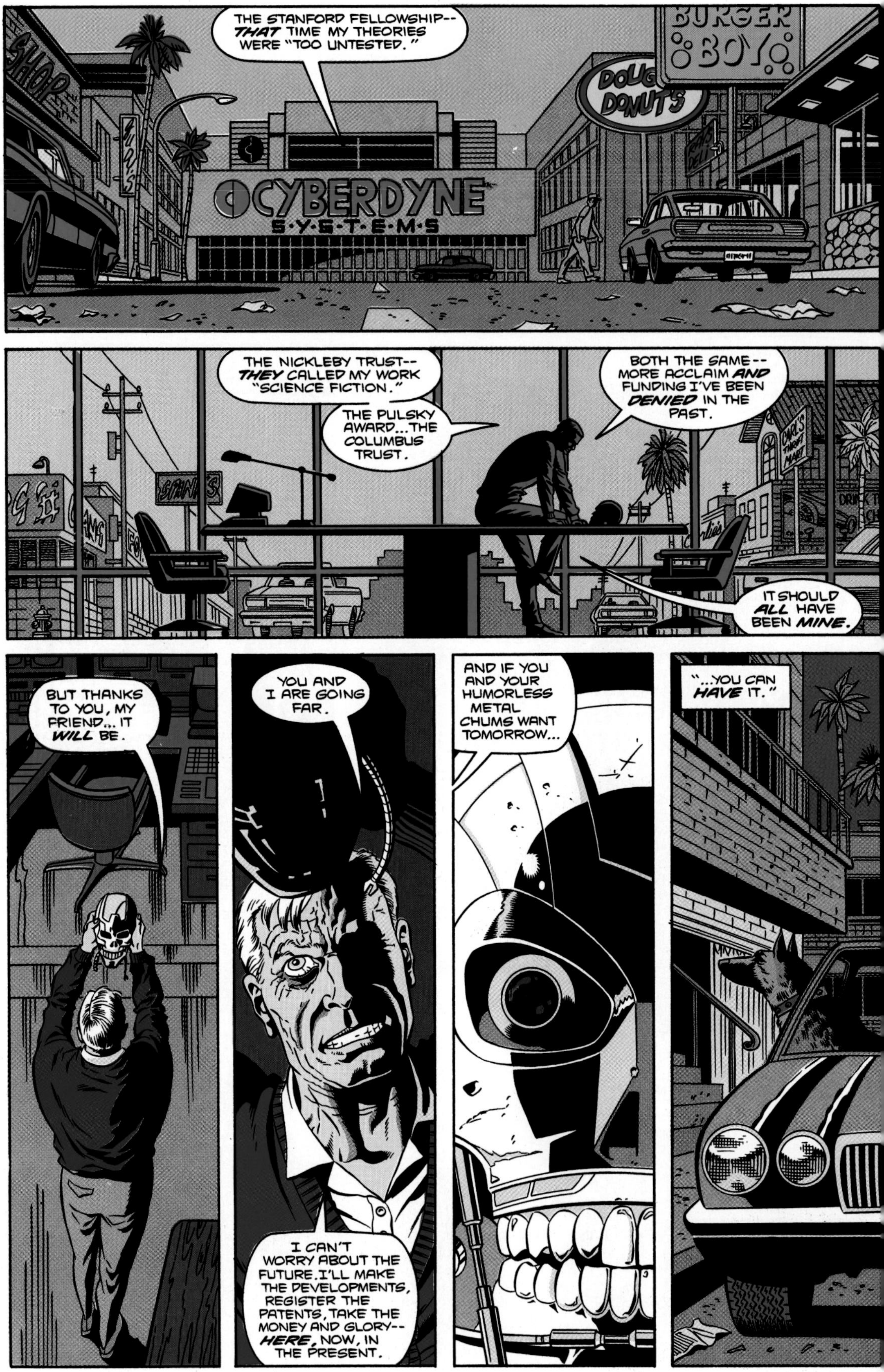
THE STANFORD FELLOWSHIP-- THAT TIME MY THEORIES WERE "TOO UNTESTED."
BURGER BOY
DOUGH DONUT'S
CYBERDYNE SYSTEMS
THE NICKLEBY TRUST-- THEY CALLED MY WORK "SCIENCE FICTION."
THE PULSKY AWARD... THE COLUMBUS TRUST.
BOTH THE SAME-- MORE ACCLAIM AND FUNDING I'VE BEEN DENIED IN THE PAST.
IT SHOULD ALL HAVE BEEN MINE.
BUT THANKS TO YOU, MY FRIEND... IT WILL BE.
YOU AND I ARE GOING FAR.
I CAN'T WORRY ABOUT THE FUTURE. I'LL MAKE THE DEVELOPMENTS, REGISTER THE PATENTS, TAKE THE MONEY AND GLORY-- HERE, NOW, IN THE PRESENT.
AND IF YOU AND YOUR HUMORLESS METAL CHUMS WANT TOMORROW...
"...YOU CAN HAVE IT."

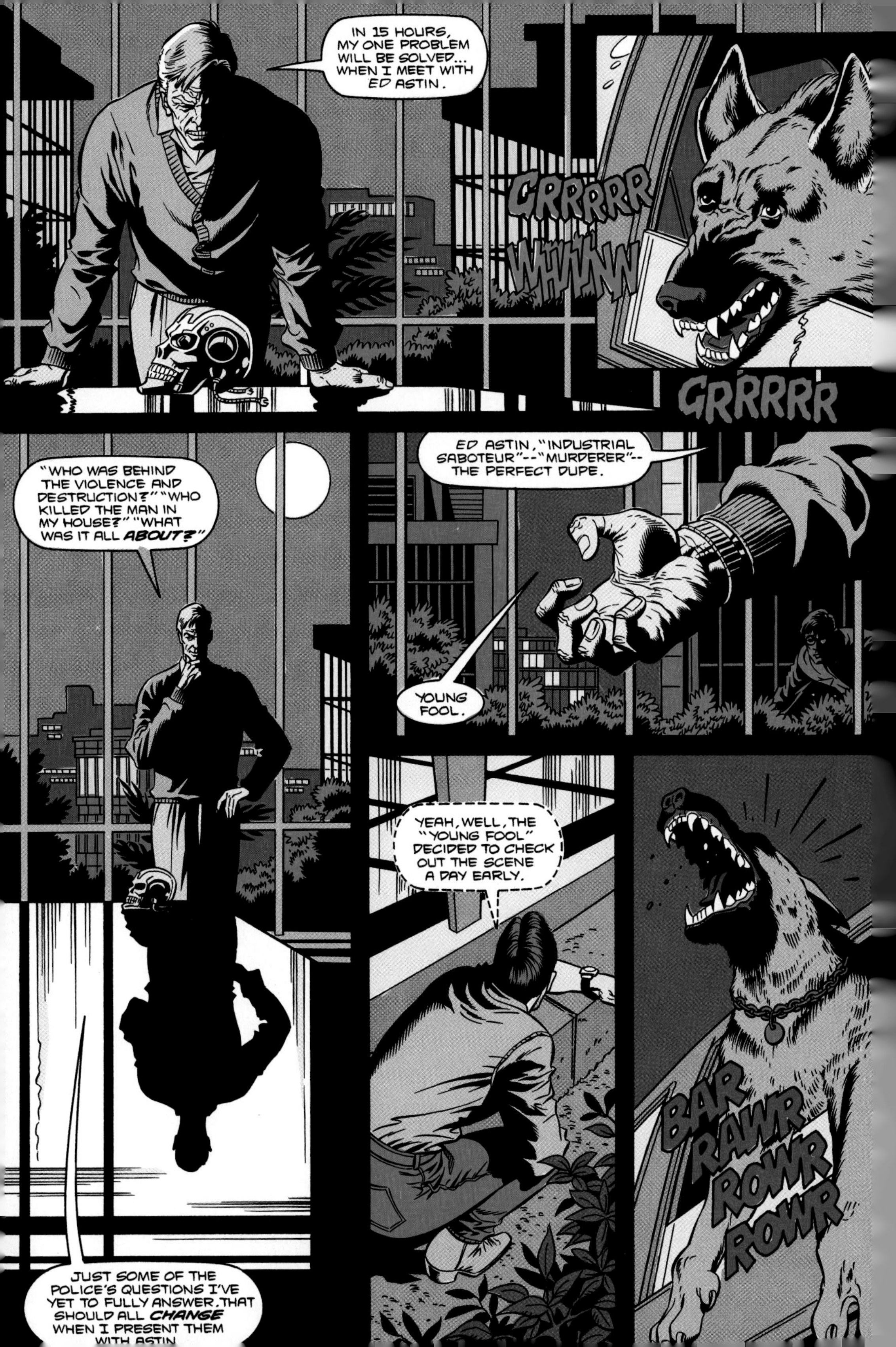
IN 15 HOURS, MY ONE PROBLEM WILL BE SOLVED... WHEN I MEET WITH ED ASTIN.
GRRRRR
WHHHNW
GRRRRR
"WHO WAS BEHIND THE VIOLENCE AND DESTRUCTION?" "WHO KILLED THE MAN IN MY HOUSE?" "WHAT WAS IT ALL ABOUT?"
JUST SOME OF THE POLICE'S QUESTIONS I'VE YET TO FULLY ANSWER. THAT SHOULD ALL CHANGE WHEN I PRESENT THEM WITH ASTIN.
ED ASTIN, "INDUSTRIAL SABOTEUR"--"MURDERER"-- THE PERFECT DUPE.
YOUNG FOOL.
YEAH, WELL, THE "YOUNG FOOL" DECIDED TO CHECK OUT THE SCENE A DAY EARLY.
BAR RAWR ROWR ROWR

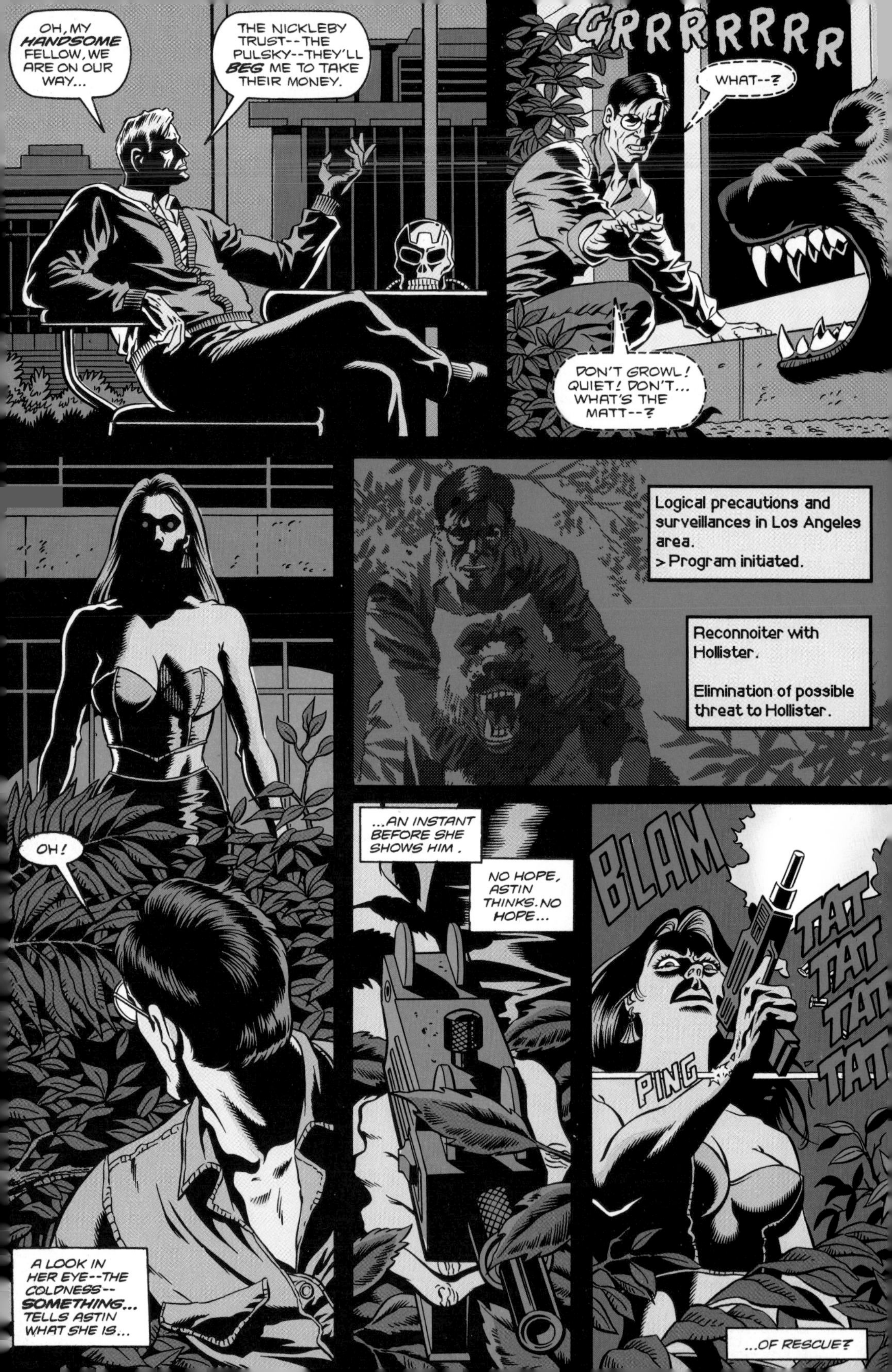
OH, MY HANDSOME FELLOW, WE ARE ON OUR WAY...
THE NICKLEBY TRUST--THE PULSKY--THEY'LL BEG ME TO TAKE THEIR MONEY.
GRRRRRRRR
WHAT--?
DON'T GROWL! QUIET! DON'T... WHAT'S THE MATT--?
Logical precautions and surveillances in Los Angeles area.
> Program initiated.
Reconnoiter with Hollister.
Elimination of possible threat to Hollister.
OH!
A LOOK IN HER EYE--THE COLDNESS--SOMETHING... TELLS ASTIN WHAT SHE IS...
...AN INSTANT BEFORE SHE SHOWS HIM.
NO HOPE, ASTIN THINKS. NO HOPE...
BLAM
TAT TAT TAT TAT
PING
...OF RESCUE?

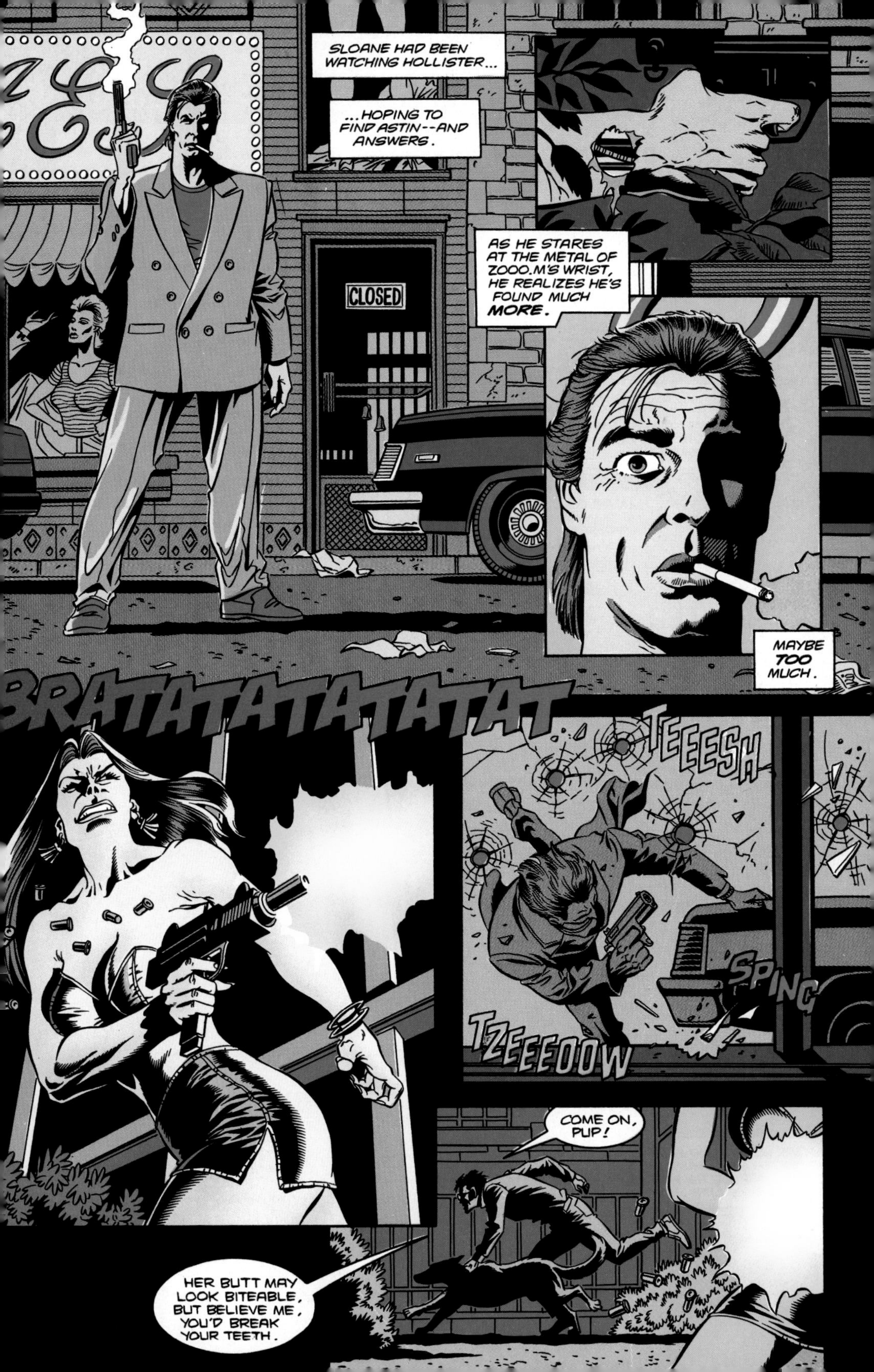

SLOANE HAD BEEN WATCHING HOLLISTER...
...HOPING TO FIND ASTIN--AND ANSWERS.
CLOSED
AS HE STARES AT THE METAL OF ZOOO.M'S WRIST, HE REALIZES HE'S FOUND MUCH MORE.
MAYBE TOO MUCH.
BRATATATATATAT
TEEESH
SPING
TZEEEOOW
COME ON, PUP!
HER BUTT MAY LOOK BITEABLE, BUT BELIEVE ME, YOU'D BREAK YOUR TEETH.

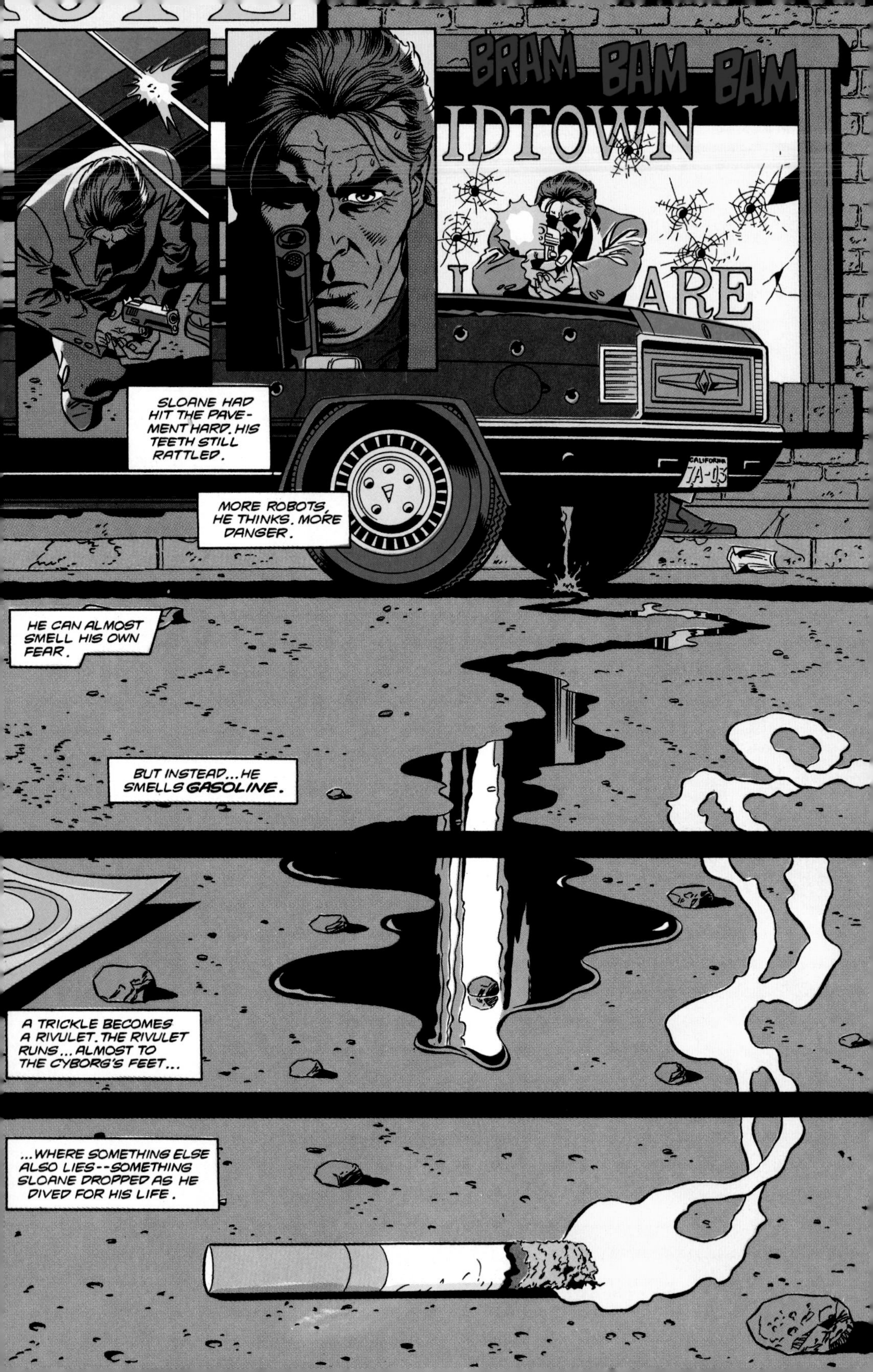
BRAM BAM BAM
IDTOWN
ARE
SLOANE HAD HIT THE PAVEMENT HARD. HIS TEETH STILL RATTLED.
CALIFORNIA
7A-03
MORE ROBOTS, HE THINKS. MORE DANGER.
HE CAN ALMOST SMELL HIS OWN FEAR.
BUT INSTEAD... HE SMELLS GASOLINE.
A TRICKLE BECOMES A RIVULET. THE RIVULET RUNS... ALMOST TO THE CYBORG'S FEET...
...WHERE SOMETHING ELSE ALSO LIES--SOMETHING SLOANE DROPPED AS HE DIVED FOR HIS LIFE.

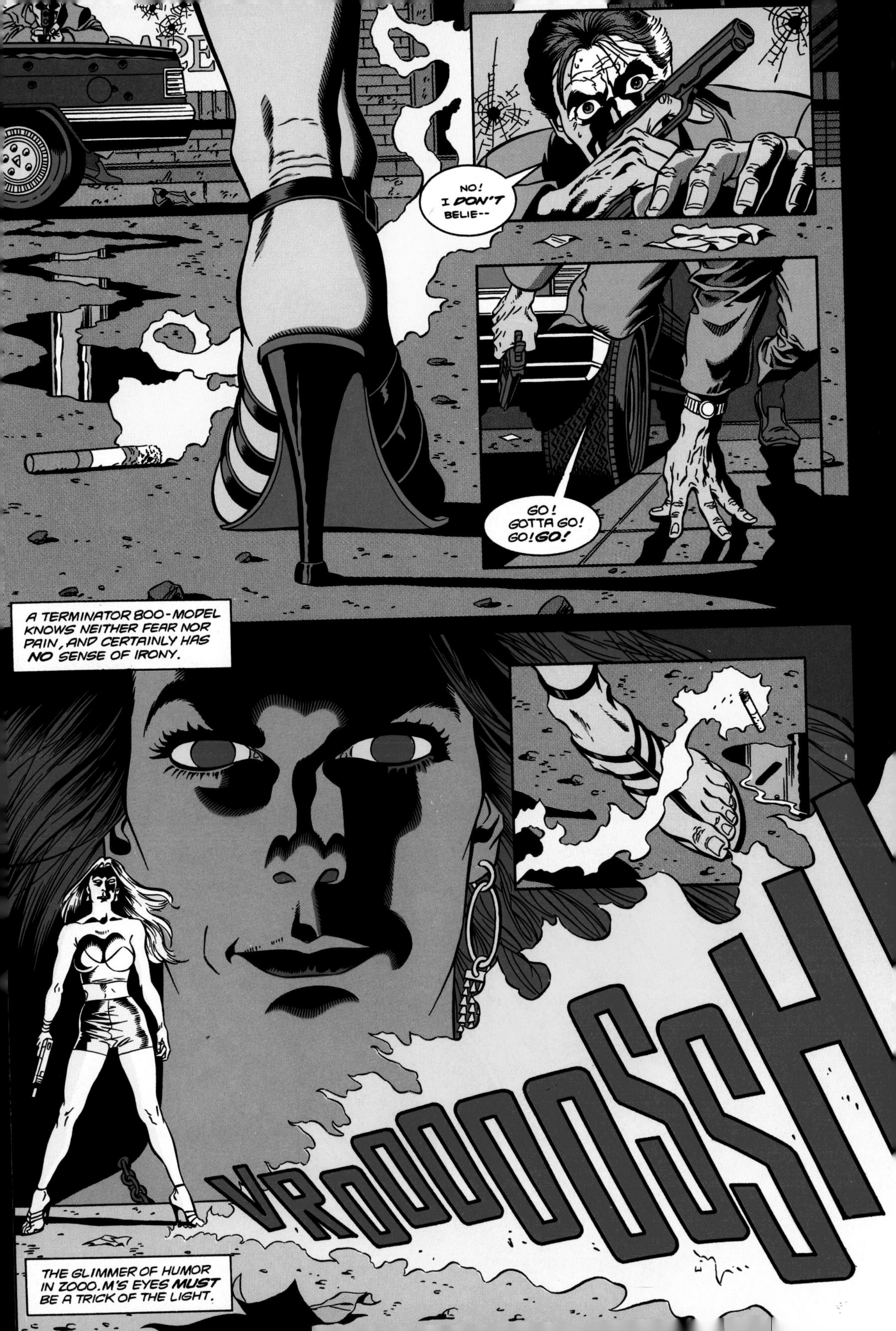
NO! I DON'T BELIE--
GO! GOTTA GO! GO! GO!
A TERMINATOR 800-MODEL KNOWS NEITHER FEAR NOR PAIN, AND CERTAINLY HAS NO SENSE OF IRONY.
VROOOOOOSSH
THE GLIMMER OF HUMOR IN ZOOO.M'S EYES MUST BE A TRICK OF THE LIGHT.

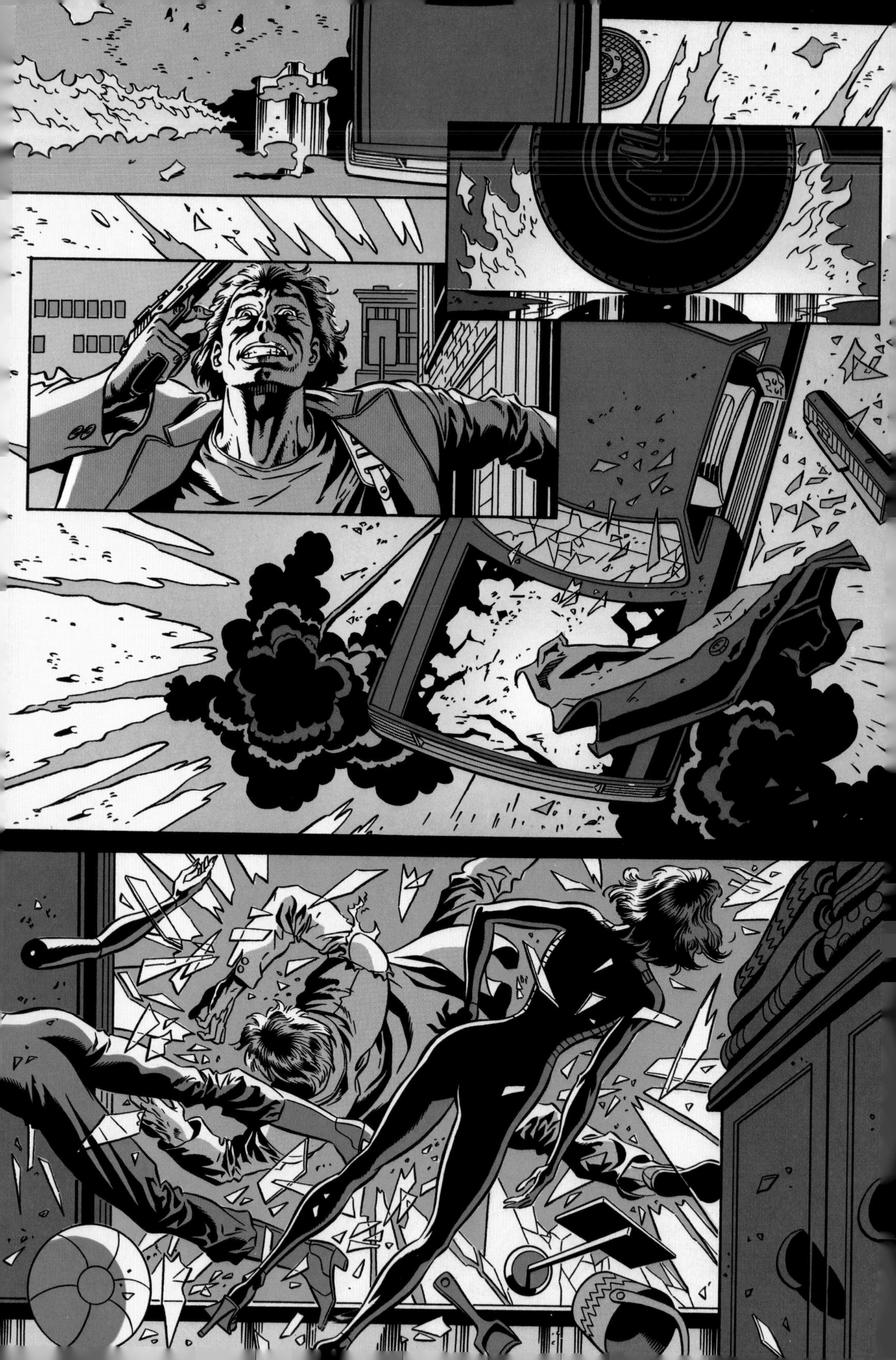

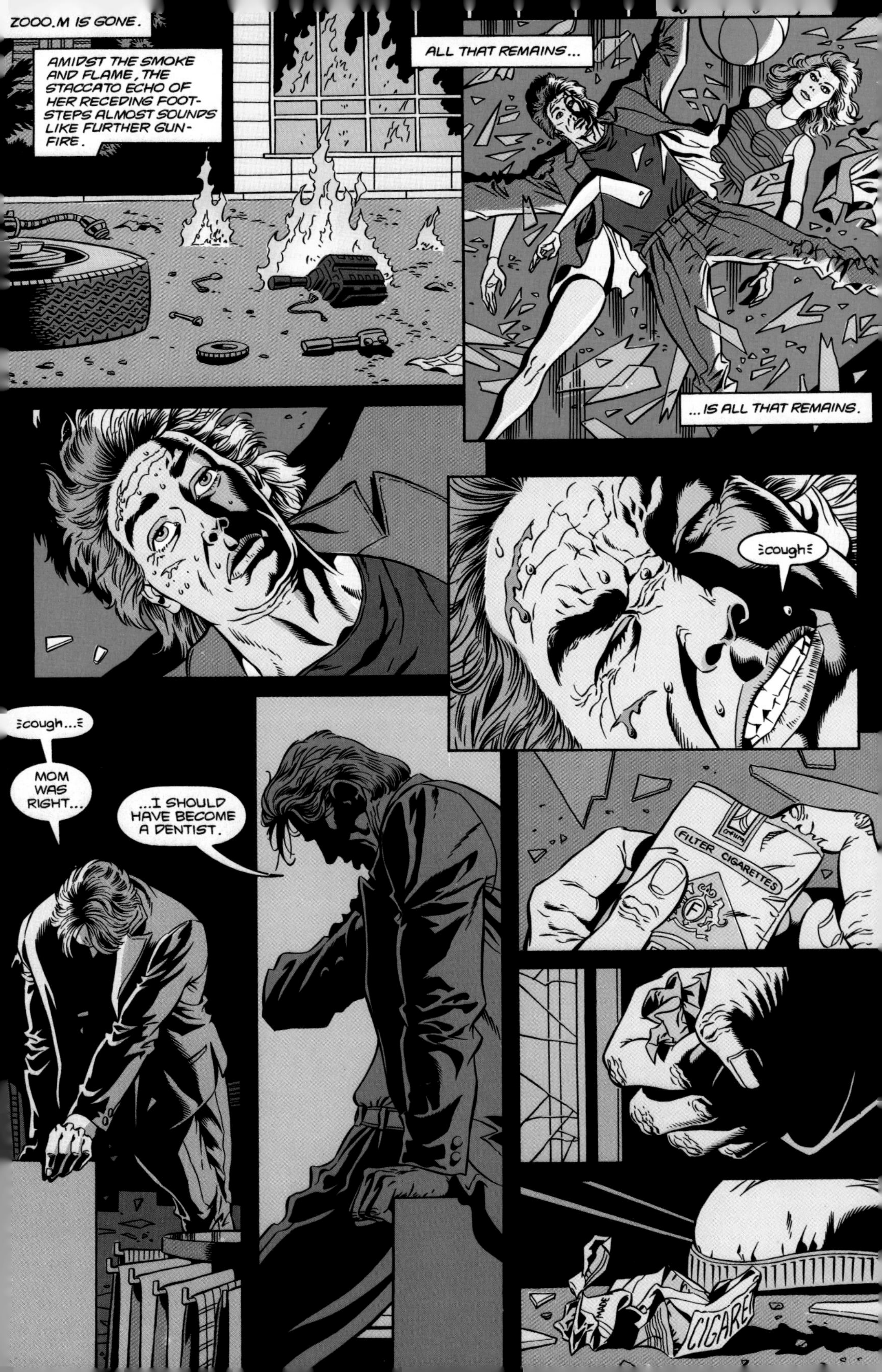
ZOOO.M IS GONE.
AMIDST THE SMOKE AND FLAME, THE STACCATO ECHO OF HER RECEDING FOOTSTEPS ALMOST SOUNDS LIKE FURTHER GUNFIRE.
ALL THAT REMAINS...
...IS ALL THAT REMAINS.
cough
cough...
MOM WAS RIGHT...
...I SHOULD HAVE BECOME A DENTIST.
FILTER CIGARETTES
CIGARE

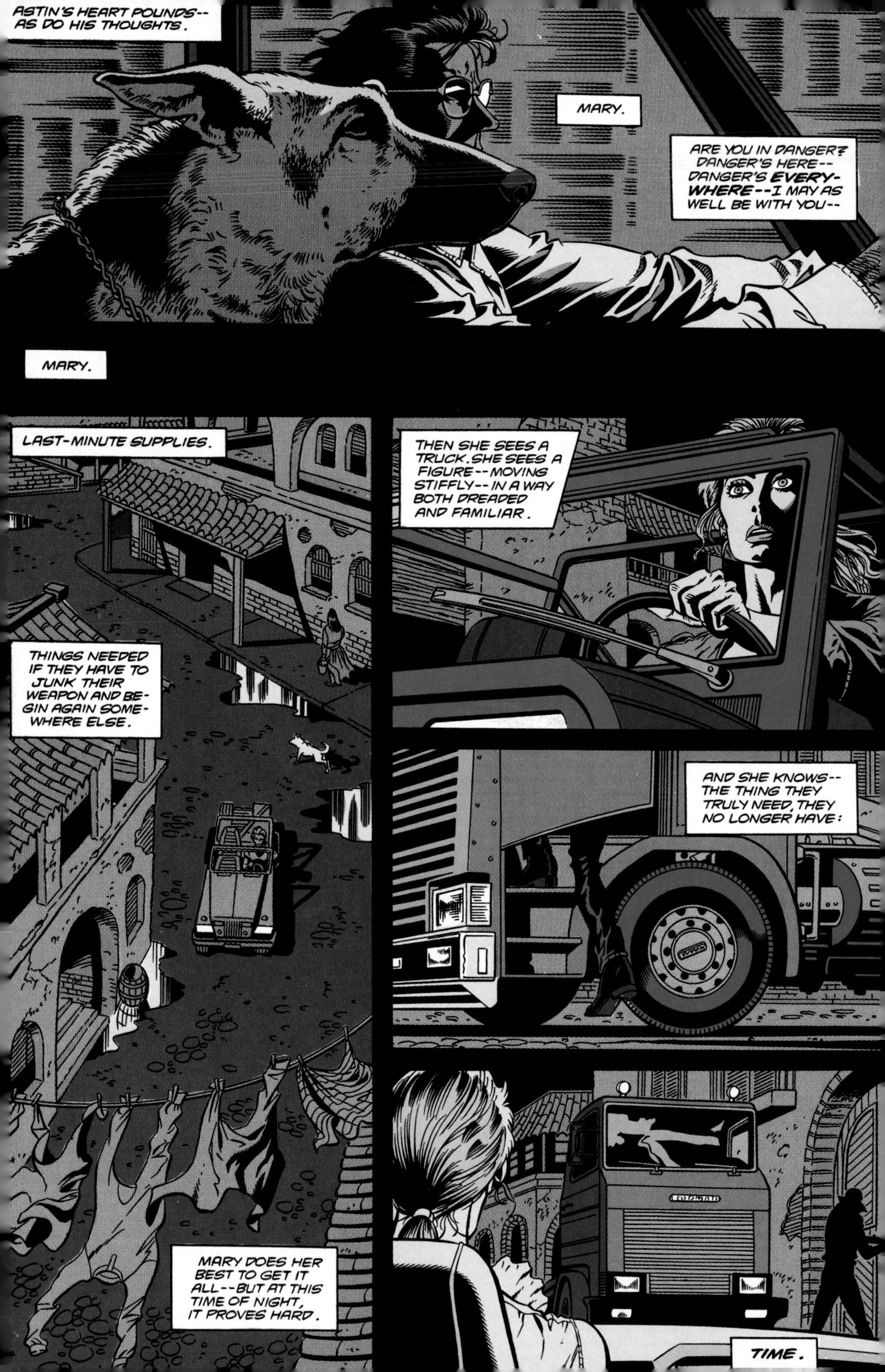
ASTIN'S HEART POUNDS-- AS DO HIS THOUGHTS.
MARY.
ARE YOU IN DANGER? DANGER'S HERE-- DANGER'S EVERY-WHERE--I MAY AS WELL BE WITH YOU--
MARY.
LAST-MINUTE SUPPLIES.
THINGS NEEDED IF THEY HAVE TO JUNK THEIR WEAPON AND BE-GIN AGAIN SOME-WHERE ELSE.
MARY DOES HER BEST TO GET IT ALL--BUT AT THIS TIME OF NIGHT, IT PROVES HARD.
THEN SHE SEES A TRUCK. SHE SEES A FIGURE--MOVING STIFFLY--IN A WAY BOTH DREADED AND FAMILIAR.
AND SHE KNOWS-- THE THING THEY TRULY NEED, THEY NO LONGER HAVE:
TIME.

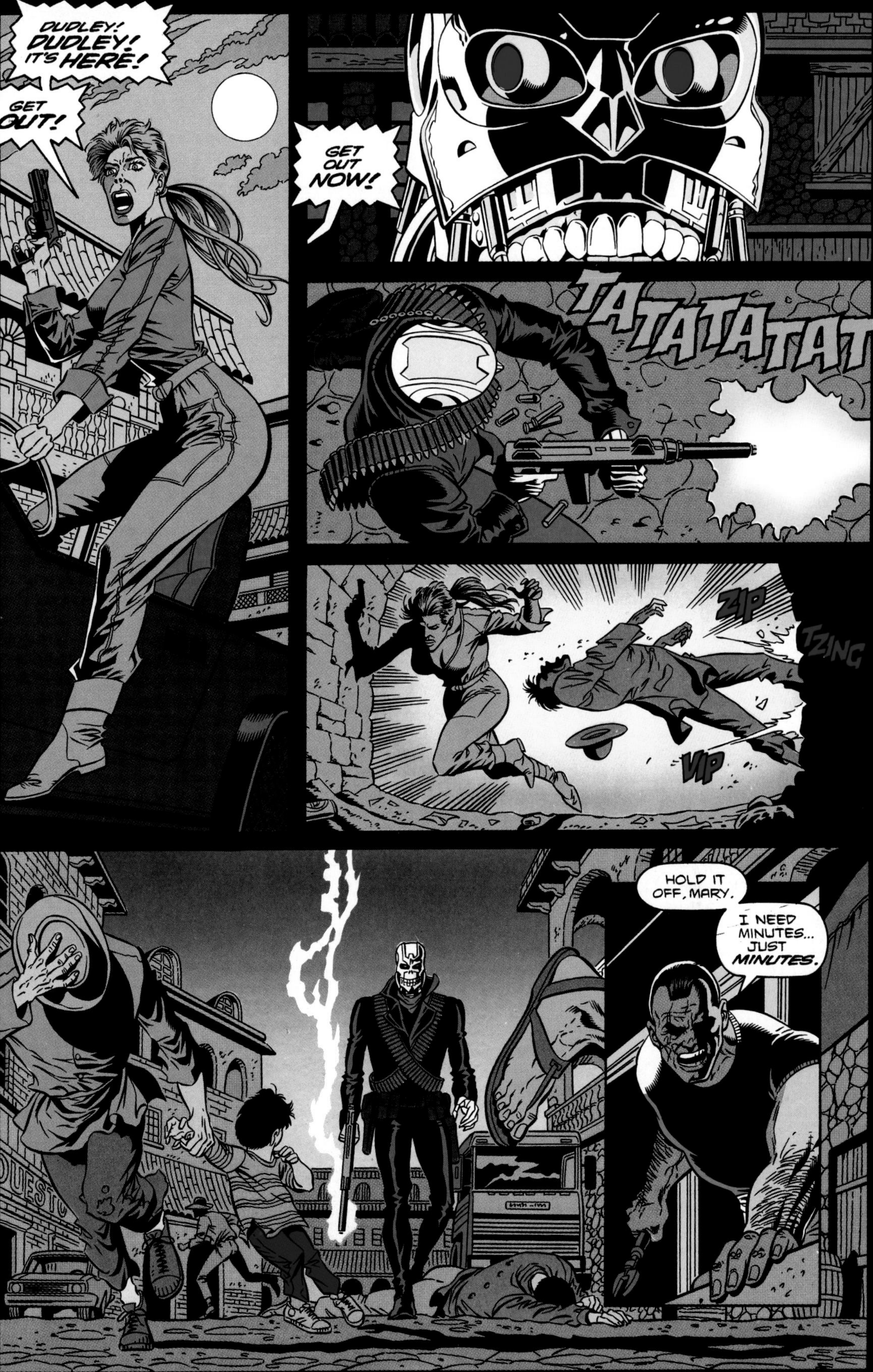
DUDLEY! DUDLEY! IT'S HERE!
GET OUT!
GET OUT NOW!
TATATATATAT
ZIP
TZING
VIP
HOLD IT OFF, MARY.
I NEED MINUTES... JUST MINUTES.

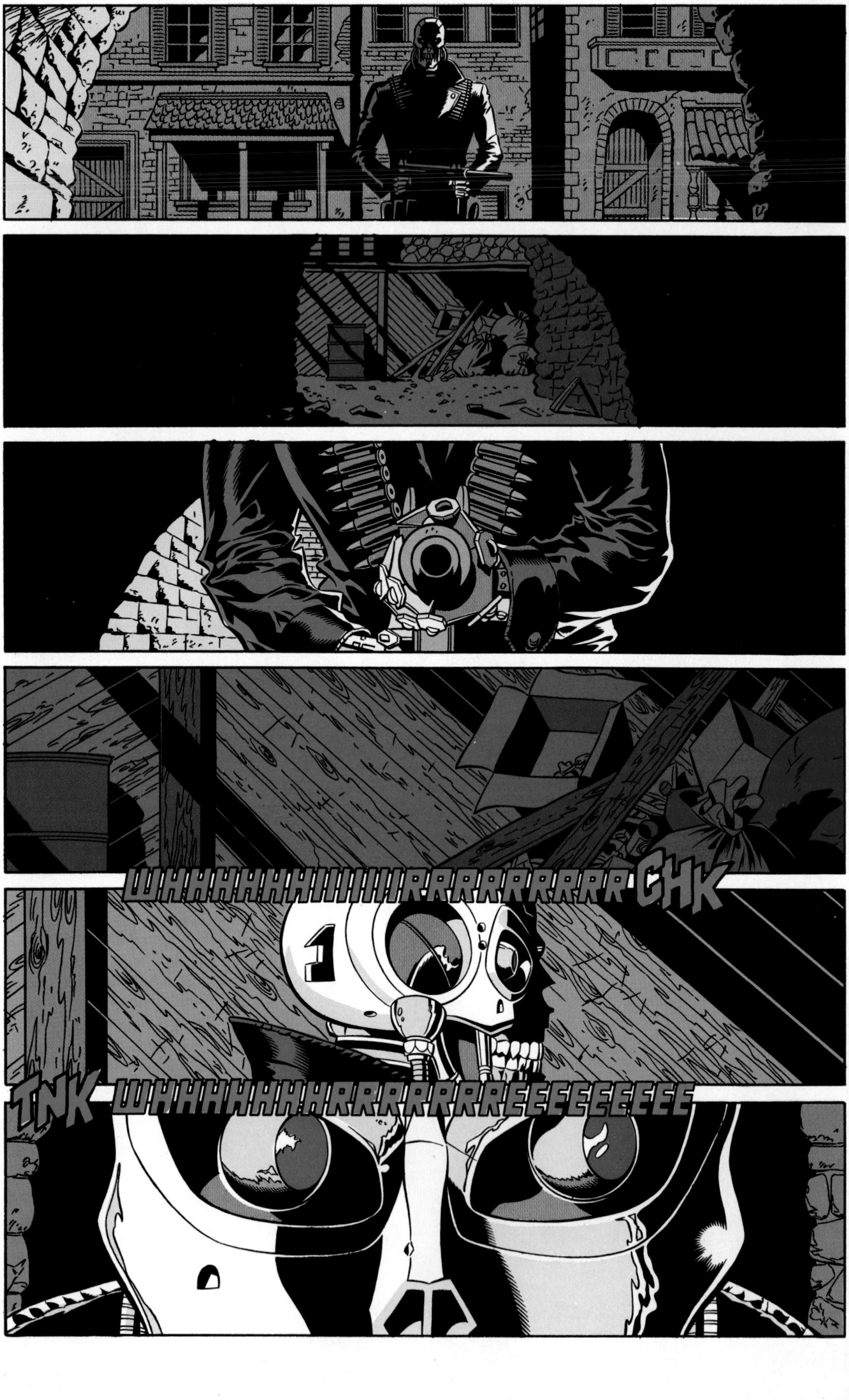
WHHHHHIIIIIIIIIRRRRRRRRRR CHK
TNK WHHHHHHHHRRRRRRREEEEEEEE

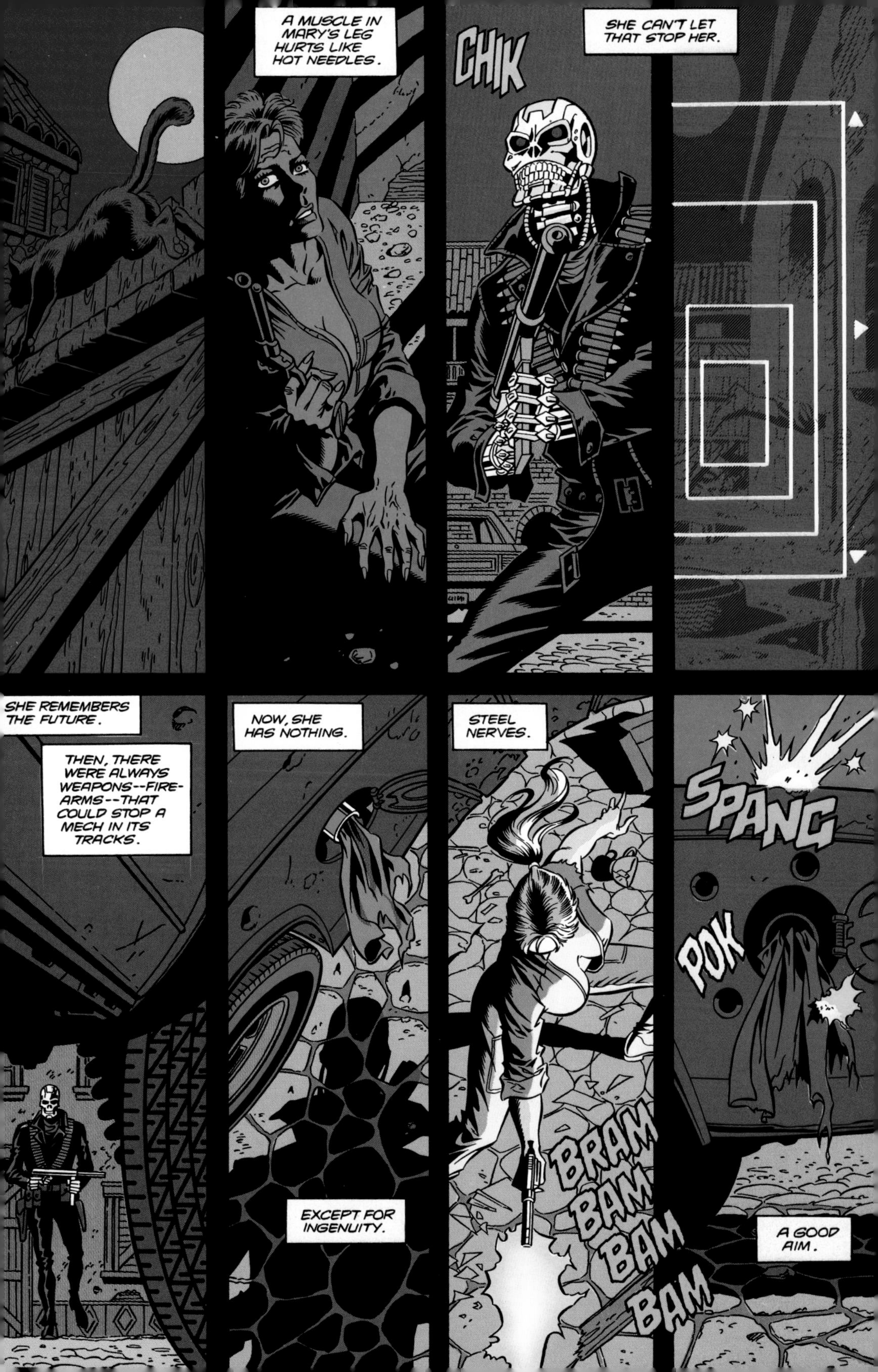
A MUSCLE IN MARY'S LEG HURTS LIKE HOT NEEDLES.
CHIK
SHE CAN'T LET THAT STOP HER.
SHE REMEMBERS THE FUTURE.
THEN, THERE WERE ALWAYS WEAPONS--FIRE-ARMS--THAT COULD STOP A MECH IN ITS TRACKS.
NOW, SHE HAS NOTHING.
EXCEPT FOR INGENUITY.
STEEL NERVES.
BRAM
BAM
BAM
BAM
SPANG
POK
A GOOD AIM.

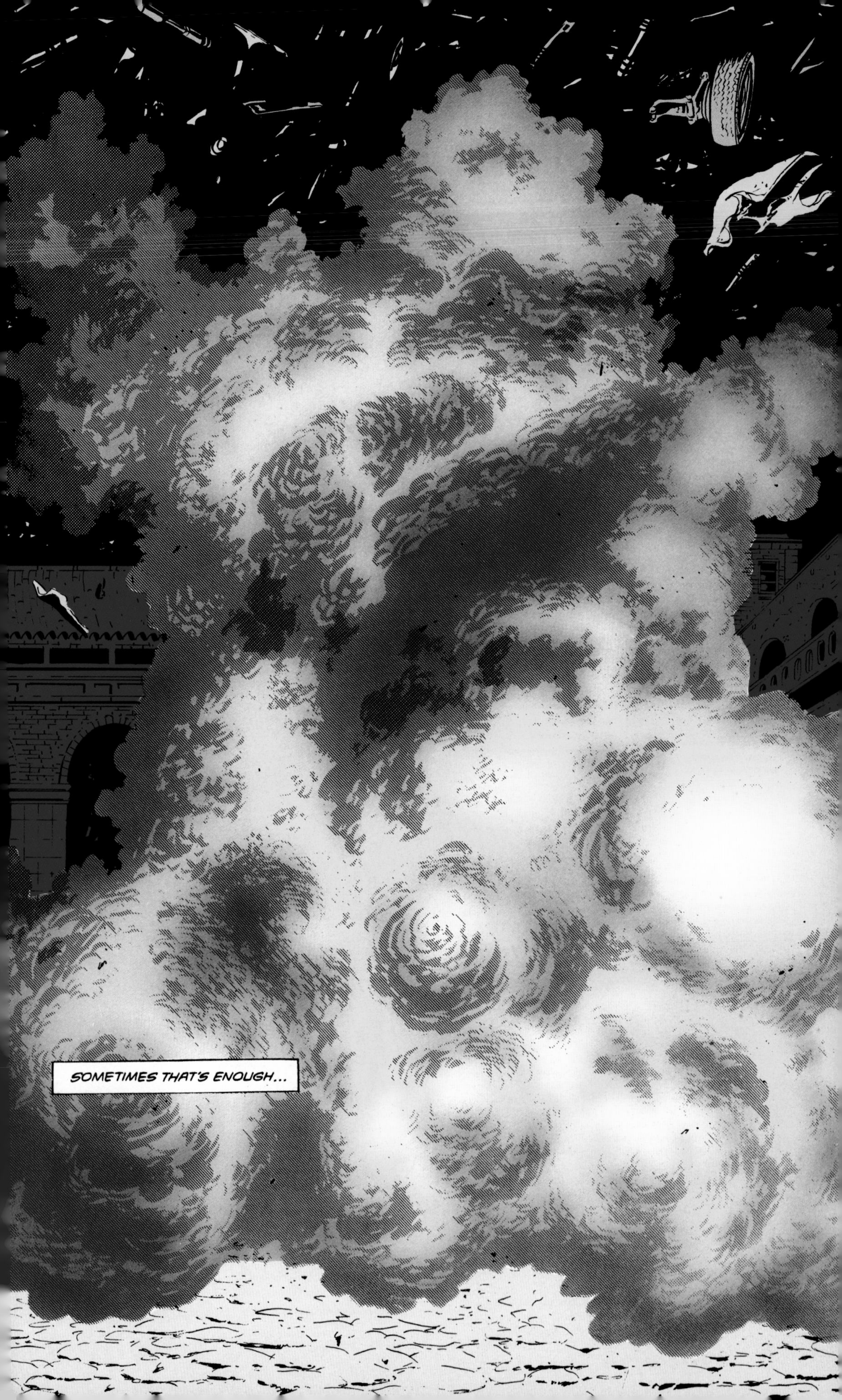
SOMETIMES THAT'S ENOUGH...

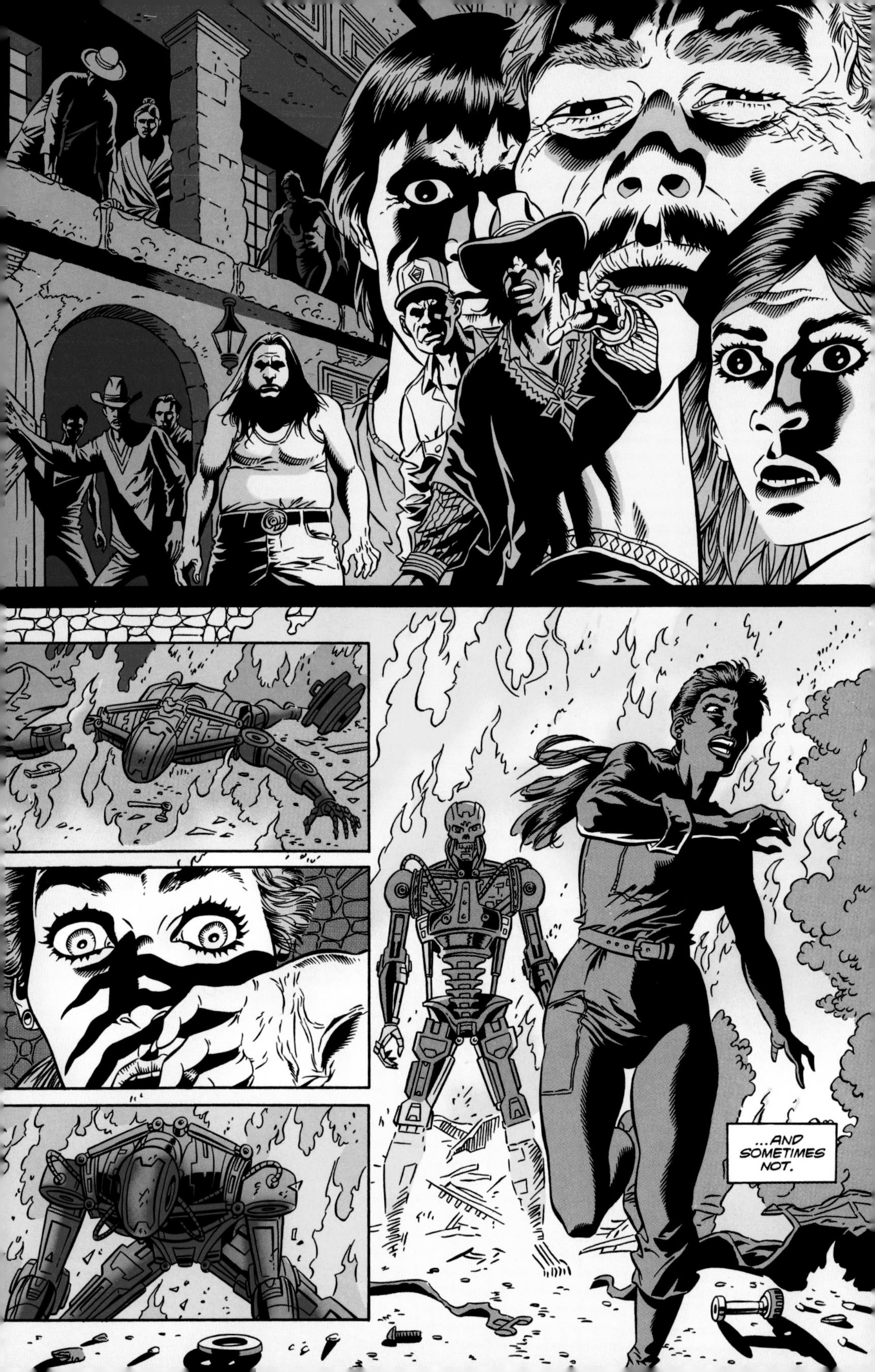
...AND SOMETIMES NOT.

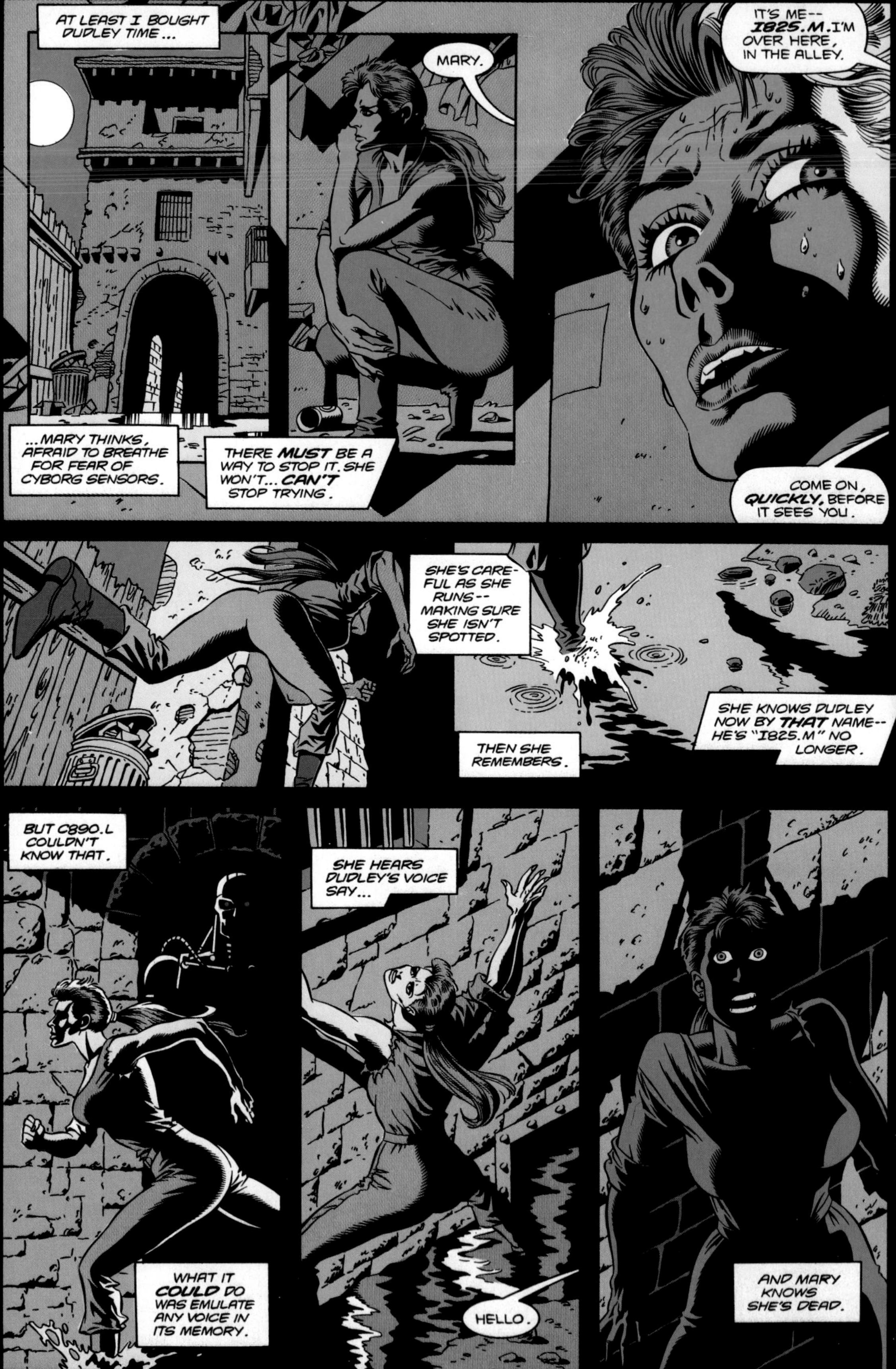
AT LEAST I BOUGHT DUDLEY TIME ...
...MARY THINKS, AFRAID TO BREATHE FOR FEAR OF CYBORG SENSORS.
MARY.
THERE MUST BE A WAY TO STOP IT. SHE WON'T... CAN'T STOP TRYING.
IT'S ME-- I825.M. I'M OVER HERE, IN THE ALLEY.
COME ON, QUICKLY, BEFORE IT SEES YOU.
SHE'S CAREFUL AS SHE RUNS-- MAKING SURE SHE ISN'T SPOTTED.
THEN SHE REMEMBERS.
SHE KNOWS DUDLEY NOW BY THAT NAME-- HE'S "I825.M" NO LONGER.
BUT C890.L COULDN'T KNOW THAT.
WHAT IT COULD DO WAS EMULATE ANY VOICE IN ITS MEMORY.
SHE HEARS DUDLEY'S VOICE SAY...
HELLO.
AND MARY KNOWS SHE'S DEAD.

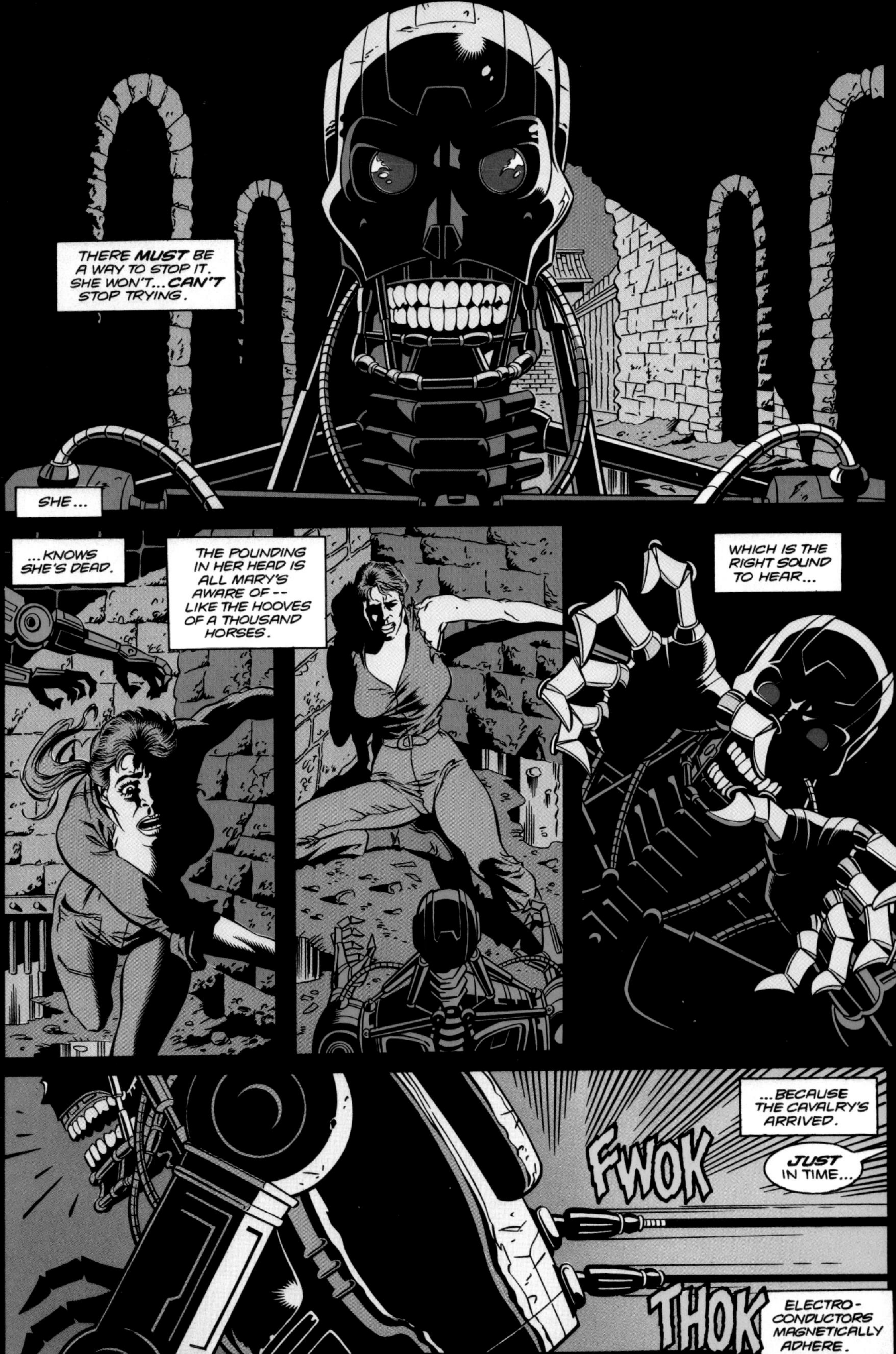
THERE MUST BE A WAY TO STOP IT. SHE WON'T... CAN'T STOP TRYING.
SHE...
...KNOWS SHE'S DEAD.
THE POUNDING IN HER HEAD IS ALL MARY'S AWARE OF -- LIKE THE HOOVES OF A THOUSAND HORSES.
WHICH IS THE RIGHT SOUND TO HEAR...
...BECAUSE THE CAVALRY'S ARRIVED.
FWOK
JUST IN TIME...
THOK
ELECTRO-CONDUCTORS MAGNETICALLY ADHERE.

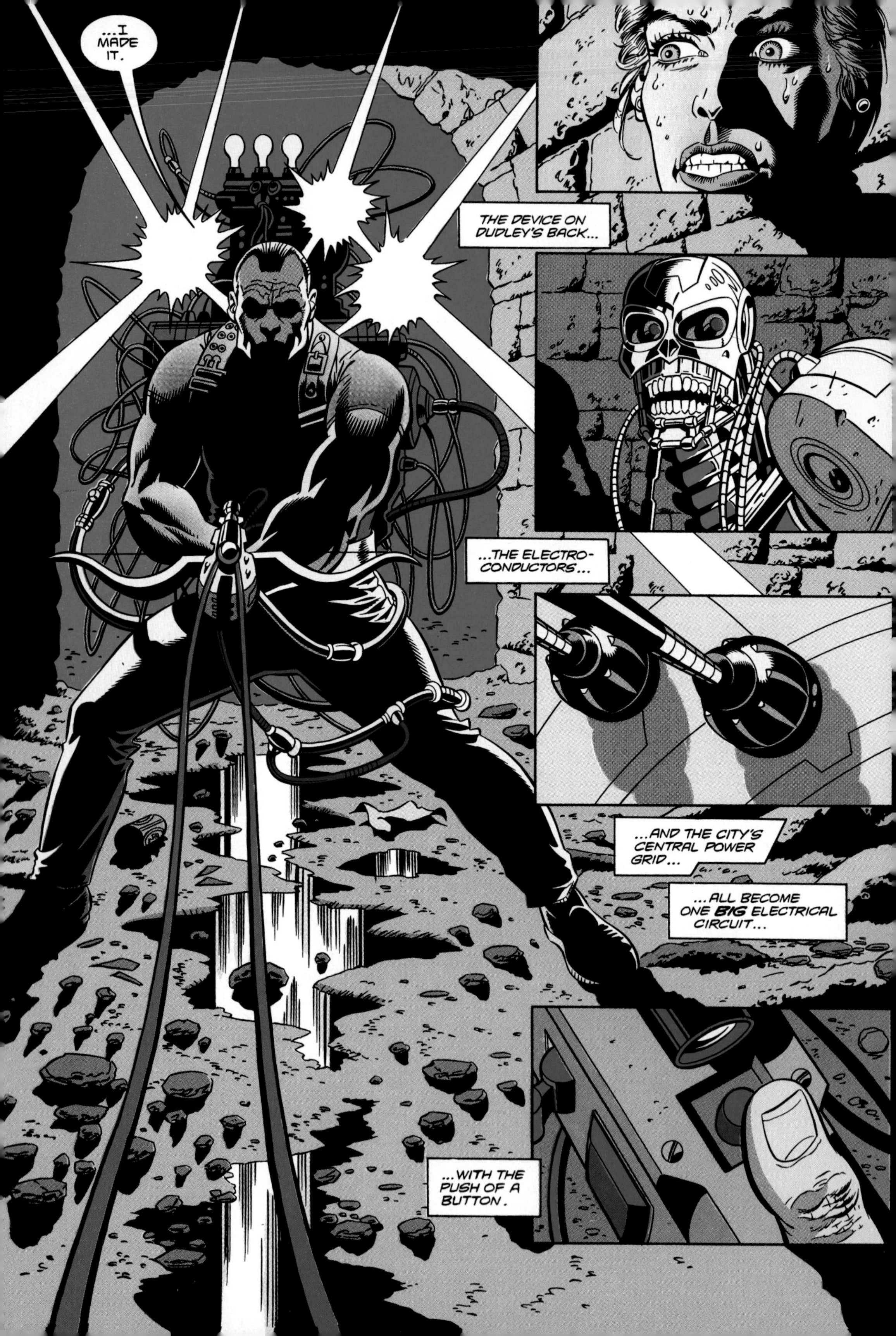
...I MADE IT.
THE DEVICE ON DUDLEY'S BACK...
...THE ELECTRO-CONDUCTORS...
...AND THE CITY'S CENTRAL POWER GRID...
...ALL BECOME ONE BIG ELECTRICAL CIRCUIT...
...WITH THE PUSH OF A BUTTON.

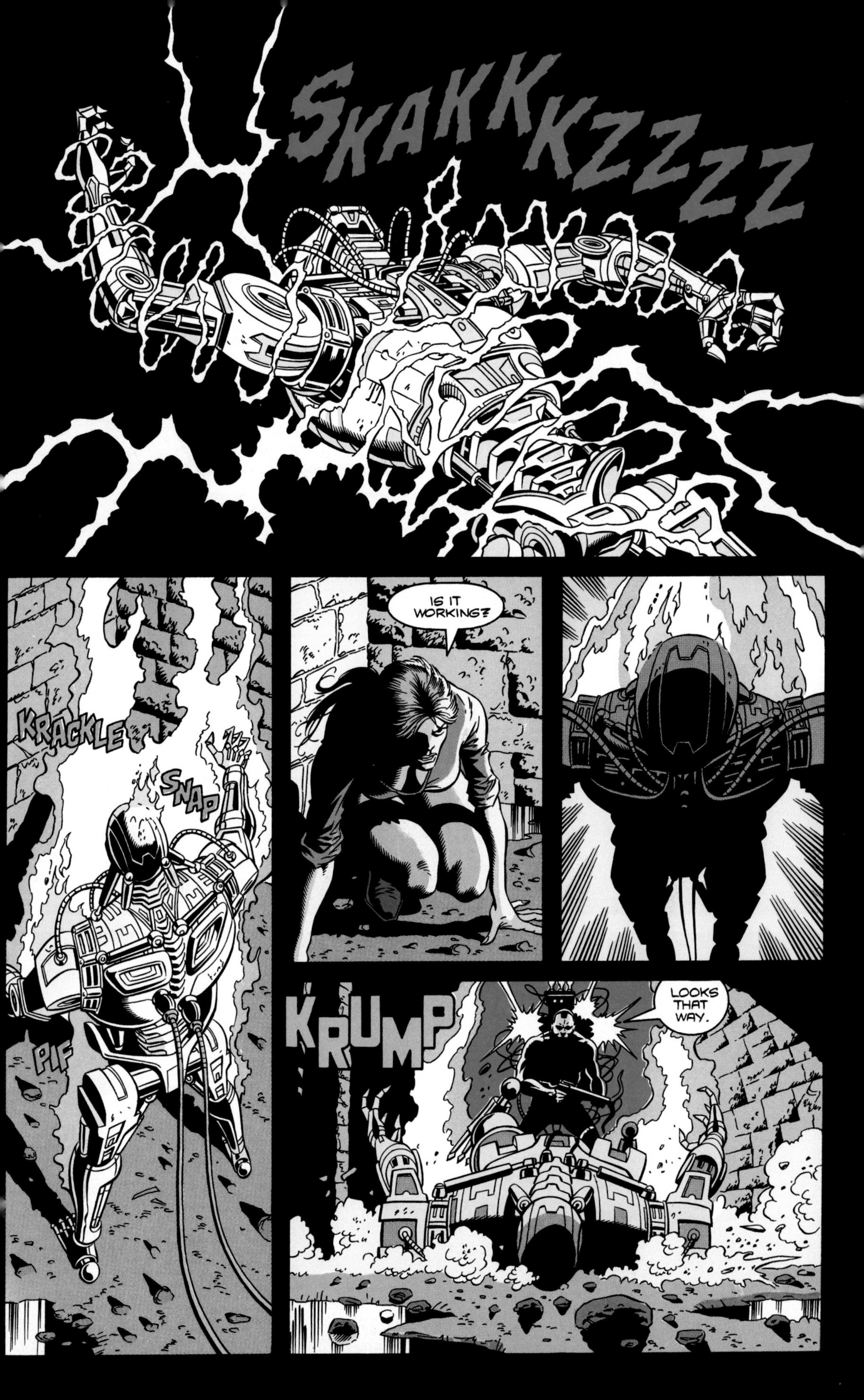
SKAKKKZZZZZ
KRACKLE
SNAP
PIF
IS IT WORKING?
KRUMP
LOOKS THAT WAY.

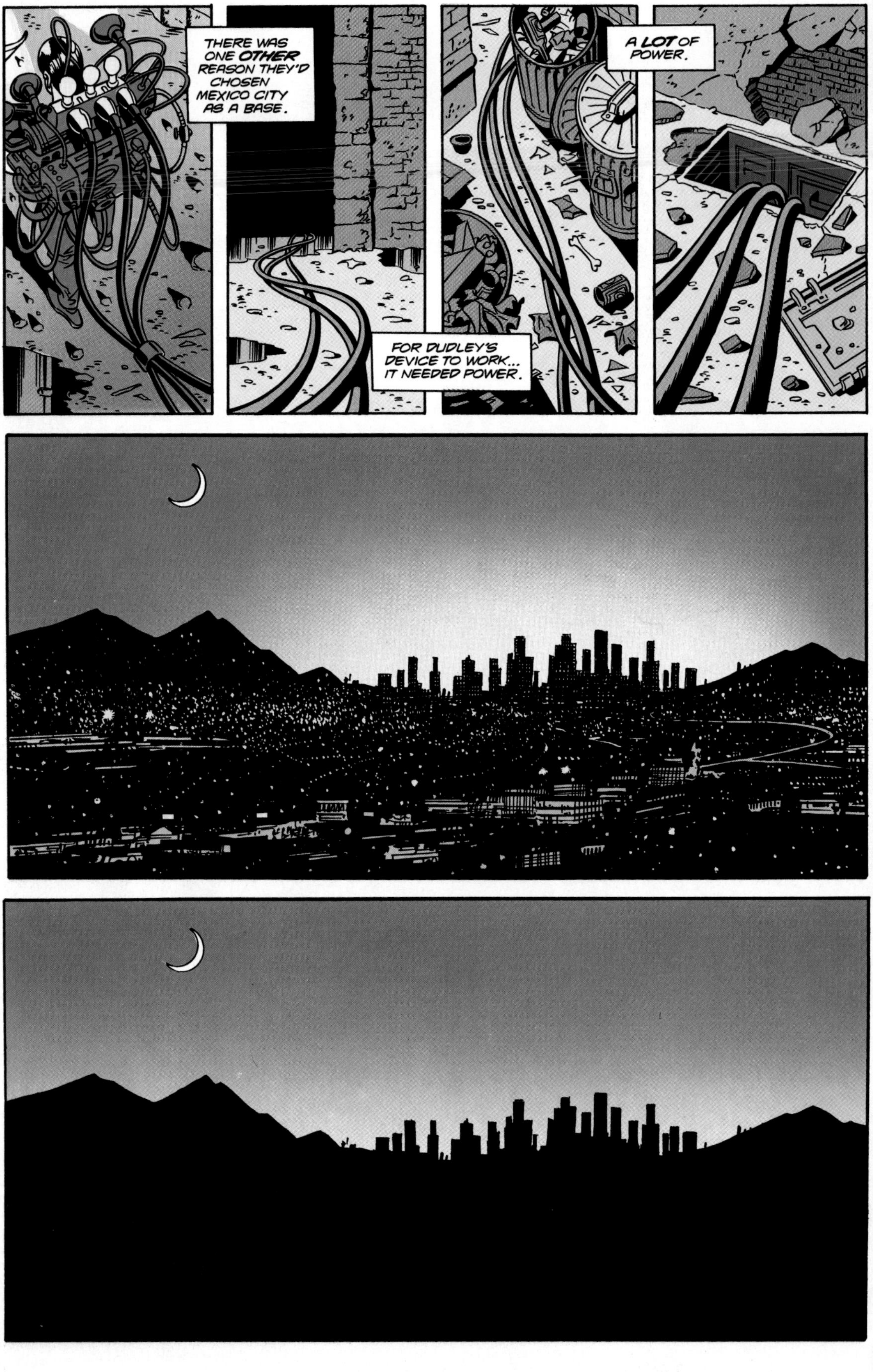
THERE WAS ONE OTHER REASON THEY'D CHOSEN MEXICO CITY AS A BASE.
FOR DUDLEY'S DEVICE TO WORK... IT NEEDED POWER.
A LOT OF POWER.

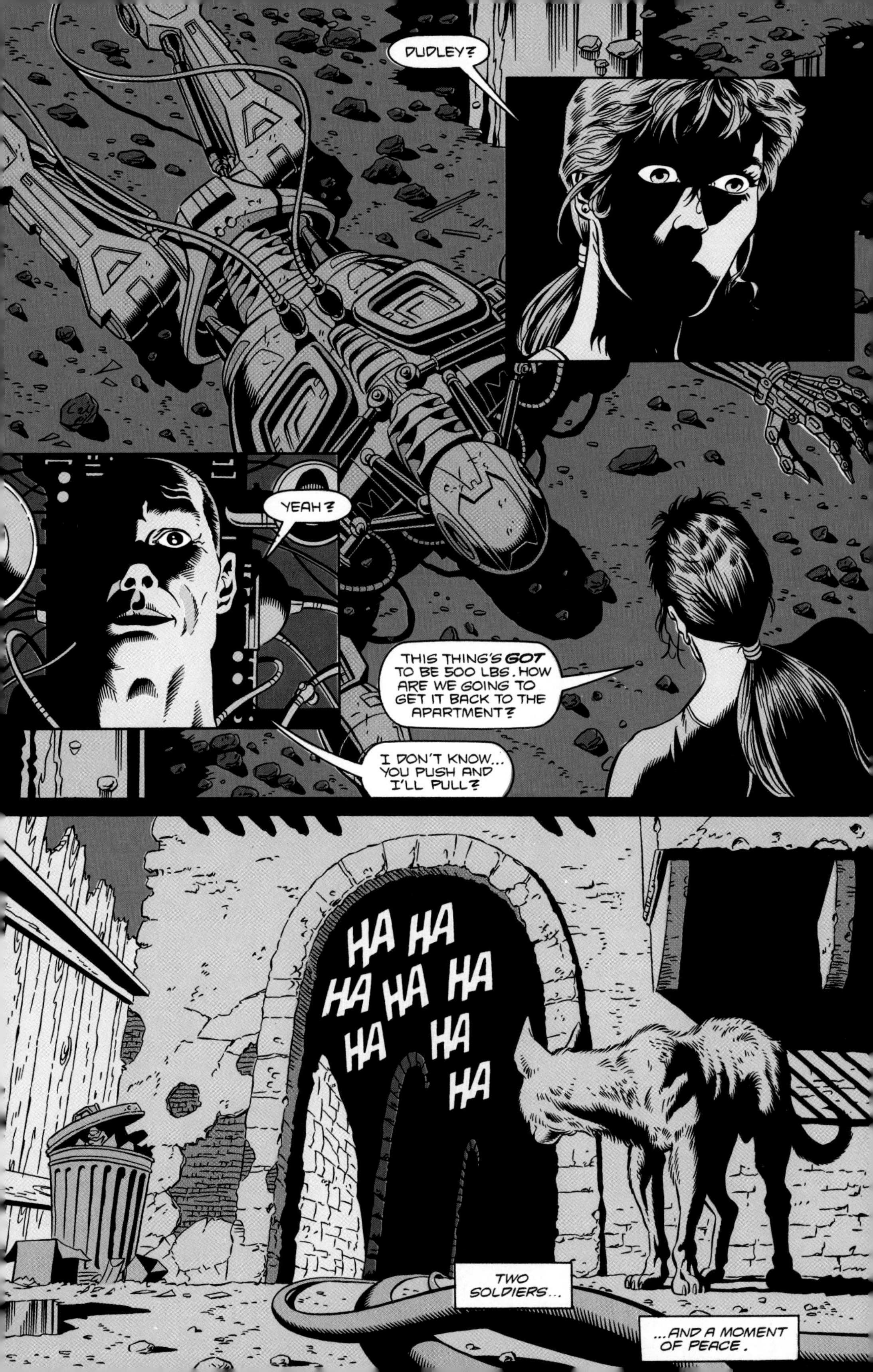
DUDLEY?
YEAH?
THIS THING'S **GOT** TO BE 500 LBS. HOW ARE WE GOING TO GET IT BACK TO THE APARTMENT?
I DON'T KNOW... YOU PUSH AND I'LL PULL?
HA HA HA HA HA HA HA HA
TWO SOLDIERS...
...AND A MOMENT OF PEACE.

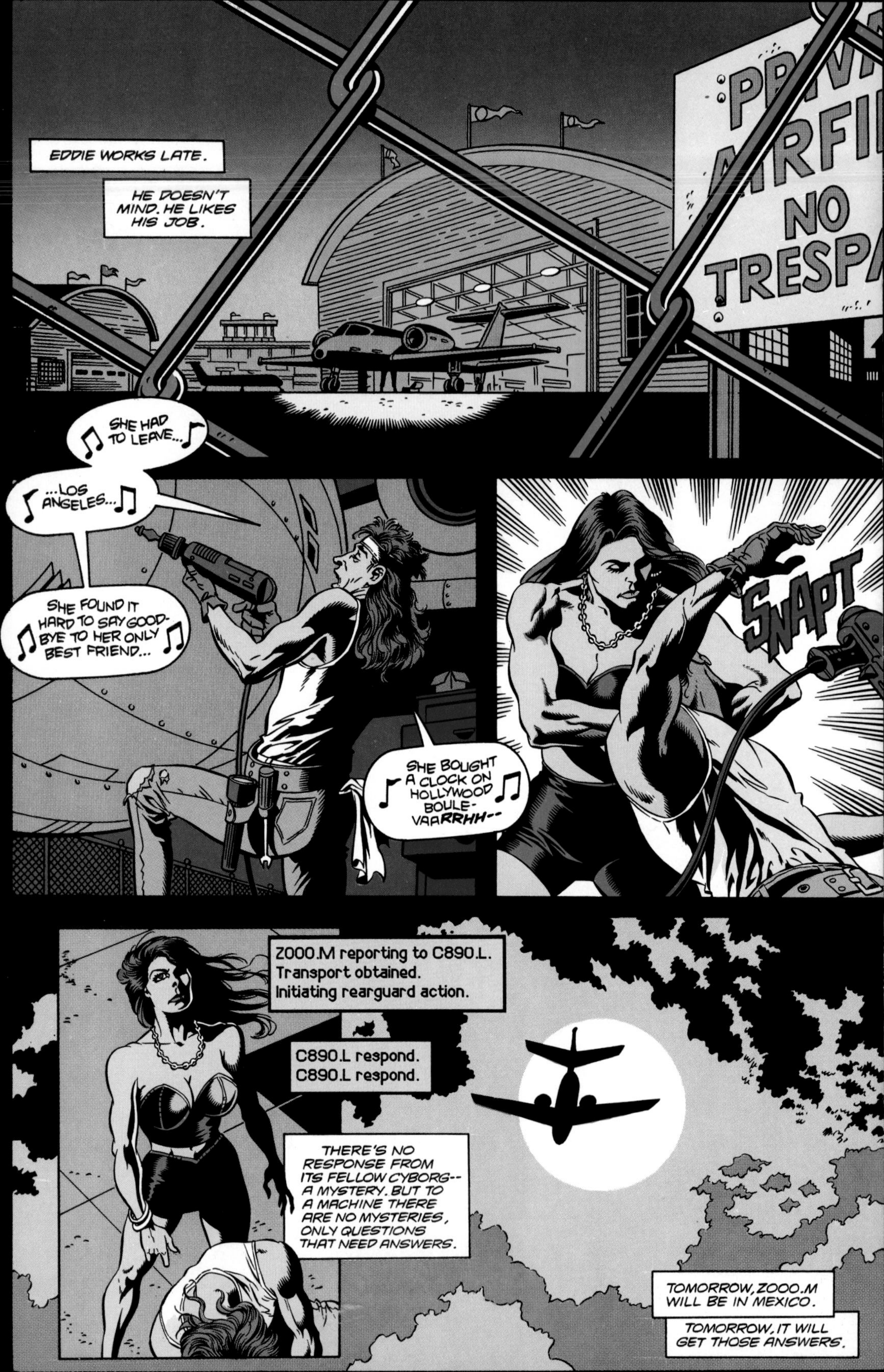

PRIVA[TE] AIRFI[ELD] NO TRESPA[SSING]
EDDIE WORKS LATE.
HE DOESN'T MIND. HE LIKES HIS JOB.
♫ SHE HAD TO LEAVE... ♪
♪ ...LOS ANGELES... ♫
SHE FOUND IT HARD TO SAY GOOD-BYE TO HER ONLY BEST FRIEND... ♫
♪ SHE BOUGHT A CLOCK ON HOLLYWOOD BOULE-VAARRHH-- ♫
SNAPT
Z000.M reporting to C890.L. Transport obtained. Initiating rearguard action.
C890.L respond. C890.L respond.
THERE'S NO RESPONSE FROM ITS FELLOW CYBORG-- A MYSTERY. BUT TO A MACHINE THERE ARE NO MYSTERIES, ONLY QUESTIONS THAT NEED ANSWERS.
TOMORROW, Z000.M WILL BE IN MEXICO.
TOMORROW, IT WILL GET THOSE ANSWERS.

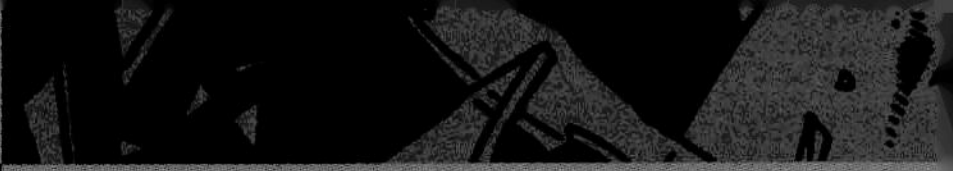

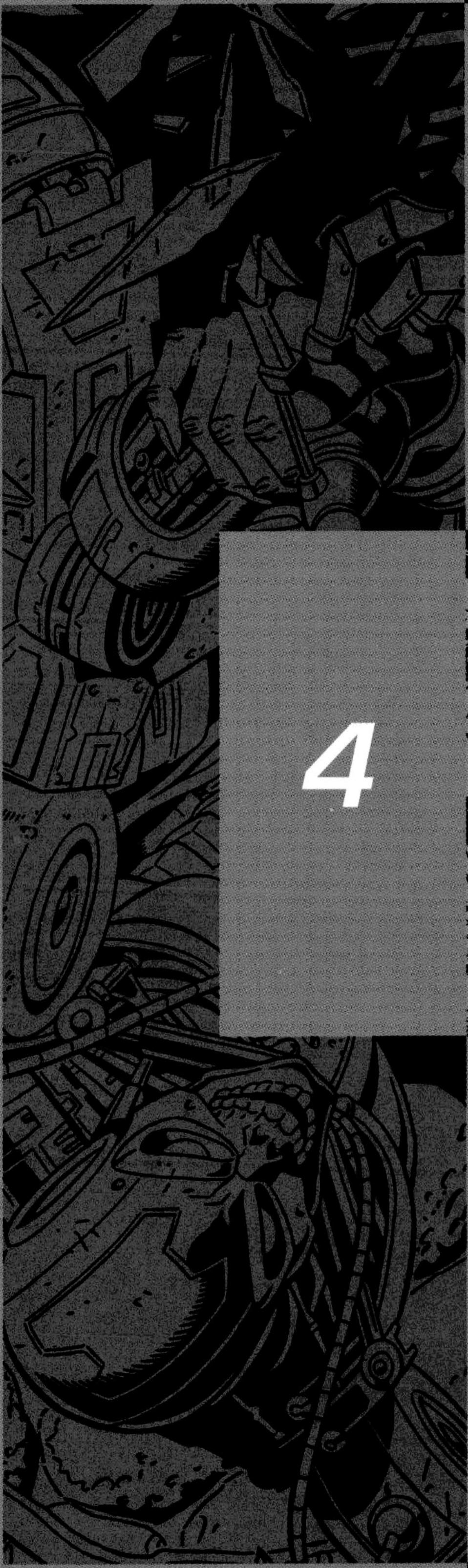

4

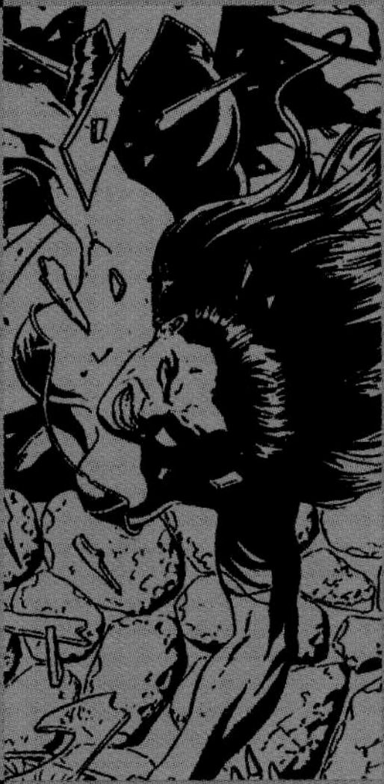

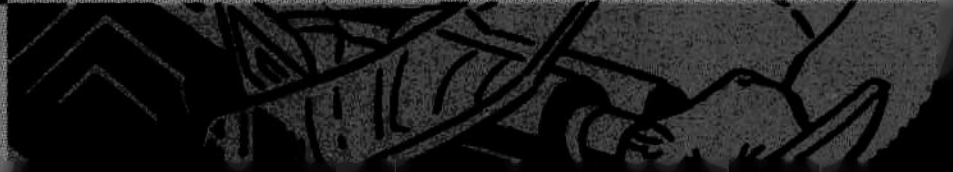

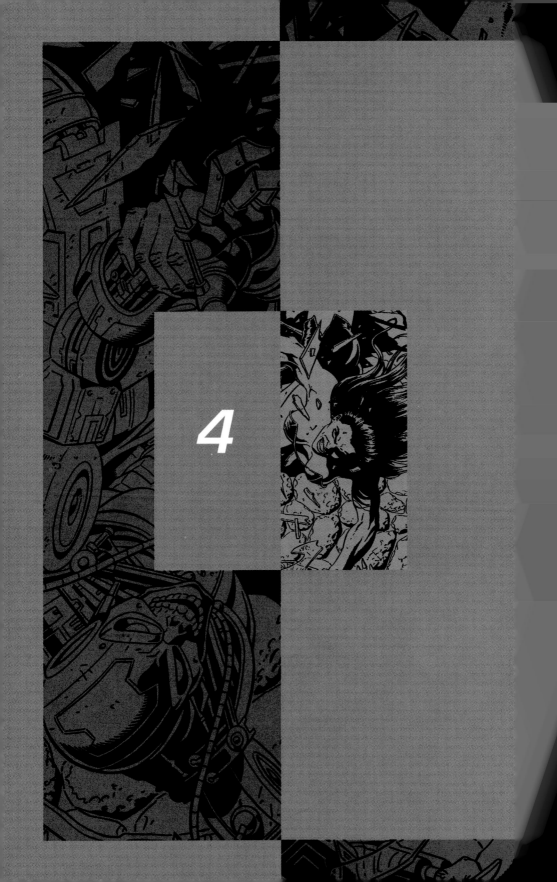

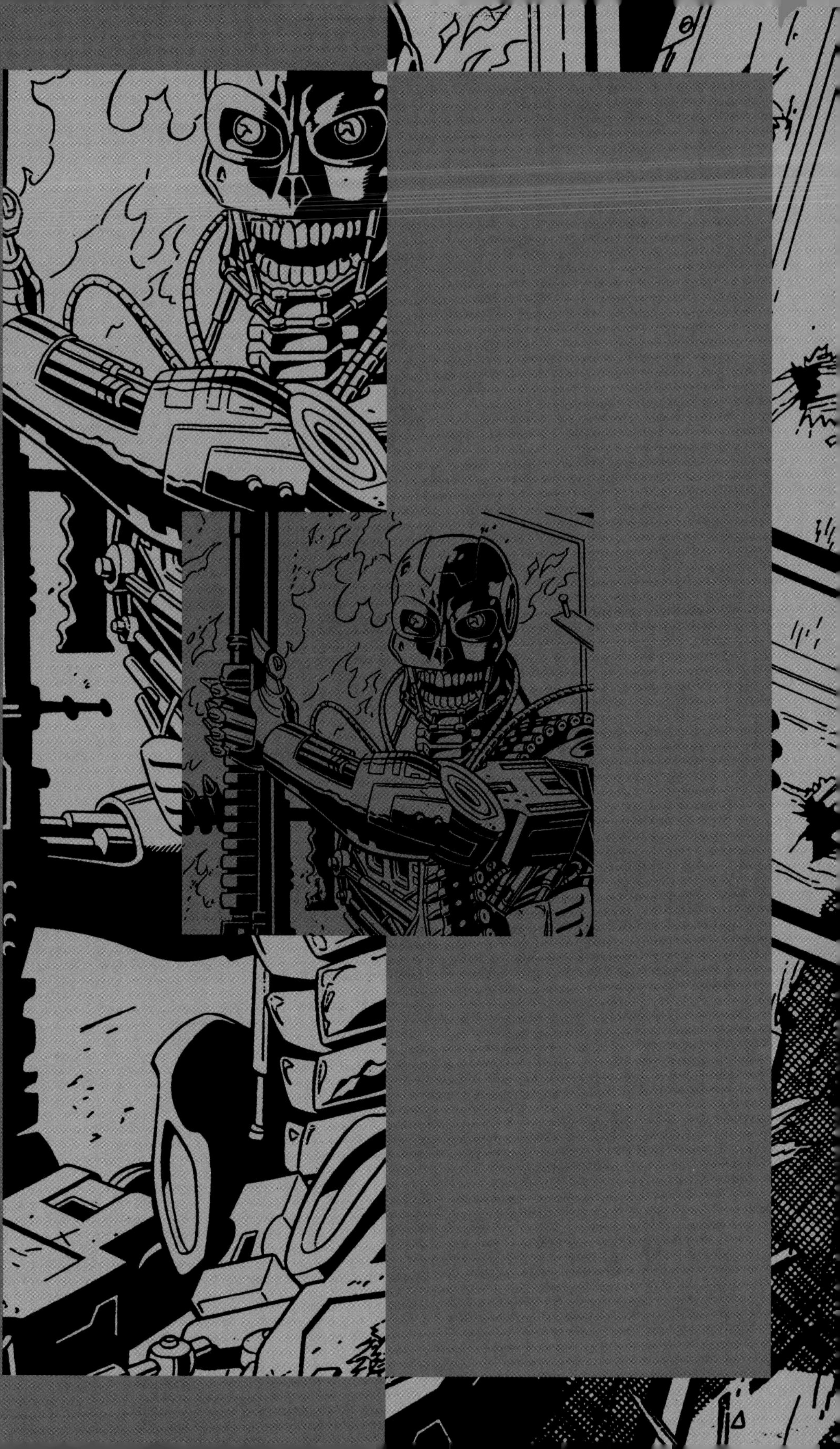

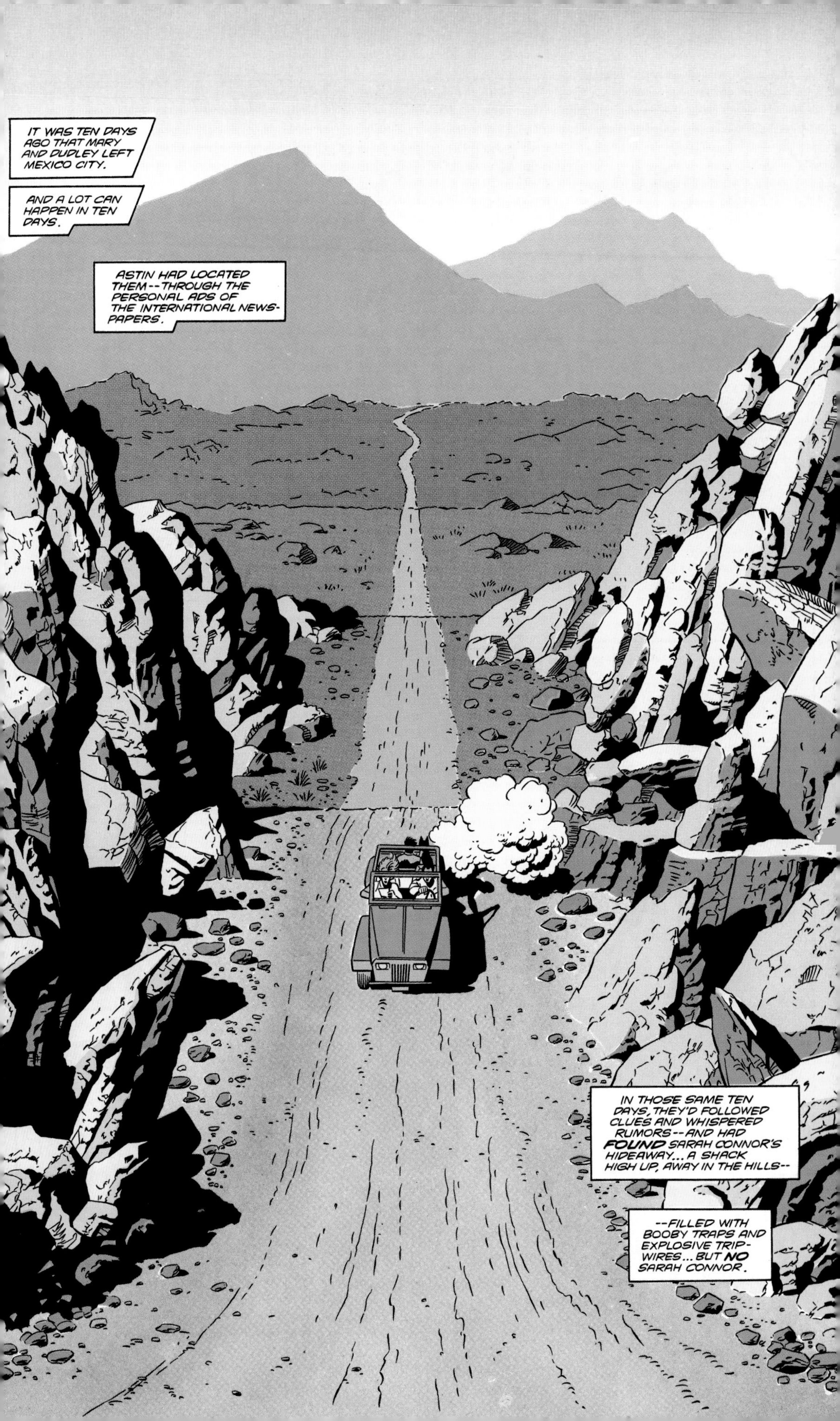
IT WAS TEN DAYS AGO THAT MARY AND DUDLEY LEFT MEXICO CITY.
AND A LOT CAN HAPPEN IN TEN DAYS.
ASTIN HAD LOCATED THEM--THROUGH THE PERSONAL ADS OF THE INTERNATIONAL NEWS-PAPERS.
IN THOSE SAME TEN DAYS, THEY'D FOLLOWED CLUES AND WHISPERED RUMORS--AND HAD **FOUND** SARAH CONNOR'S HIDEAWAY... A SHACK HIGH UP, AWAY IN THE HILLS--
--FILLED WITH BOOBY TRAPS AND EXPLOSIVE TRIP-WIRES... BUT **NO** SARAH CONNOR.

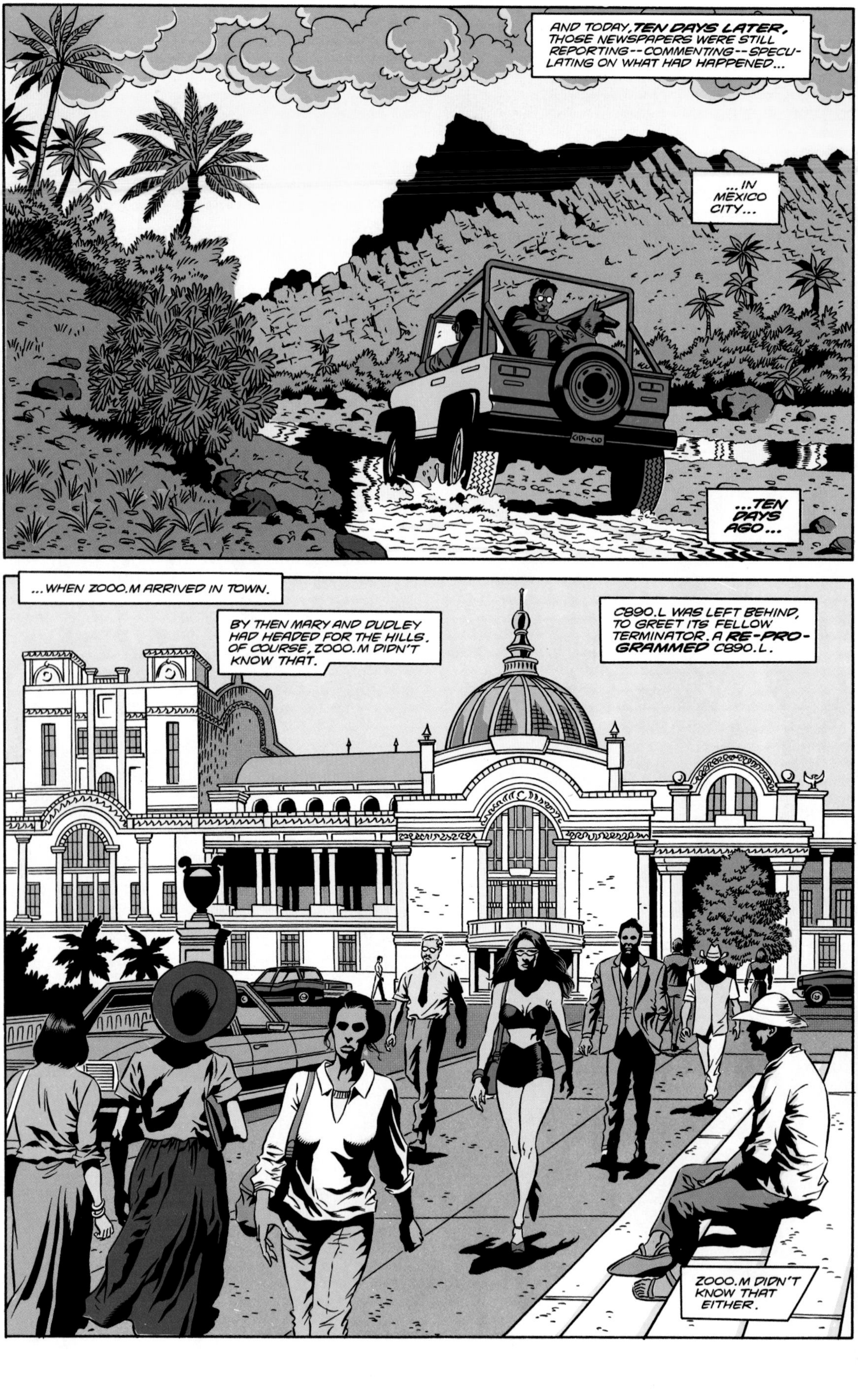

AND TODAY, **TEN DAYS LATER,** THOSE NEWSPAPERS WERE STILL REPORTING--COMMENTING--SPECULATING ON WHAT HAD HAPPENED...
...IN MÉXICO CITY...
...TEN DAYS AGO...
...WHEN ZOOO.M ARRIVED IN TOWN.
BY THEN MARY AND DUDLEY HAD HEADED FOR THE HILLS. OF COURSE, ZOOO.M DIDN'T KNOW THAT.
C890.L WAS LEFT BEHIND, TO GREET ITS FELLOW TERMINATOR. A **RE-PROGRAMMED** C890.L.
ZOOO.M DIDN'T KNOW THAT EITHER.

IT DIDN'T KNOW WHAT DUDLEY HAD DONE...

...INSIDE C890.L'S SKULL-- WITH A SCREWPRIVER AND THE RIGHT KNOWLEDGE.

"AN 800- MODEL'S BRAIN," DUDLEY TOLD MARY, "IS JUST A COMPUTER."

"ITS INBUILT PROGRAMS ARE IMPOSSIBLE TO COMPLETELY DE-LETE...BUT THEY CAN BE *TEMPO-RARILY* OVER-RIDDEN."

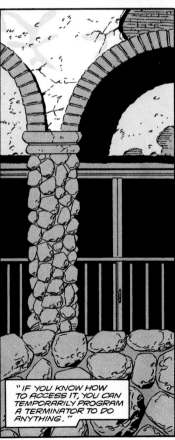

"IF YOU KNOW HOW TO ACCESS IT, YOU CAN TEMPORARILY PROGRAM A TERMINATOR TO DO ANYTHING."

ANYTHING.

INCLUDING...

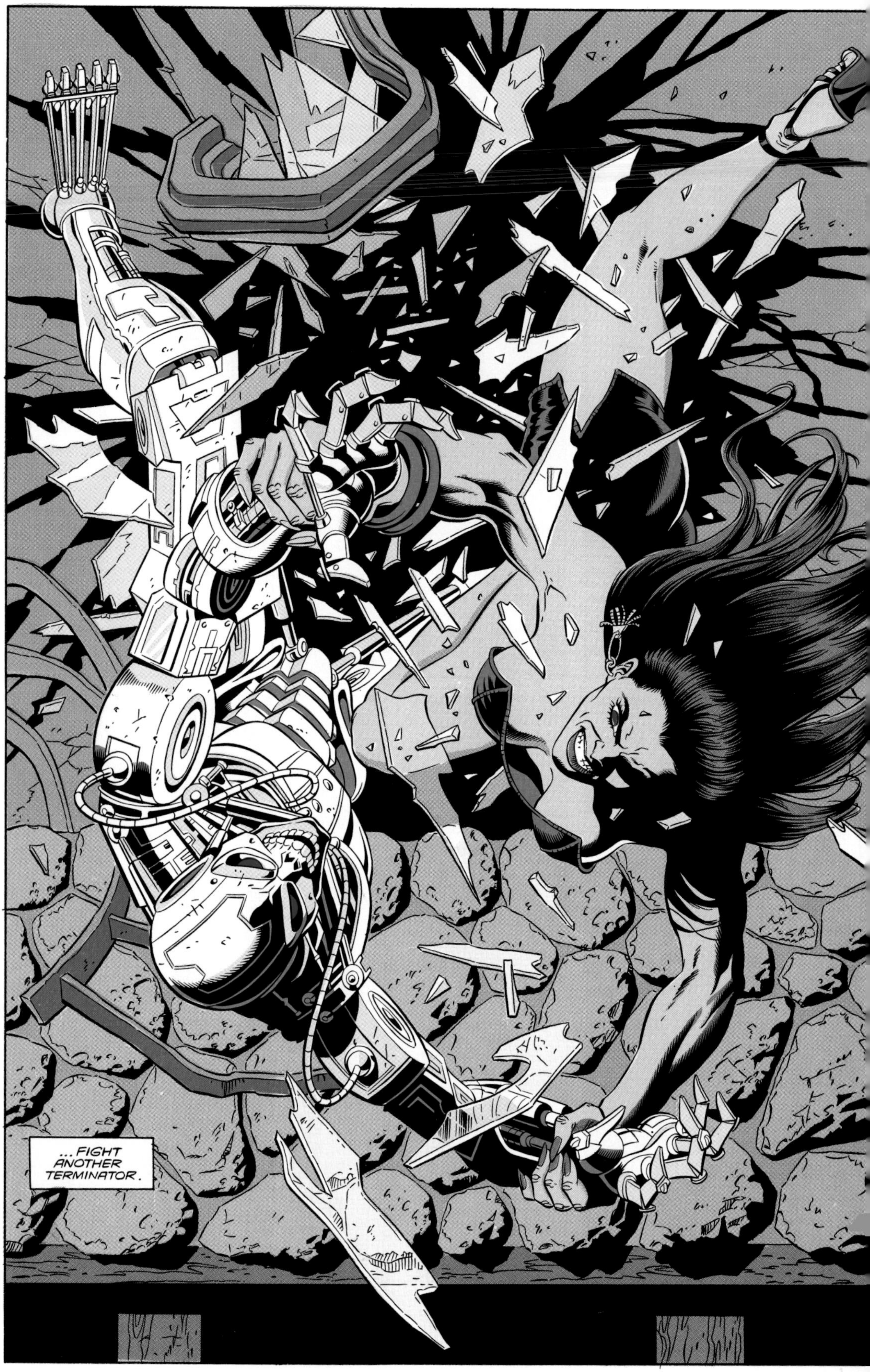
...FIGHT ANOTHER TERMINATOR.

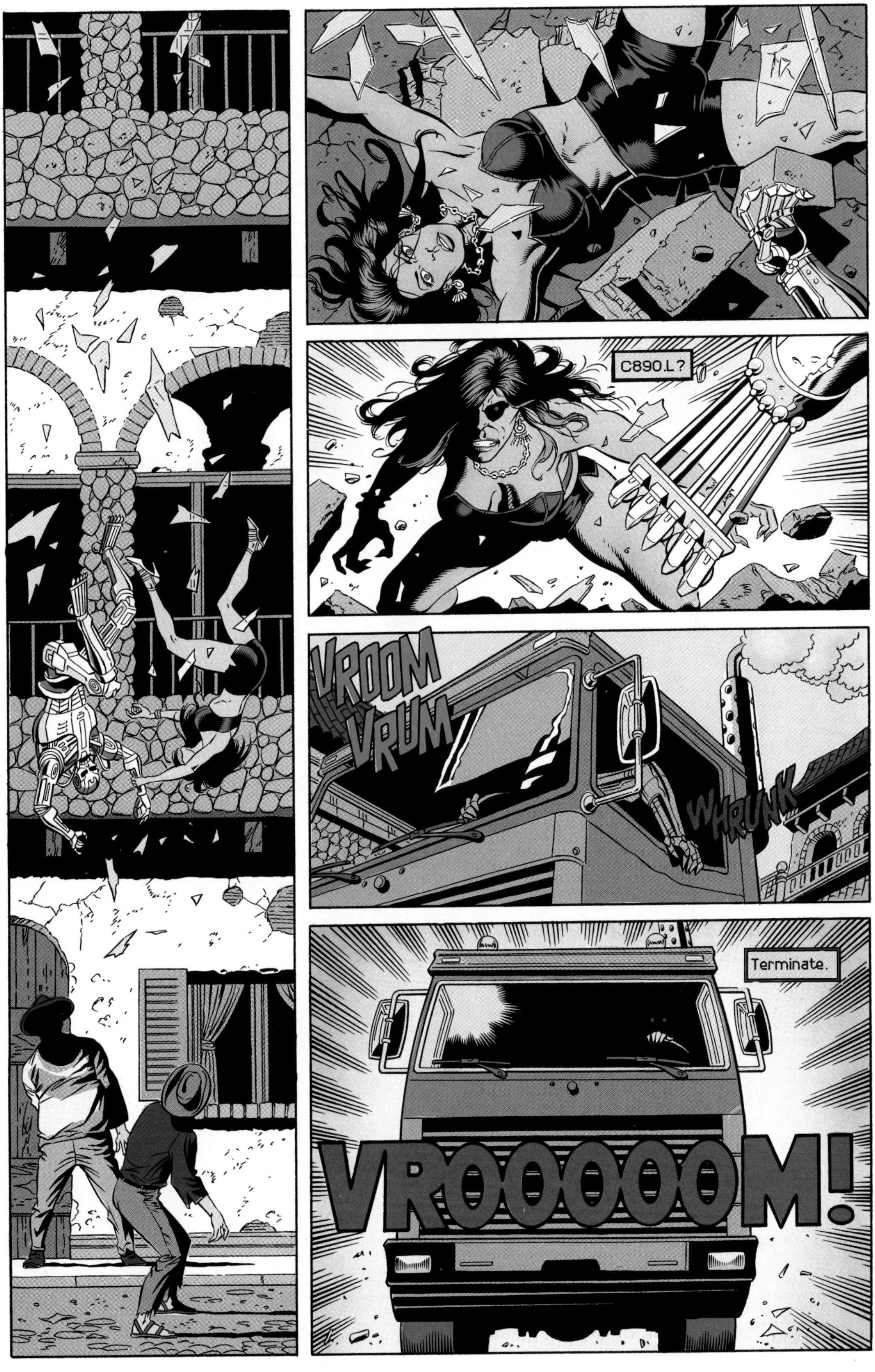
C890.L?
VROOM
VRUM
WHRUNK
Terminate.
VROOOOOM!

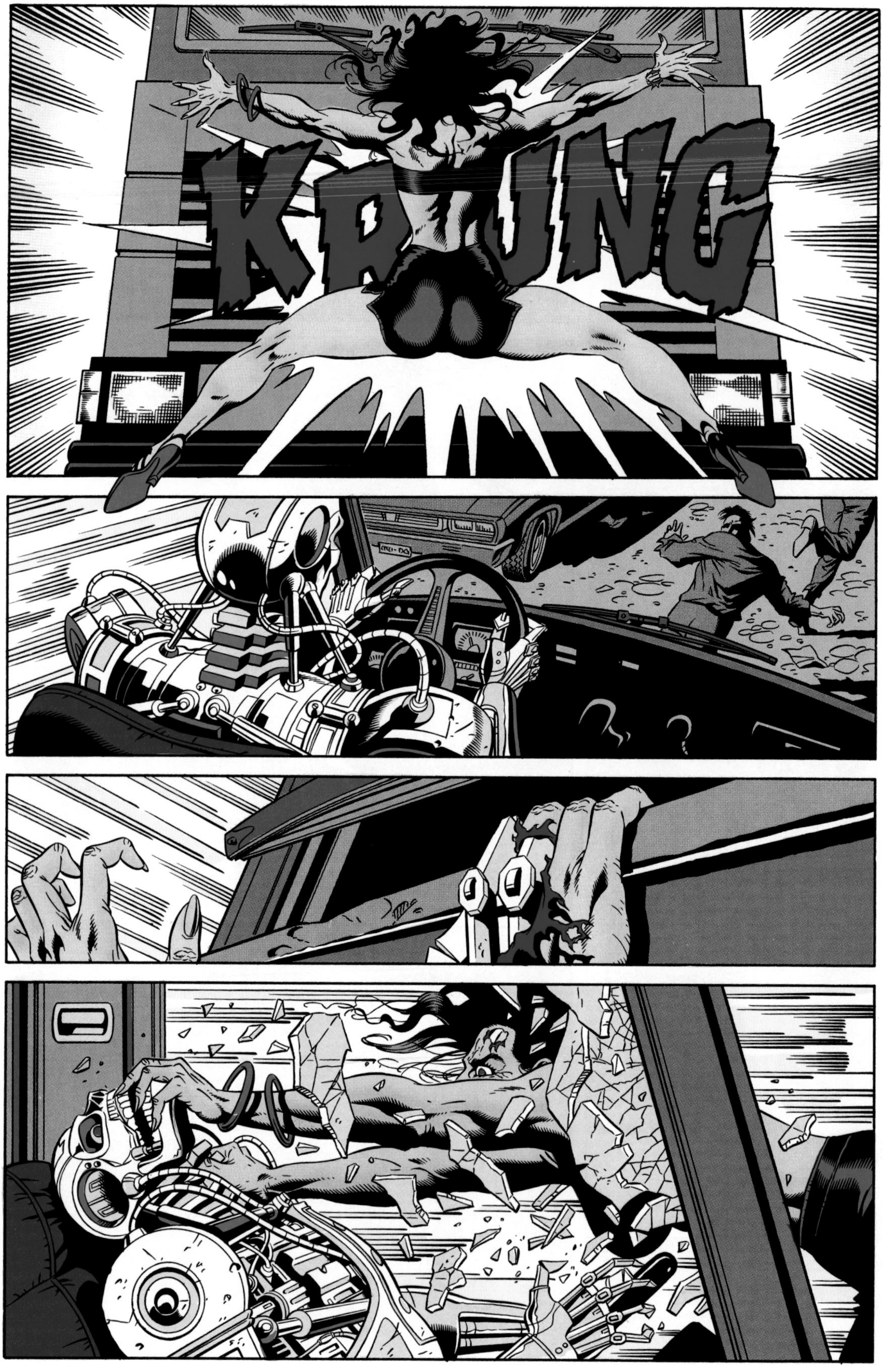
KRUNG

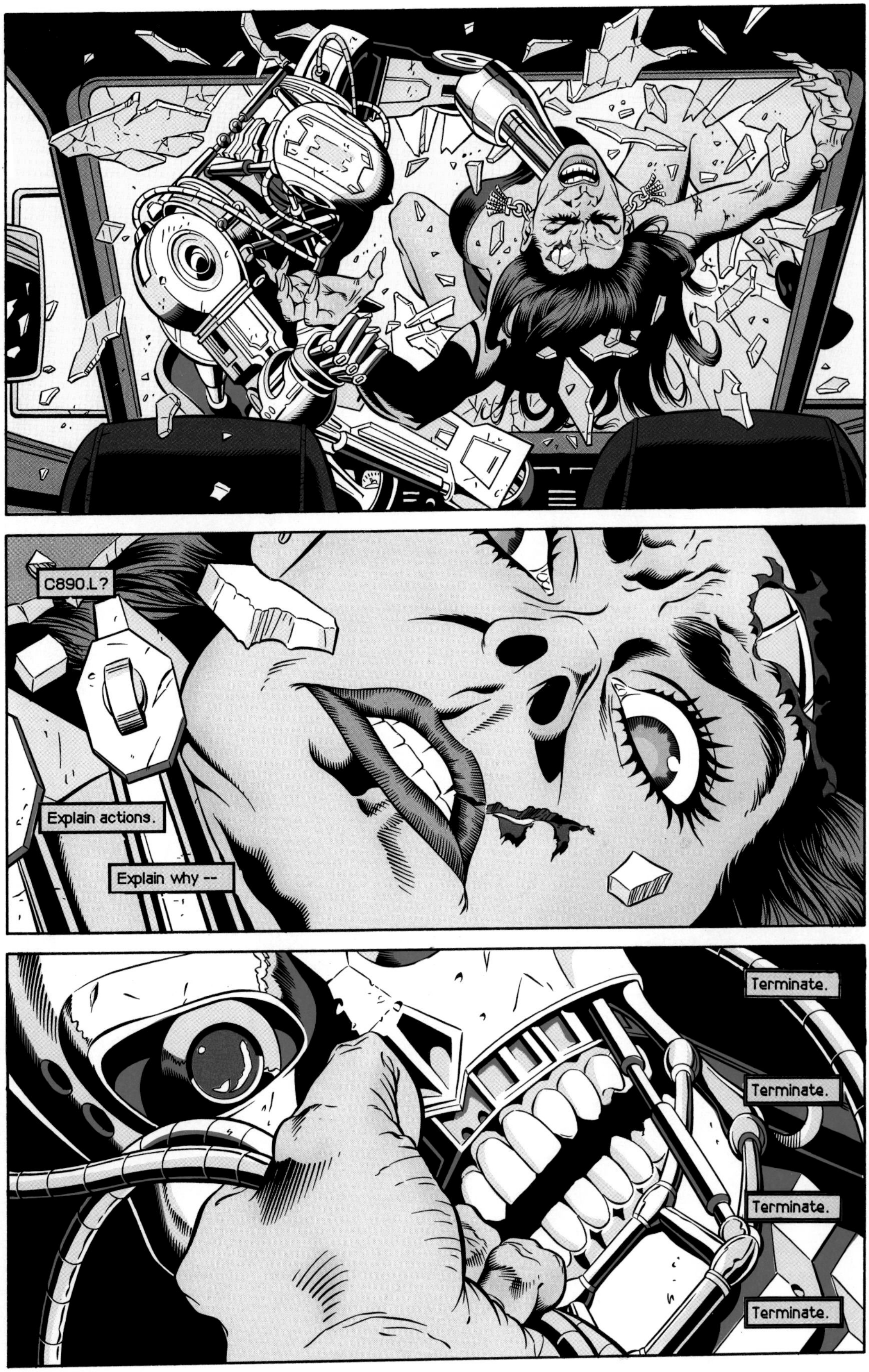
C890.L?
Explain actions.
Explain why --
Terminate.
Terminate.
Terminate.
Terminate.

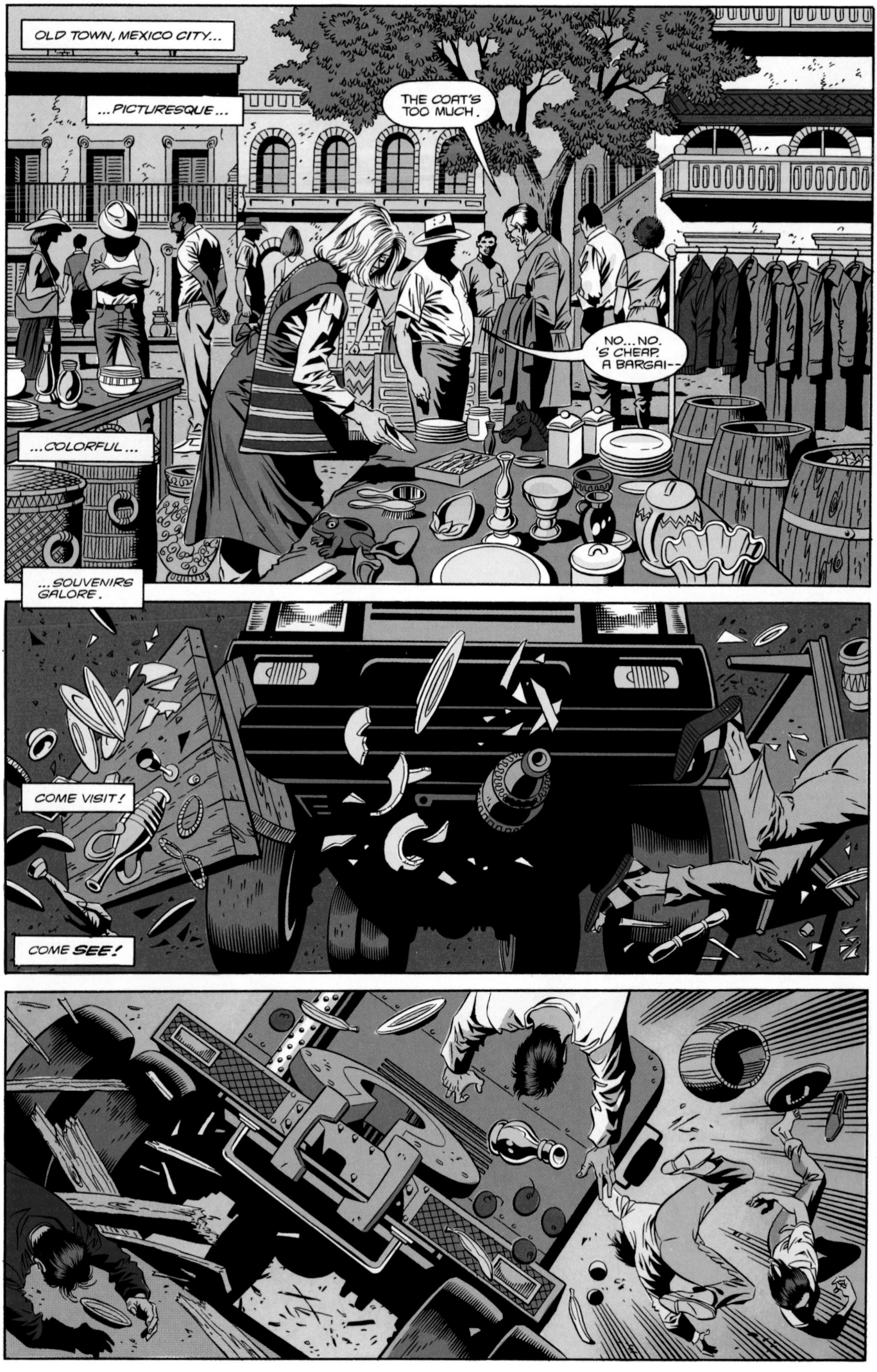
OLD TOWN, MEXICO CITY...
...PICTURESQUE...
THE COAT'S TOO MUCH.
NO...NO. 'S CHEAP. A BARGAI--
...COLORFUL...
...SOUVENIRS GALORE.
COME VISIT!
COME SEE!

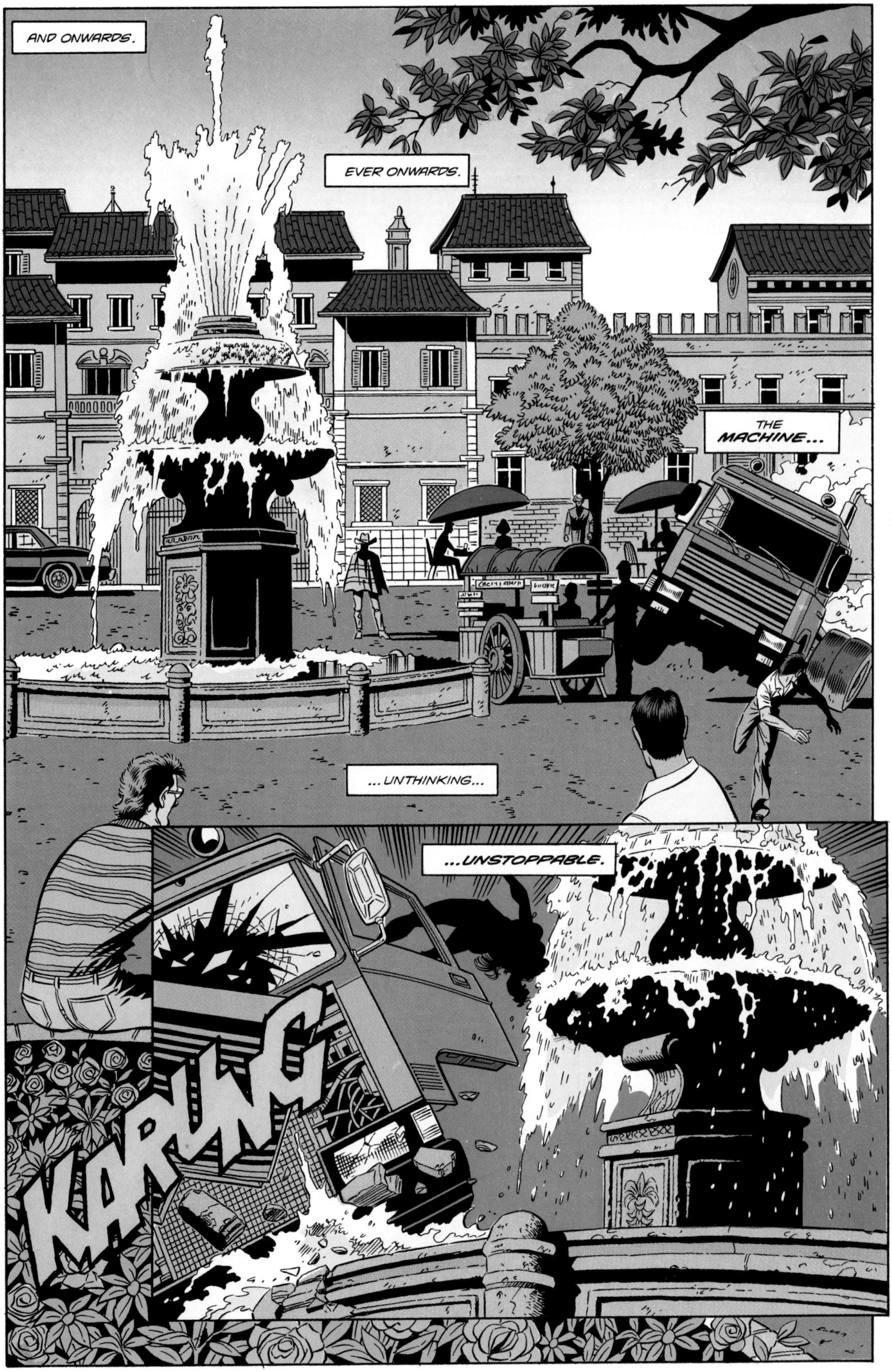
AND ONWARDS.
EVER ONWARDS.
THE MACHINE...
...UNTHINKING...
...UNSTOPPABLE.
KARUNG

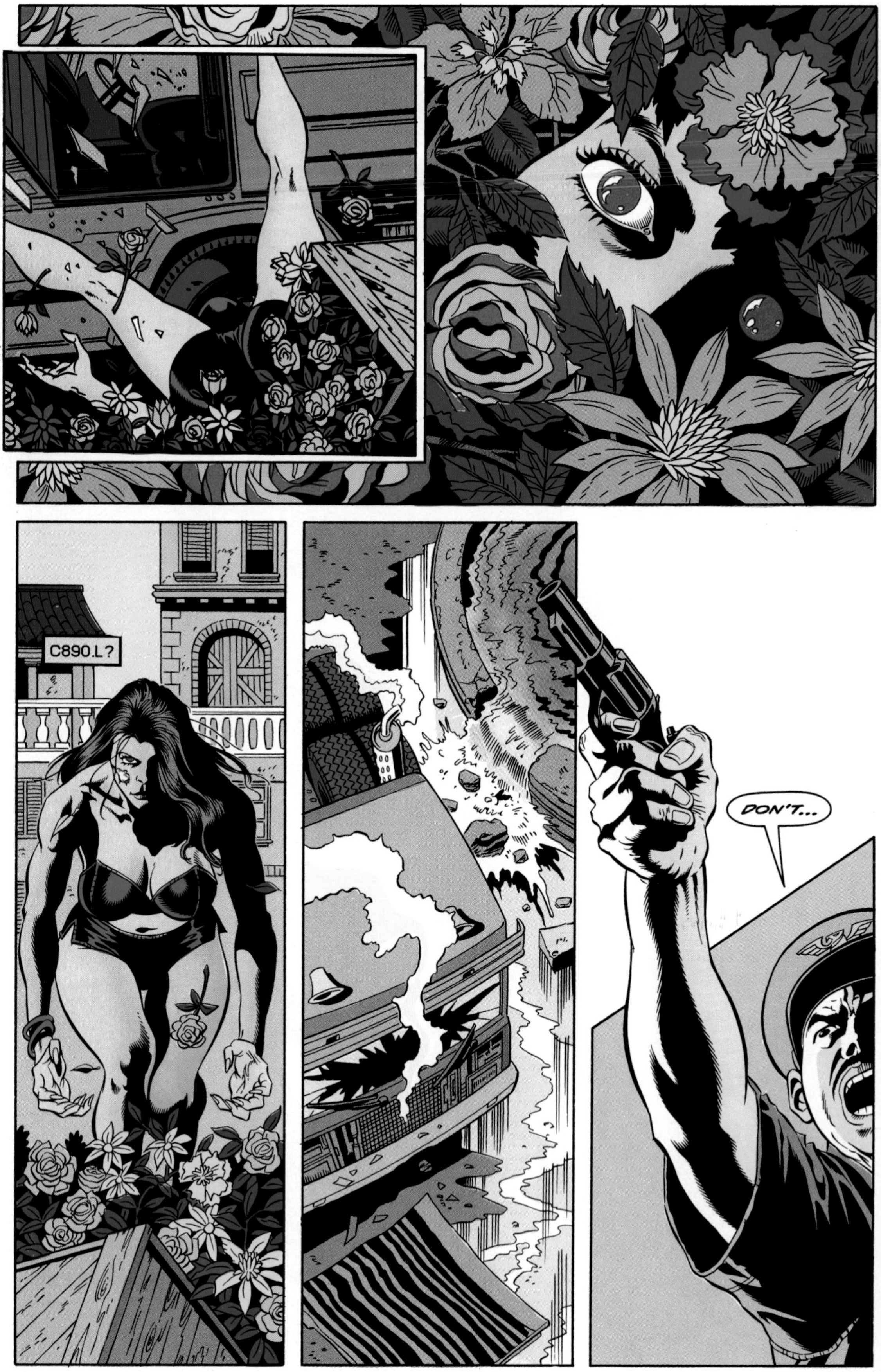
C890.L?
DON'T...

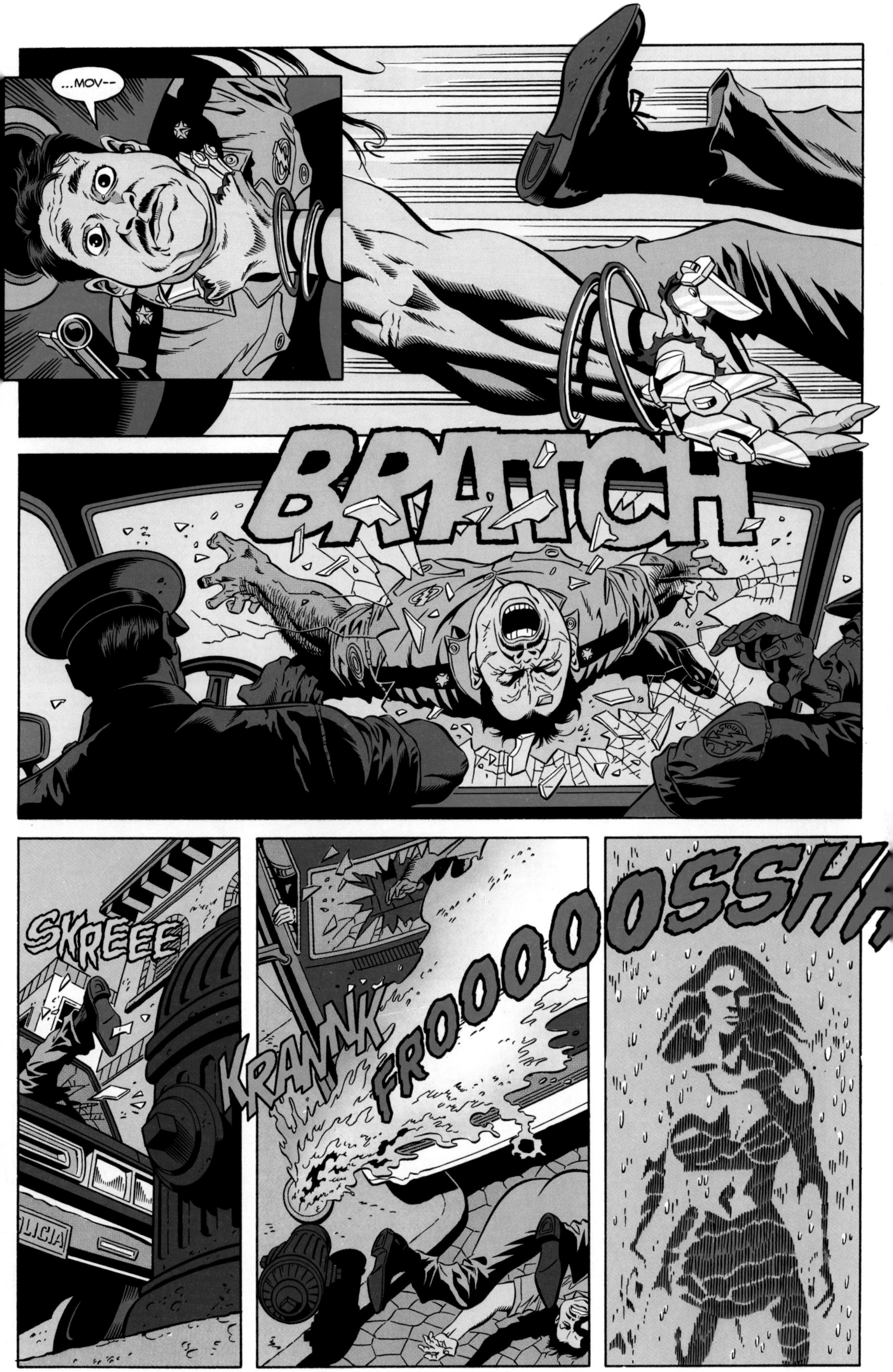
...MOV--
BRATCH
SKREEE
POLICIA
KRANNK
FROOOOOOOSSHH

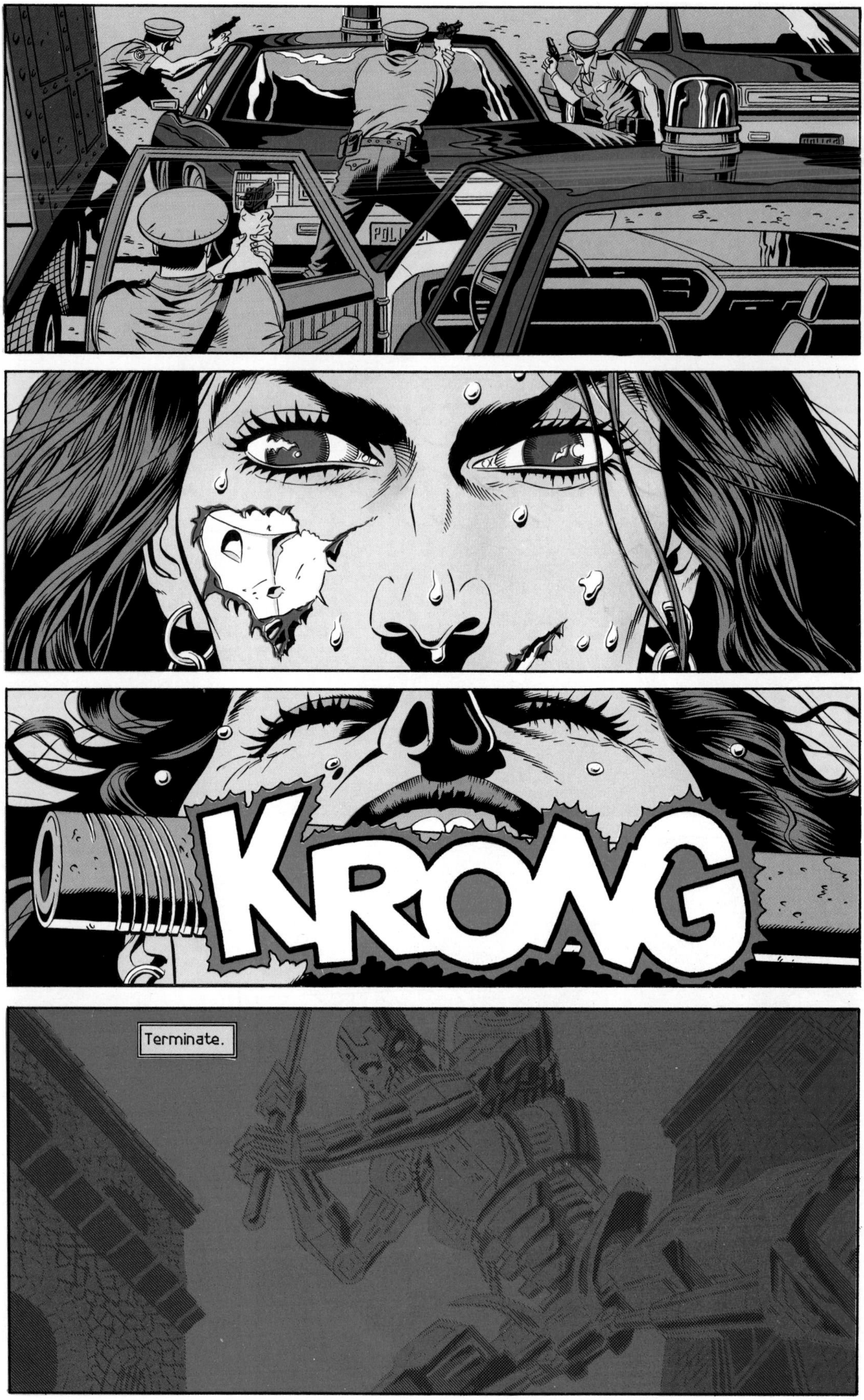
KROAG
Terminate.

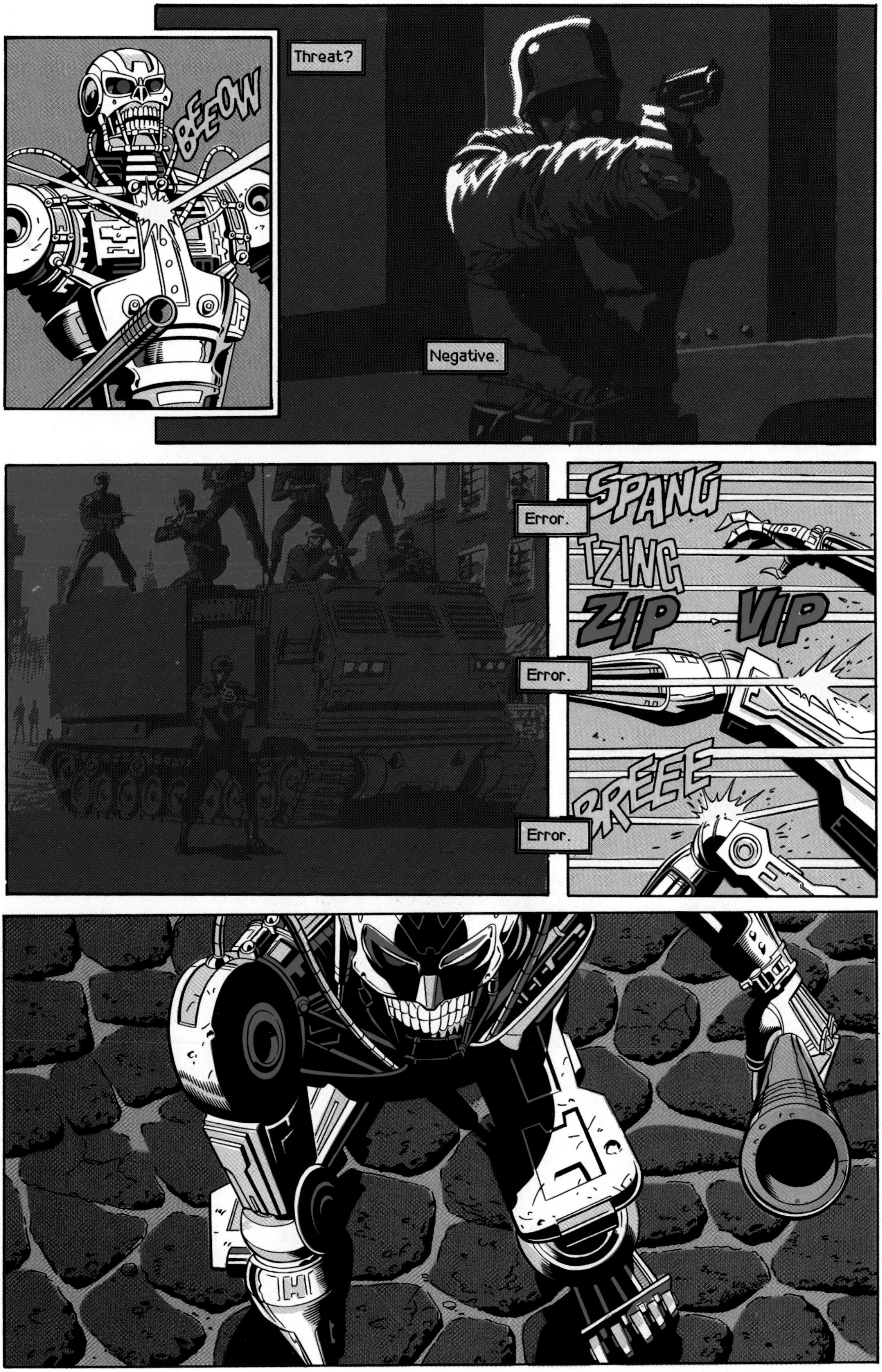
BEEOW
Threat?
Negative.
Error.
SPANG
TZING
ZIP
VIP
Error.
BREEE
Error.

TAT
TATAT

TAT
TAT ATATATAT

Arms. Arsenal.

KRUNK

Stored within
armored carrier.

Requirement:
explosive
charges.

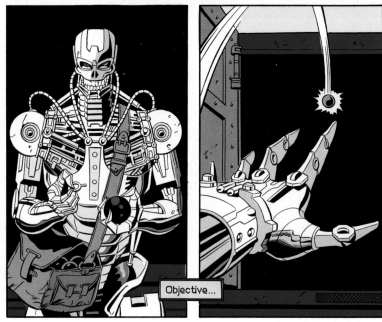

Objective...

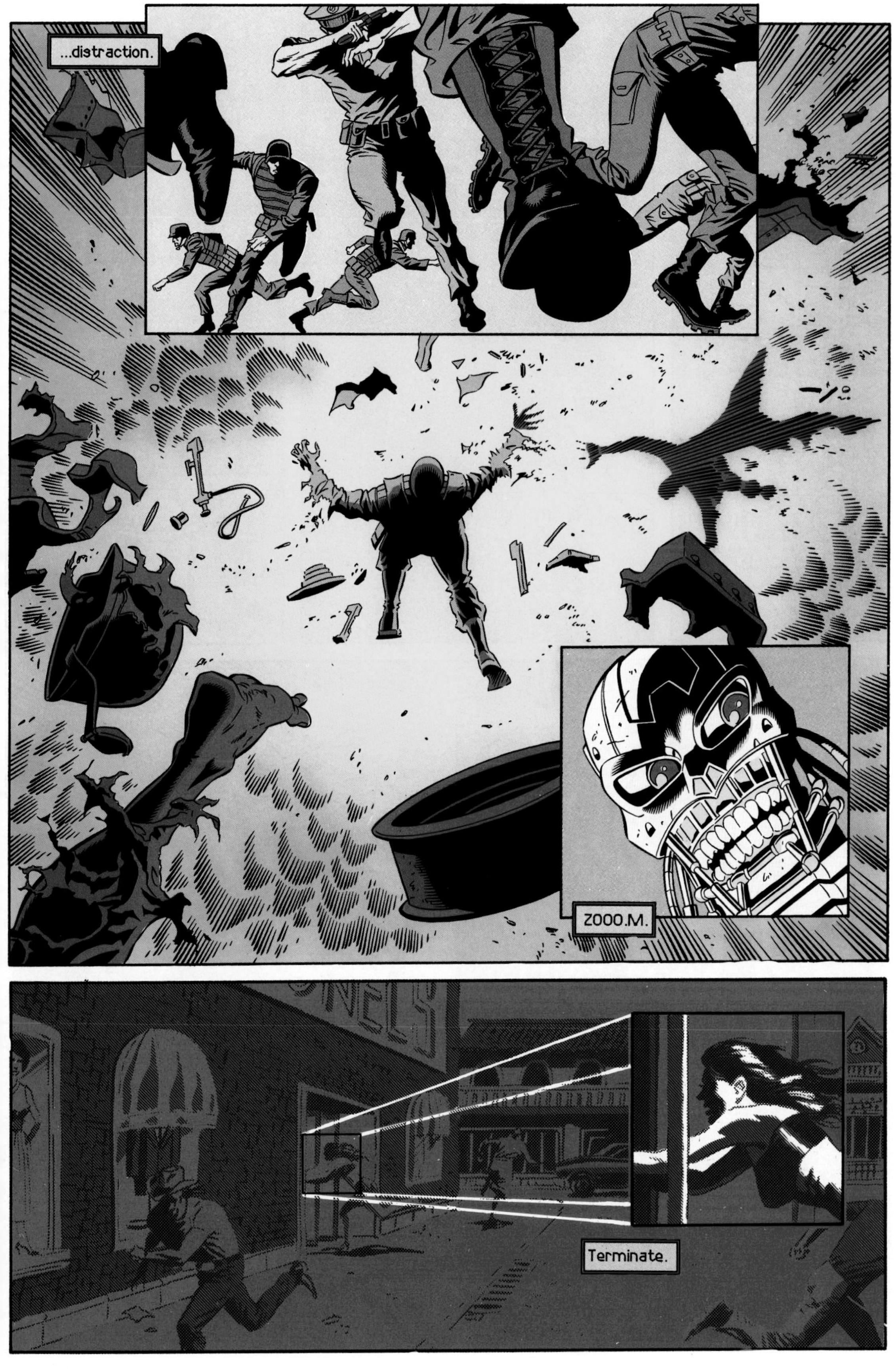
...distraction.
ZOOO.M.
Terminate.

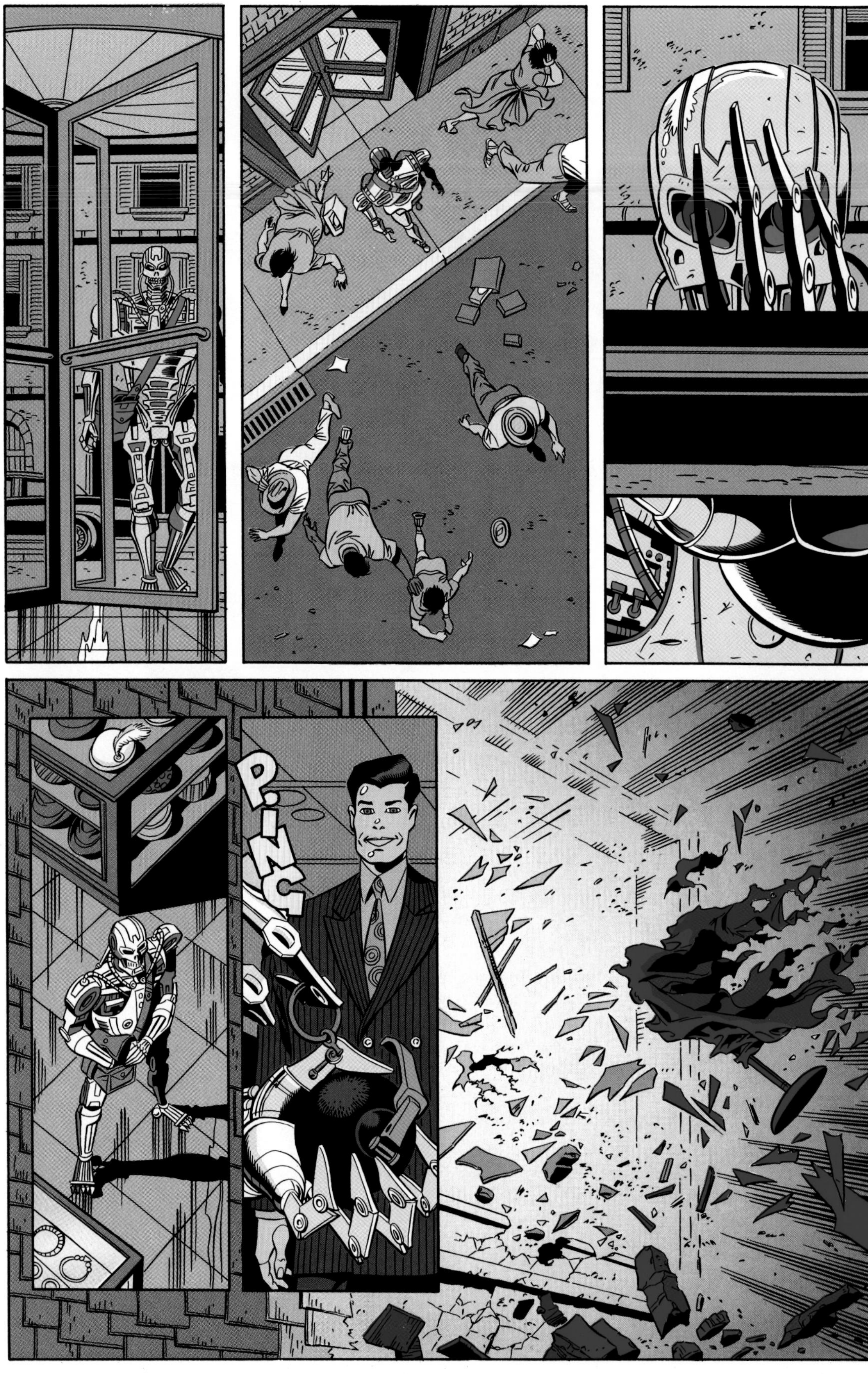
PING

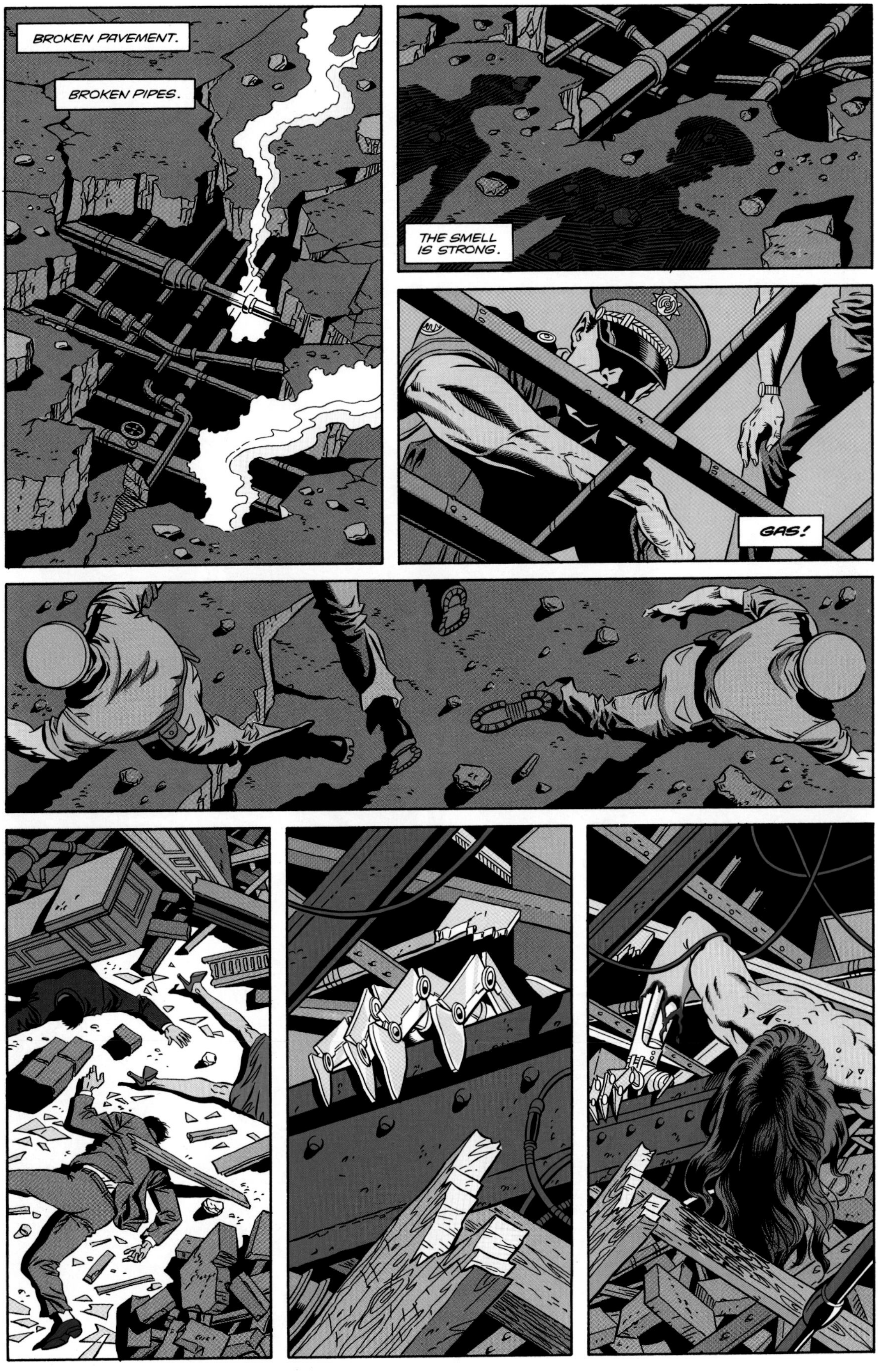
BROKEN PAVEMENT.
BROKEN PIPES.
THE SMELL IS STRONG.
GAS!

MUCH ARISES...

...FROM THE RUBBLE.

DUST.

SMOKE.

CHILLING THE PEOPLE'S HEARTS.

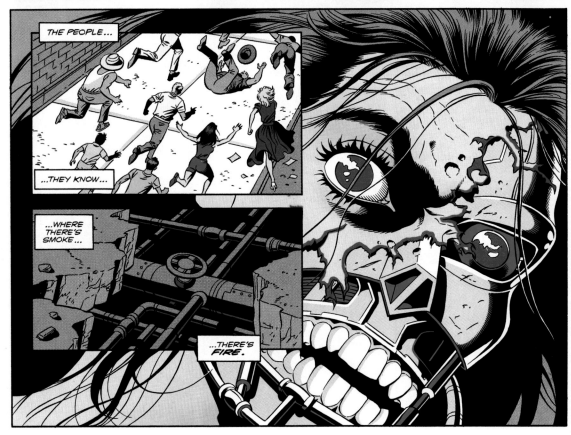

THE PEOPLE...

...THEY KNOW...

...WHERE THERE'S SMOKE...

...THERE'S FIRE.

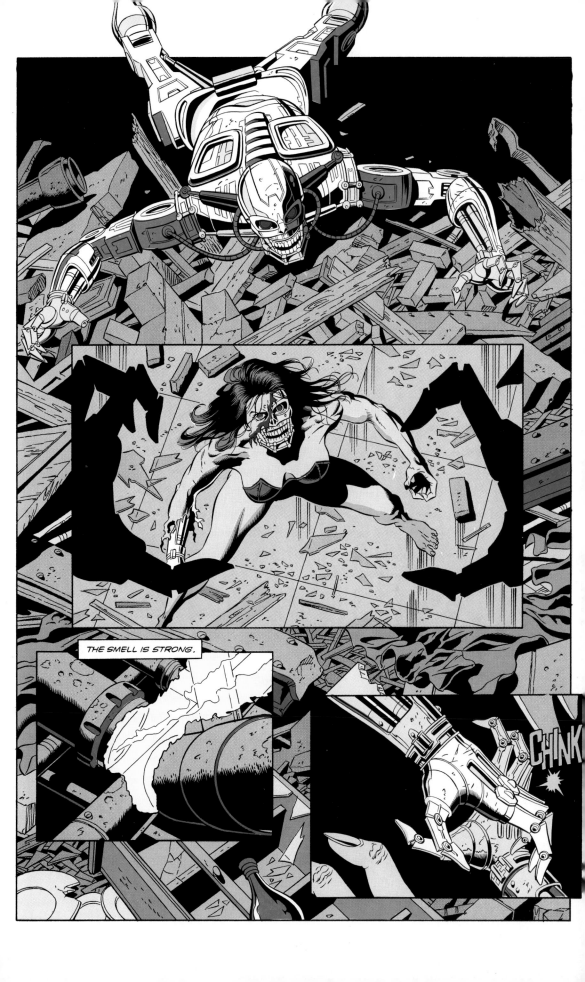

THE SMELL IS STRONG.

CHINK

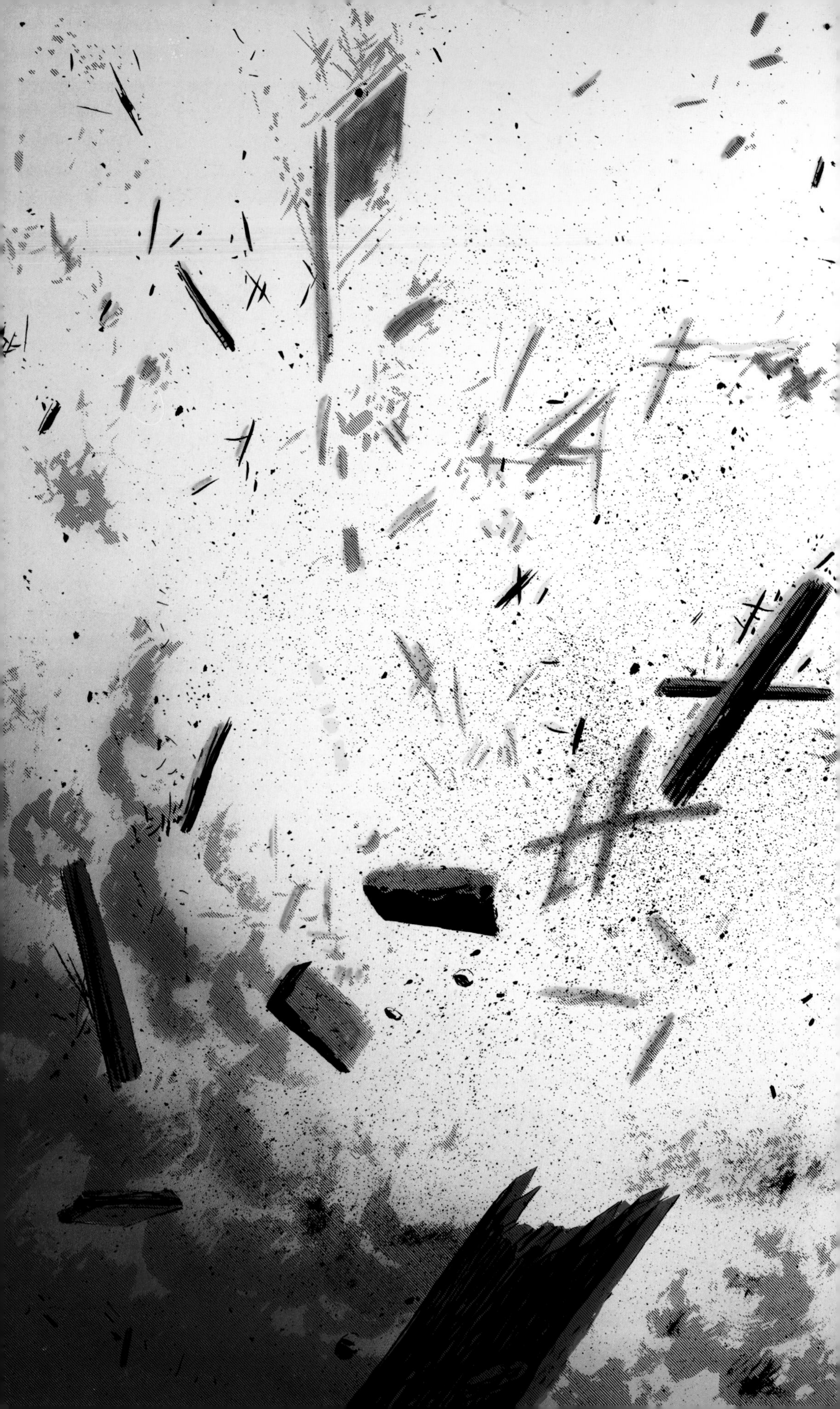

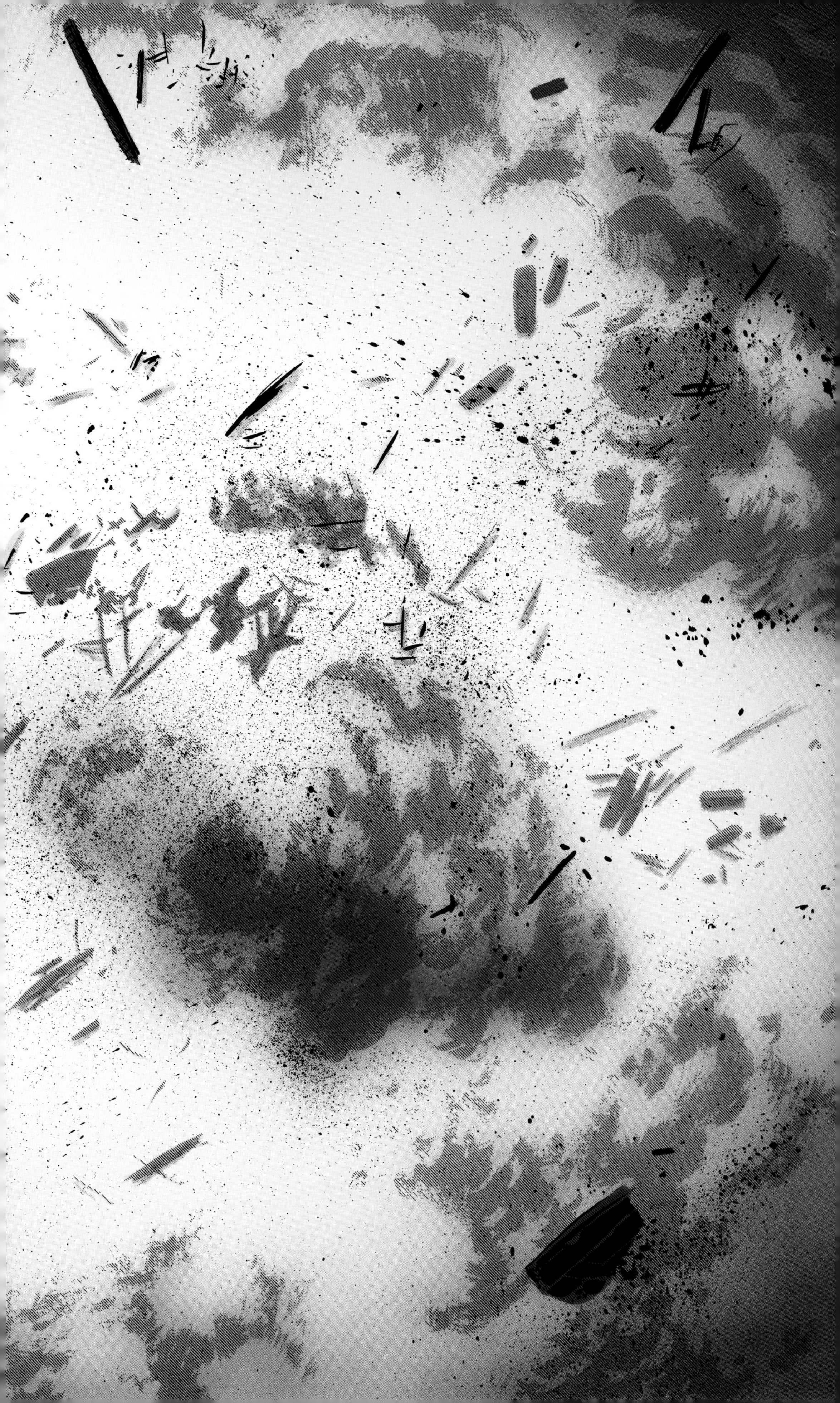

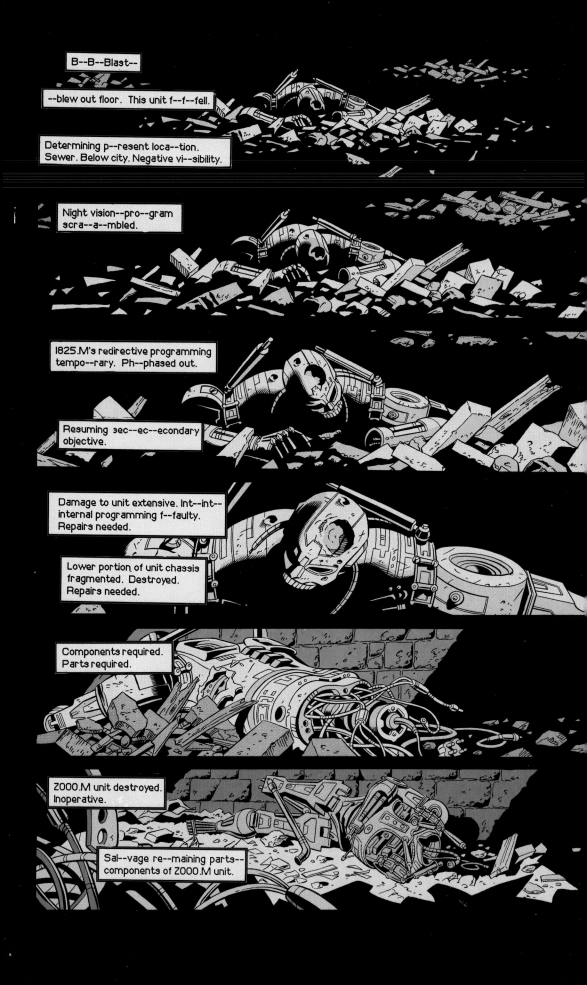

B--B--Blast--

--blew out floor. This unit f--f--fell.

Determining p--resent loca--tion.
Sewer. Below city. Negative vi--sibility.

Night vision--pro--gram
scra--a--mbled.

1825.M's redirective programming
tempo--rary. Ph--phased out.

Resuming sec--ec--econdary
objective.

Damage to unit extensive. Int--int--
internal programming f--faulty.
Repairs needed.

Lower portion of unit chassis
fragmented. Destroyed.
Repairs needed.

Components required.
Parts required.

Z000.M unit destroyed.
Inoperative.

Sal--vage re--maining parts--
components of Z000.M unit.

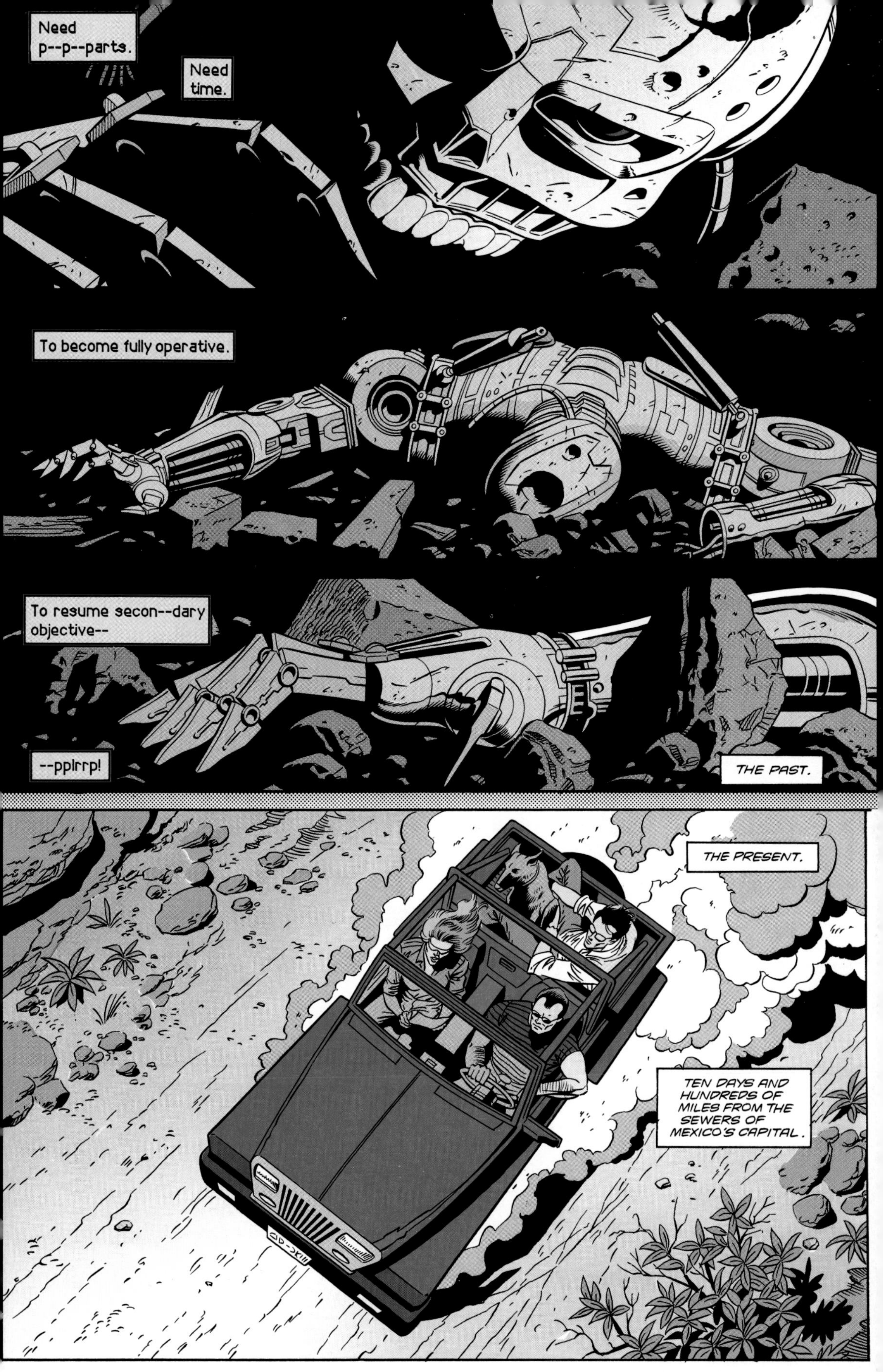
Need
p--p--parts.
Need
time.
To become fully operative.
To resume secon--dary
objective--
--pplrrp!
THE PAST.
THE PRESENT.
TEN DAYS AND
HUNDREDS OF
MILES FROM THE
SEWERS OF
MEXICO'S CAPITAL.

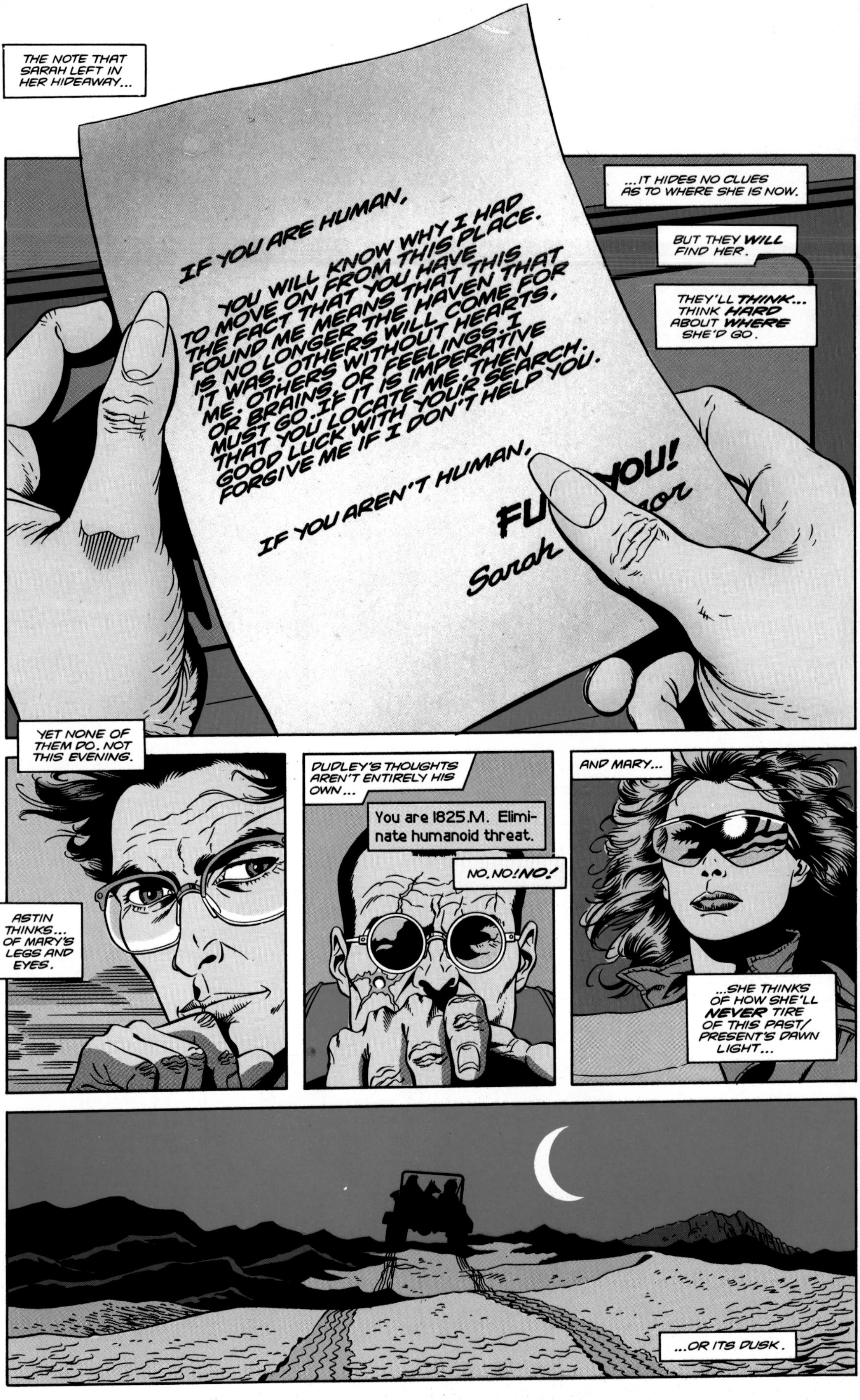
THE NOTE THAT SARAH LEFT IN HER HIDEAWAY...
IF YOU ARE HUMAN,
YOU WILL KNOW WHY I HAD TO MOVE ON FROM THIS PLACE. THE FACT THAT YOU HAVE FOUND ME MEANS THAT THIS IS NO LONGER THE HAVEN THAT IT WAS. OTHERS WILL COME FOR ME. OTHERS WITHOUT HEARTS, OR BRAINS, OR FEELINGS. I MUST GO. IF IT IS IMPERATIVE THAT YOU LOCATE ME, THEN GOOD LUCK WITH YOUR SEARCH. FORGIVE ME IF I DON'T HELP YOU.
IF YOU AREN'T HUMAN,
Sarah
...IT HIDES NO CLUES AS TO WHERE SHE IS NOW.
BUT THEY WILL FIND HER.
THEY'LL THINK... THINK HARD ABOUT WHERE SHE'D GO.
YET NONE OF THEM DO. NOT THIS EVENING.
ASTIN THINKS... OF MARY'S LEGS AND EYES.
DUDLEY'S THOUGHTS AREN'T ENTIRELY HIS OWN...
You are 1825.M. Eliminate humanoid threat.
NO. NO! NO!
AND MARY...
...SHE THINKS OF HOW SHE'LL NEVER TIRE OF THIS PAST/PRESENT'S DAWN LIGHT...
...OR ITS DUSK.

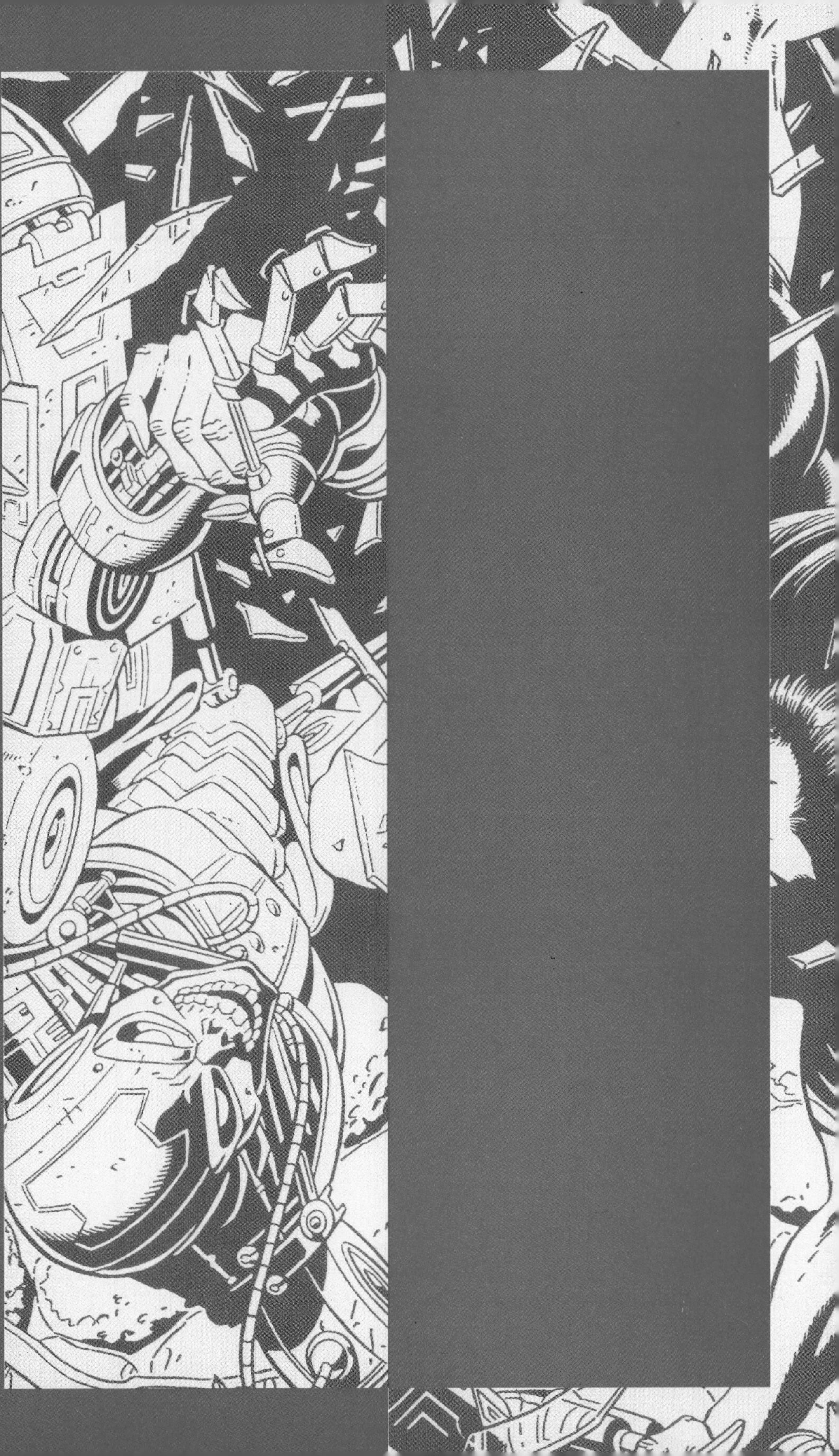

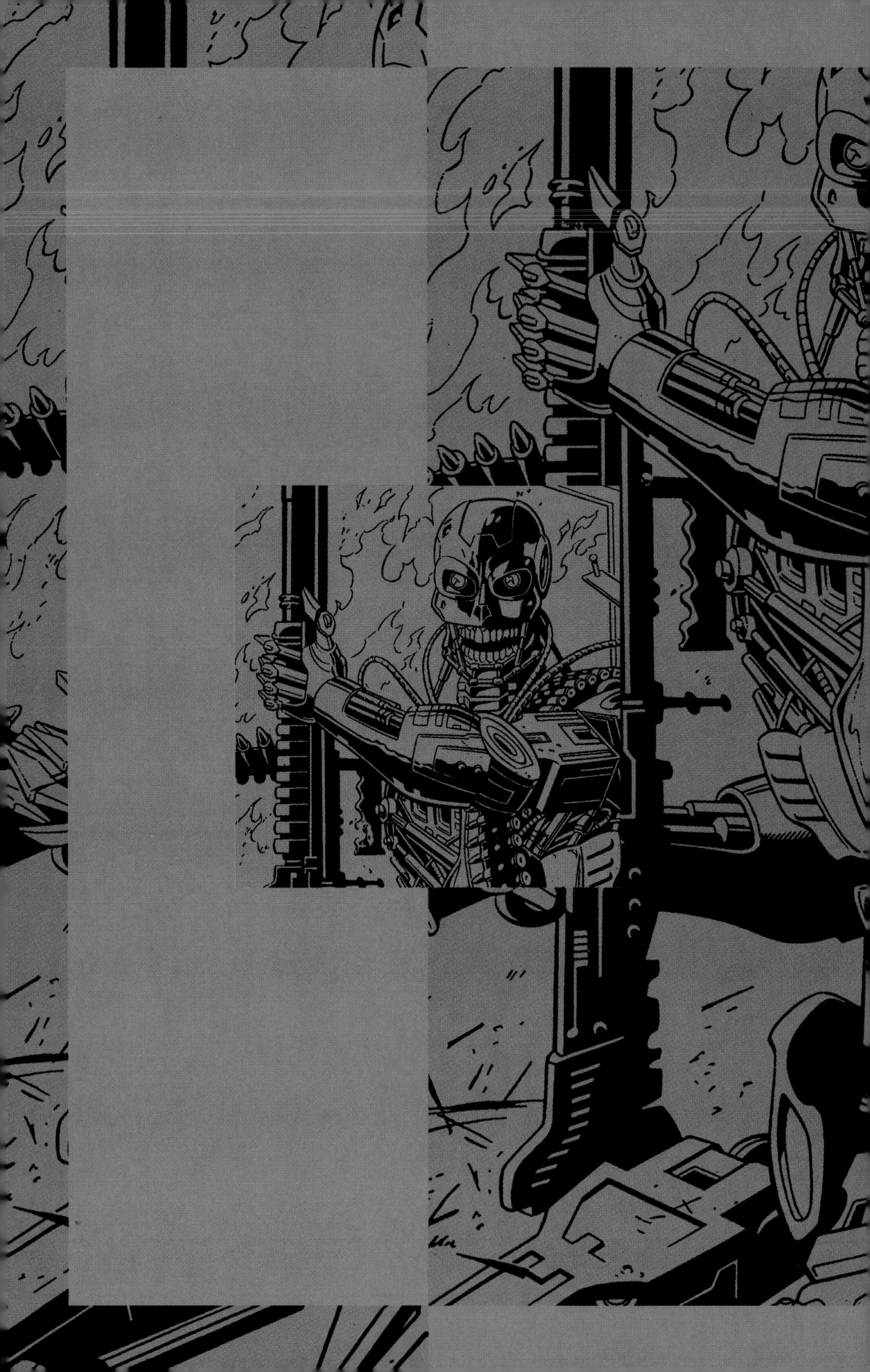

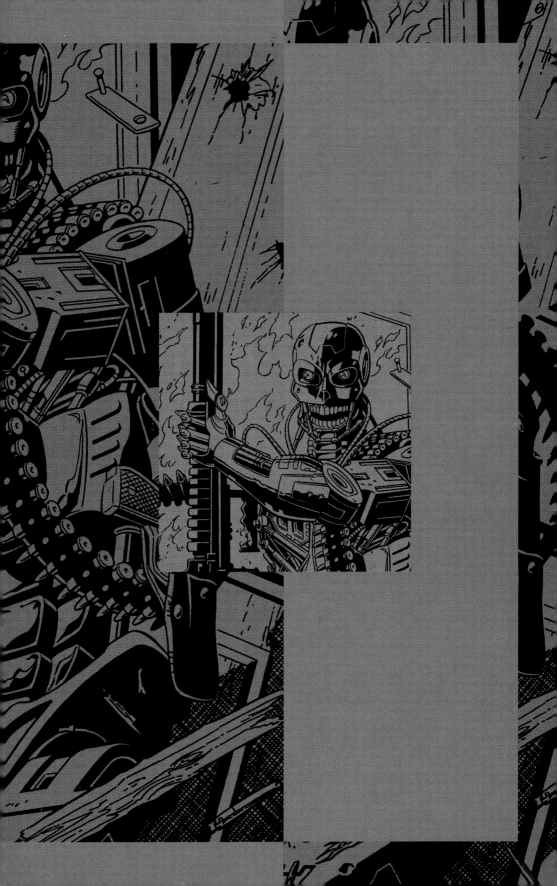